THE GODLESS
GOSPEL

Also by Julian Baggini

How the World Thinks: A Global History of Philosophy

Freedom Regained: The Possibility of Free Will

The Virtues of the Table: How to Eat and Think

The Ego Trick

*Should You Judge This Book by Its Cover?: 100 Fresh
Takes on Familiar Sayings and Quotations*

*Do They Think You're Stupid?: 100 Ways of Spotting Spin
& Nonsense from the Media, Pundits & Politicians*

Welcome to Everytown: A Journey into the English Mind

*The Pig That Wants to be Eaten: And 99
Other Thought Experiments*

What's It All About? – Philosophy and the Meaning of Life

By Julian Baggini and Jeremy Stangroom

Do You Think What You Think You Think?

THE GODLESS GOSPEL

Was Jesus a Great Moral Teacher?

Julian Baggini

GRANTA

Granta Publications, 12 Addison Avenue, London W11 4QR
First published in Great Britain by Granta Books, 2020

A CIP catalogue record for this book
is available from the British Library.

1 3 5 7 9 10 8 6 4 2

ISBN 978 1 78378 231 4 (hardback)
ISBN 978 1 78378 669 5 (trade paperback)
ISBN 978 1 78378 233 8 (ebook)

Typeset in Janson by M Rules
Printed and bound by CPI Group (UK) Ltd, Croydon, CRO 4YY

To everyone at Granta over the last sixteen years who has supported me in my writing and helped build a relationship that feels more than just professional

CONTENTS

PART ONE:

The Moral Philosophy of Jesus of Nazareth

PART TWO:

The Godless Gospel

PART ONE

The Moral Philosophy of Jesus of Nazareth

INTRODUCTION

'JESUS WAS A GREAT MORAL TEACHER.'

Richard Dawkins

Signs of a long Christian history are found across huge swathes of the earth. Churches and chapels have been built on remote islands, deep in forests and across sparsely populated plains and mountain ranges as well as in all the major cities of the world. Nearly a third of the global population identifies as Christian, significantly more than the quarter who belong to the next largest religion, Islam.[1] Yet in most advanced industrial societies, the faith's buildings are half empty, derelict or have been converted for secular purposes. In many countries, fewer and fewer people accept the divinity of Christ. In the Christian USA, for instance, one survey suggested that a majority of millennials either think Jesus was a mortal or are unsure of his divinity, whereas 62 per cent of older people believe he is God.[2] Even a sizeable minority in the clergy interpret his resurrection and description as 'the son of God' in metaphorical terms. Early this century, one survey of Church of England clergy found a third doubted or disbelieved the physical resurrection.[3]

Nonetheless, a great deal of respect is still given to this fallen Messiah. Even today's most notorious atheist, Richard Dawkins, has said that 'Jesus was a great moral teacher'.[4] In many nominally Christian countries, few believe he literally raised the dead or fed five thousand people with only five loaves and two fishes. In the UK, only one in ten believe biblical accounts of his miracles and nearly half say they do not believe that Jesus performed any miracles at all.[5] But many do believe in loving your neighbour, forgiveness and doing as you would be done by, all principles they attribute to Jesus of Nazareth.

Faith in the Christ may be declining but belief in the moral teaching of Jesus of Nazareth seems to be as strong as ever. Many believe that Christian morality provides the moral glue that holds our society together, shared values which secularisation threatens to undermine. Unsurprisingly, Christian leaders express this view most forcefully. Former Archbishop of Westminster Cardinal Cormac Murphy-O'Connor has claimed that 'the inability to believe in God and to live by faith is the greatest of evils. You see the things that result from this are an affront to human dignity, destruction of trust between peoples, the rule of egoism and the loss of peace.'[6] Pope Benedict XVI blamed secularisation for the paedophilia uncovered in his own church. 'Ultimately, the reason is the absence of God,' he wrote.[7]

Even some non-Christians think society needs the morality of the religion they reject. The eighteenth-century Enlightenment philosopher Voltaire was a deist who believed the creator God took no interest in human affairs yet he worried that godlessness weakened 'the sacred bonds of society', concluding that 'If God did not exist, it would be necessary to invent him.'[8] As the British current affairs magazine the *Spectator* put it in a leader column, 'While fewer of us call ourselves Christian, we remain a country steeped in Christian values.'[9] Most have given up Christian worship and Christian creeds, but fewer seem prepared to give up Christian morality. This is despite the fact that most people today have only a vague sense of what Jesus actually taught, a thin recollection from childhood education.

But does it make sense to reject Jesus as a divine figure and hold on to his teaching? Not if we take the Gospels to be the definitive record of Christ's teaching. The religious aspects of Christ's mission are central, not incidental. Reading the Gospels closely, it becomes clear that the 'supernatural' elements make up almost half. If one focuses only on Jesus's teachings, then almost nothing of Jesus's early life prior to taking up his ministry survives and the story ends with his burial. Along the way are pages of healings and miracles, a raising of the dead, references to God and numerous verses telling us how Jesus's actions fulfil prophecies. Hardly any of John's Gospel, often described as the most 'spiritual', remains. Whatever we may think of the Gospels, they are certainly not tracts of secular moral philosophy. The divine and supernatural are everywhere.

Christians have never seen Jesus as a man like any other. For almost all who fill the pews, Jesus remains, in the words of the Nicene Creed, 'the only Son of God' who 'for us and for our salvation ... came down from heaven' and 'by the power of the Holy Spirit he became incarnate from the Virgin Mary, and was made man'. He was crucified, 'suffered death and was buried' but 'on the third day he rose again', then 'ascended into heaven and is seated at the right hand of the Father. He will come again in glory to judge the living and the dead, and his kingdom will have no end.' If Jesus was just a moral teacher, he is a very different character from the dominant Christ of Christendom.

The children's author and theologian C. S. Lewis dismissed as 'really foolish' the common statement 'I'm ready to accept Jesus as a great moral teacher, but I don't accept his claim to be God.' He wrote, 'A man who was merely a man and said the sort of things Jesus said would not be a great moral teacher ... he would either be a lunatic – on the level with the man who says he is a poached egg – or else he would be the Devil of Hell.' For Lewis, if we relegate Jesus from the divine to the merely mortal we undermine his sanity. 'You can shut him up for a fool, you can spit at him and kill him as a demon or you can fall at his feet and call him Lord and God, but let us not come with any patronising nonsense about his being a great human teacher. He has not left that open to us. He did not intend to.'[10]

Lewis is surely right, if we take the Gospels to be accurate history. But most people who don't believe Jesus was the Messiah do not believe he was mad either. They believe the more plausible alternative: that Jesus was a human teacher who was mythologised after his death. The authors of the Gospels added supernatural adornments to their confabulated version of his life. He was neither crazy nor divine, he was simply misrepresented.

If this is correct, the Gospels are historically unreliable and we are left ignorant of what Jesus actually said. We have no other major source for his teachings than the distorted accounts of the Gospels. The only other historical texts that provide evidence even for his existence are the Jewish historian Josephus's *Antiquities of the Jews* (c. 93–4 CE) and the Roman historian Tacitus's *Annals* (c. 109 CE). There has been quite an industry in scholars attempting to reconstruct the historical Jesus, but none can justly claim to have found him. Assessing his moral philosophy would appear to be impossible. If Jesus was simply a great moral teacher, his teachings have been lost to history and remade by myth.

There is still, however, a way we can extract a secular moral philosophy from the religious teachings of the Gospels. We can strip away the religious elements of the accounts of Jesus's life and teachings and see what secular ethics remains. This is not an attempt to reconstruct a historically authentic version of his teachings, simply an exercise in seeing whether there are important moral insights to be found in the Gospels as they are, ones that speak to a secular society as well as to a Christian one.

This is the approach I have taken. I went through the four Gospels and deleted all the supernatural elements, such as miracles, healings and claims to have fulfilled prophecies. The only category of religious sayings I retained were those that refer to 'the Kingdom of Heaven', which I understand as referring to an ideal or inner state rather than to a supernatural realm – perhaps, as some theologians argue, how it was intended to be understood. With the supernatural laid to one side, I created one, hybrid, godless Gospel, combining different versions of the same stories and teachings to avoid repetition. The resulting 22,000-word Gospel is a fascinating document which distils Jesus's ethical teachings and is reproduced in full in Part Two.

This isn't the first such reduced Gospel. Tolstoy published *The Gospel in Brief* in 1892, synthesising the four Gospels and eliminating miracles and the resurrection. Tolstoy's Jesus is still, however, the son of God and the Messiah. Thomas Jefferson attempted something similar in 1820 when he cut and pasted with razor and glue the passages from the Gospels which he believed best represented the ethical teachings of Jesus. *The Life and Morals of Jesus of Nazareth*, commonly known as *The Jefferson Bible*, was presented to new members of the US Congress every year from 1904 to the 1950s. Like *The Godless Gospel*, *The Jefferson Bible* excludes all of Jesus's miracles, claims of divinity and his resurrection. It is far from a fully secular-ised gospel since it leaves in talk of devils and angels, Jesus's healings, and frequent mentions of God, including the injunc-tion to fear him. Jefferson's project is, however, indicative of a long tradition of wanting to save New Testament ethics from religion and put the humanity rather than the divinity of Jesus centre stage.

To help me in my attempt to extract a secular moral philos-ophy from the teachings of Jesus, I have had discussions with several theologians and philosophers. Almost all of them are Christians, and I have included many of their observations and comments in this book. One thing they helped to clarify was that Jesus did not leave us a set of plain, simple and unequivocal moral teachings or a fully formed moral theory. 'He actually left pretty abruptly without any kind of book or set of rules or instructions. They had to just get on with it,' says Lucy Winkett, a regular contributor to BBC Radio Four's *Thought for the Day*, in which religious figures have nearly three minutes to offer edifying food for thought to listeners of all faiths and none.

One reason why it's difficult to extract a complete and coherent moral system from the Gospels is that they are not anything like a moral or philosophical tract. 'The Gospels are narratives,' says Nick Spencer, a theologian at the Christian think tank Theos, which combines strong religious conviction with a commitment to intelligent, open discussion. 'With the Sermon on the Mount as a possible exception, most of what we understand of Jesus's ethical commands comes from particular encounters. So what he says inevitably depends on whether he is talking to a priest, a Levite, a woman, a leper and so on.'

Another obstacle to clarity is that Jesus taught in parables, many of which are cryptic or ambiguous. Nor are his teachings entirely consistent. Jesus is not the exact same character in all four Gospels. Each biographer has a different take on him, John's being markedly different from the more similar versions portrayed in Matthew, Mark and Luke.

It would be easy to pick up on these contradictions and dismiss the moral philosophy of Jesus as incoherent. I prefer to adopt the principle of trying to understand what others say in the way that makes it most reasonable: interpreting the various teachings so that they stand together as coherently as possible. Apparent contradictions should be made compatible without bending interpretation so far that it breaks – a common theological vice. Too often I find that religious apologists use one convenient, idiosyncratic verse of scripture to explain away more numerous, awkward ones. My view is that the right approach is the opposite of this: where there appear to be contradictions, we have to take what is most dominant and recurrent as primary.

One final problem with extracting a moral philosophy fit for now is that some specific teachings are out of kilter with what most of us would believe to be good ethics today. These could be lazily used as sticks to beat Jesus with. But the same can be said of almost any moral teacher from an earlier era, such as one of Western philosophy's foundational thinkers, Aristotle. We are able to separate off his repugnant views on women and slaves from his broader system. If we are to treat Jesus as a moral teacher, we owe him the same charity of interpretation.

These preliminary cautions show that any moral theory extracted from the Gospels has to be an interpretation. No one can avoid using their personal judgement. That is why there has been so much room for disagreement about what Jesus commanded. I offer my own reflections more as promising ways to start thinking about Jesus as a secular moral philosopher than as a definitive interpretation. I urge you to read *The Godless Gospel* yourself and see if you can make better sense of it.

In *The Quest of the Historical Jesus* Albert Schweitzer wrote, 'each successive epoch of theology found its own thoughts in Jesus; that was, indeed, the only way in which it could make Him live. But it was not only each epoch that found its reflection in Jesus; each individual created Him in accordance with his own character.'[11] Aware of this tendency, I have tried not to create the image of Jesus that would most please me, nor for that matter the straw-man version that I could most easily discredit. At the same time, believers or not, we can only see him from where we are now. I have tried to rise to the challenge of understanding Jesus in a way that makes sense for us today without so updating him that his capacity to question and overturn the assumptions of the modern world is lost.

The prospects for a secular moral philosophy based on the Gospel teachings of Jesus might look rather unpromising. I was surprised to find that most of the thinkers I consulted doubted Jesus was essentially a moral teacher at all. The theologian Keith Ward was particularly clear about this. 'There aren't many very clear moral teachings in the Gospels,' he told me. 'The only one that seems clear is love God and love your neighbour, which is very vague. If you make a list of great moral teachers and miss out the bit about the Holy Spirit changing your life I'd probably put Confucius above Jesus.' Karen Kilby, a Catholic theologian, agrees with Ward, saying that 'If you limit yourself to what Jesus said, you wouldn't be able to construct a moral system to live by.'

Despite their words of caution, I have discovered that interesting and important moral ideas can be found in Jesus's life and words. Indeed, what emerges is richer and more interesting than I anticipated. I admit that when I started out I expected his stripped-down moral philosophy to consist of little more than a call for charity and forgiveness, neither of which is particularly original or controversial in today's world. What I actually found is a belief system which goes against the gentle image of Jesus as an advocate of homely moral truths that we can all easily and warmly embrace. Much of his teaching is discomforting, and quite a bit is objectionable. Yet this is something even many believers might welcome. It rescues Jesus from the literally infantilising image of the meek and mild baby in the manger who comes to bring peace. It recasts him as an iconoclastic revolutionary so threatening that he was crucified. The moral philosophy of Jesus is often challenging and radical, for believers and infidels alike.

I

A REVOLUTION
OF THE SOUL

After the tale of the baby born in a Bethlehem manger, the second most famous Christmas story in the world is surely Charles Dickens's *A Christmas Carol*. It's a folksy tale of a mean and miserly curmudgeon, Ebenezer Scrooge, who is forced to confront the truth about his past, present and future selves by three spirits who visit him on Christmas Eve. When the last of these spirits shows him his own unloved, neglected grave, Scrooge is filled with anxiety that it is too late to change, too late to be redeemed: 'Good Spirit . . . Assure me that I yet may change these shadows you have shown me, by an altered life!'

Despite its chocolate-box sentimentality, the central message of the book is a faithful but family-friendly version of one of the Gospels' main teachings. What we need above all else is a *change of heart*. The Greek word used in the New Testament for this is *metanoia*, a compound of *meta* ('after' or 'with') and *noeo* ('to perceive' or 'to think'). Most translators render this as 'change of mind and heart' or 'change of consciousness'. That is what Scrooge experiences. He is transformed from a mean-spirited person into a kind and generous one, heartless to compassionate, selfish to selfless. His actions change completely as a result of his change of heart.

Reading *The Godless Gospel*, it seems clear to me that *metanoia* is at its core. Jesus is calling for nothing less than a revolution of the soul. It is unfortunate that in the traditional lexicon of Christianity *metanoia* has morphed into repentance, with its suggestion of the primacy of confessing one's sins. This obscures the original meaning of a transformation of the self.

We might think of repentance as a matter of 'inner trans-formation', but Nick Spencer warns that this is potentially misleading. Spencer argues that the now common-sense idea of the self as essentially inner and private is anachronistic if applied to biblical teachings. Many have argued that it only became widespread in the West after Descartes, who in the seventeenth century identified the self with a private, con-scious essence: 'I think, therefore I am.' There is good reason to believe that in many cultures across history, the private and subjective aspects of experience have not been given the same emphasis. People have more commonly thought of themselves primarily as beings who exist in relation to others, not as self-contained, atomised units. This is important to bear in mind when thinking about how Jesus sought a transformation of the self. For Jesus and his contemporaries, this self is never purely inner. It is essentially linked with the outer, in particular our social relations.

With that in mind, we should understand *metanoia* not only as a change of your inner being but as a transformation that affects how you behave and how you relate to others. What we call inner and outer are two sides of the same coin. If you believe you have good intentions but still behave badly, that shows your moral cultivation has a long way to go. If you perform the right acts without the right intentions, you have only the appearance of virtue, not the reality. It's like the difference between giving a gift out of genuine affection and doing it because you know you're expected to. The physical act is the same but its nature and meaning are completely different. For Jesus, you have to do the right things because you are motivated to do so for the right reasons. Your good actions should flow from your state of self, one which, as we will see, is never perfectly good (not even Jesus is that) but is striving towards perfection as an unattainable goal.

When Jesus washes his disciples' feet, it is as though he is enacting a parable about the importance of achieving true purity that expresses itself in action (5:21–30). The literal cleaning involved is not the point. Indeed, the act of washing purifies the washer more than the washed as it enables them to practise humility and service. That this is a symbolic act is made plain when Simon Peter, who initially didn't want his master to serve him, changes his mind and pleads, 'Lord, not my feet only, but also my hands and my head.' Jesus replies, 'He that is washed needeth not save to wash his feet, but is clean every whit: and ye are clean, but not all.' The cleanliness he is referring to is clearly spiritual, intimating at the treachery Judas is soon to enact.

For many Christians, the idea of *metanoia* is linked to the idea of being 'born again'. There is some sense in this, since the radical change of heart is a deep transformation that requires letting go of our past life. But being 'born again' has come to refer to a life-changing *event*, whereas for Jesus it was a *process* without end. As the philosopher John Cottingham explains, it is 'what the Benedictines call conversion of life, which is a lifelong project. It's not *boom* and then you're saved.'

Cottingham taught me as an undergraduate at Reading in the late 1980s and we've stayed in touch ever since. Cottingham has an intellectual generosity that I have always tried to emulate. I remember a lecture in which someone asked him a question that I thought was so stupid it was hard to believe the questioner had been paying any attention at all. Cottingham did not swipe the student away like a bothersome fly, as he could easily have done. He stopped and thought, and then gave an answer that made the question look more sensible than it was. As he later confirmed to me, it is his practice to ask himself what serious and genuine concern a questioner might be incompetently grappling to articulate. This was the best demonstration I've seen of the principle of charity in action. If only more people employed it in their discussions about religion we'd have more mutual understanding and respect, less mutual incomprehension and ridicule.

The paradox of *metanoia* is that it requires acute attention to one's self but the result is that we become more selfless. Versions of this paradox appear in many religions and wisdom traditions, most obviously several Indic and Buddhist ones. They share the goal of becoming less attached to one's ego. The only way to do this is to work very hard on your self in order to loosen this attachment.

Christian thought also has its versions of loss of self. The word that best expresses this is *kenosis*, which literally means 'emptying'. Christians are required to follow the example of Jesus, who had to empty himself of his own will in order to follow the will of God. In his second letter to the Philippians, Paul says Jesus 'emptied himself ... humbled and became obedient to the point of death' (Philippians 2:7–8).[1] *Kenosis* is a particularly important concept in Orthodox Christianity, but the basic idea resonates in other denominations.

For Lucy Winkett, *kenosis* is what makes the Christian message distinctive and special. Many traditions have versions of the golden rule – do to others as you would have them do to you – but she sees these as tending to be forms of an 'ethic of mutuality, which is more transactional than sacrificial. The focus for Jesus is not so much "do to others as you would have them do to you", but "do as I have done to you". That's the new commandment on Maundy Thursday [the day of the Last Supper before his crucifixion] when he washes his disciples' feet. That whole paradigm of foot washing is the *kenosis* that St Paul talks about, the self-emptying ethic, which is not the same as do as you would be done by. That's what captures me: a free person, with dignity, choosing to kneel to wash the feet of another person.'

Although *kenosis* appears to be a theologically laden concept, it is not difficult to make sense of it in secular terms. Secular *kenosis* requires emptying ourselves of our egotistical desires and doing the right thing. For instance, it is not too much of a stretch to see the philosopher Immanuel Kant's injunction to follow our moral duties or the utilitarian command to maximise the welfare of all as this kind of *kenosis*.

The Christian image of self-emptying and changing our hearts is extremely powerful, suggesting a kind of spiritual evisceration. At one point Jesus runs with this metaphor with extreme results, instructing us to pluck out our right eye or cut off a hand or a foot if any cause us to sin (2:28–30). It's obvious that these comments should not be taken literally. It's not your limbs or organs that cause you to do wrong. It is simply a graphically vivid way of driving home how deep *metanoia* needs to go. 'It is better for thee to enter life halt or maimed, than having two feet to be cast into hell.' Given the figurative nature of the passage, it is not difficult to take hell non-literally here too. In hell we are alienated from our best selves, trapped in a lower form of existence. To escape we need to recognise that living a good life is more important than living a healthy or prosperous one. And although we would stop short of self-mutilation as a means to prevent sin, we're not a million miles from doing just that when we consider chemical castration or medication to curb violent impulses.

These metaphors of self-mutilation are good examples of Jesus's use of hyperbolic language. His tendency to deliberately overstate is something many theologians warn we need to be careful of. His style was not that of the cool seminar room. 'You have to understand him in the context of a whole line of Jewish prophets,' says Cottingham. 'Throughout the Hebrew Bible people come and really tear people off a strip.'

Vicar Brian Mountford agrees with Cottingham that 'The prophetic tradition often takes an extreme position and exaggerates its point. Speaking truth to power in a prophetic way can also require action that seems unreasonable to many.' He compared it to the people who had been protesting against climate change in London around the time of our conversation. 'They can't really justify holding up the whole of London's traffic but they're going to do it because they know it's going to make people sit up and listen. I think there's an element of that in Jesus's teaching.'

I wasn't surprised to hear Mountford speaking up for radical disrupters. When he was vicar of the University Church, Oxford, he had the habit of inviting the occasional atheist to give a sermon – on one occasion he chose me. As the title of his book *Christian Atheist* suggests, Mountford is at the very liberal end of the Christian spectrum.

The vivid and sometimes violent imagery of some of Jesus's language is not just a stylistic quirk. It is also an indication of how challenging and countercultural his teachings are. The revolution of the soul is a difficult one which questions our normal priorities, including our moral ones. *Metanoia* and *kenosis* both require us to focus on developing a purity of spirit that is in tension with Jesus's emphasis on love and compassion.

Consider the story of the sisters Martha and Mary. When Jesus visits them, Martha does all the hard work of being the host while Mary just sits around talking to him. Martha understandably complains but Jesus tells her that Mary has her priorities right. 'Martha, Martha, thou art careful and troubled about many things. But one thing is needful: and Mary hath chosen that good part, which shall not be taken away from her' (6:28–30). Martha is too concerned about looking after Jesus well and not enough about her own self-cultivation. Mary looks to herself, Martha to her guests, but it is Mary whom Jesus praises, dismissing Martha's seeming kindness as excessive anxiety and concern.

This aspect of Jesus's teaching arguably contains one of the seeds of the individualism that has gradually taken over in Christendom. Judaism was centred on the group, the chosen people. Rituals and rules may not always have served a high moral purpose but they were part of the fabric that held society together. Jesus focused less on the relationship between God and his people and more on that between God and each individual. 'Your relationship with God is finally independent of all the other relationships you have around you,' as Nick Spencer puts it.

Jesus has little positive to say about any of the things that focus on the group rather than the moral health of the individual. Indeed, he repeatedly told people that *metanoia* required them to turn their back on tradition, their families and tribal loyalties and focus on what we would now call 'personal growth', albeit of a very different kind. For Cottingham, *metanoia* means that 'For each of us there is a task we are called on to undertake. This is in one part a matter of purification, discarding the damaging and unfulfilling and self-oriented impulses, and in another part orienting ourselves towards an objective good. In so doing, we are finding the soul or the self we are meant to be.' If we turn away from this task of becoming who we ought to be, we in effect lose who we truly are. This is what Jesus warns when he says, 'For what shall it profit a man, if he shall gain the whole world, and lose himself or be cast away? Or what shall a man give in exchange for his soul?' (4:15). As Cottingham puts it, 'There is a core self that you're called on to be and no amount of success, money or whatever will compensate for the loss of that self.'

To say Jesus helped give birth to modern individualism is not to say Jesus promoted selfish egocentrism. The degree of our progress in self-development is measured by what difference it makes to how we act and in particular how we treat others. Still, it is not too fanciful to suggest that Jesus's emphasis on the individual helped create the conditions in which the wrong kind of egoism could flourish. That is no reason to reject the original teaching which gave rise to modern individualism. If anything, it is a reason to return more carefully to the source and to see more clearly the difference between egotistical self-cultivation and the more selfless alternative.

Of course, people ask what the point of *metanoia* is if there is no God or transcendent source of moral values. Why would we even be motivated to seek a change of heart without God? Are human beings even capable of it without divine assistance? We will consider all these questions in due course.

I've been somewhat surprised to find just how easy it is to describe Jesus's ideas about self-transformative *metanoia* without struggling to disentangle them from their usual religious context. That is not to say that Jesus saw himself as a secular moral teacher. It's not even clear that such a concept would have made sense in his time. Nonetheless, we can all understand what is noble about seeking to purify yourself of your baser desires, to empty yourself of egotistical thoughts and to focus on being a good person. We can also understand that a selfish life is not a desirable life, as it leaves us trapped in the world of our own unfulfillable desires. All this can be understood without God or heaven coming into it. Jesus's teachings about moral self-cultivation can be uprooted from the Jewish soil in which they grew and take root even in godless ground.

2

A QUESTION OF CHARACTER

In May 2018, a man was walking through the streets of Paris on his way to watch a football match. His attention was caught by a crowd of people looking up at the fourth floor of an apartment block. A small boy was desperately hanging on to a balcony edge, sometimes only by one hand. The man did not join the watchers. Instead, with incredible strength and dexterity, he scaled the building, scooped the boy up under his arm and placed him safely inside the balcony. The man, Mamadou Gassama, was an illegal migrant from Mali. Such was the admiration for his heroism that he was fast-tracked to French citizenship by President Macron and given a job in the fire department.

None of the reports mentioned Gassama's religion or which ethical theory, if any, he endorsed. That is because it was irrelevant. As he would later say, he had no time to think about what to do. He did not need to ask what Jesus or, more likely, Muhammad would have done (Mali is an overwhelmingly Islamic country). Nor would he have calculated which of the actions available to him was most likely to maximise the greatest happiness of the greatest number, or what principle of action could be willed as a universal law. He just acted.

That, I think, is precisely why we find Gassama and people like him so praiseworthy. Our admiration reflects an important truth about ethics. Truly good people are not guided by rules or principles. They do not need precepts to stop them murdering, thieving or lying. They don't do such things simply because they have strong moral characters and do what is right almost automatically.

This idea of moral character as the core of ethics is the central claim of what has come to be known as virtue ethics. It is most associated with Aristotle's articulation in the *Nicomachean Ethics* but was also advocated in some form by many ancient Greek and Roman thinkers. The focus in virtue ethics is not on lists of right and wrong actions but on the cultivation of moral character. Our primary moral task is to practise acting virtuously in all our daily actions so that doing the right thing becomes second nature. With continual practice we develop a kind of moral skill which enables us to see what is right and what is wrong. This same skill means that in the rare cases when killing, stealing or lying is actually the right thing to do, the person of good moral character will be willing to make an exception to the usual rule.

Jesus's emphasis on *metanoia* (change of heart and mind) and the reform of character chimes with this. When he attacks the scribes and Pharisees, both kinds of legal experts, he sounds very much like a virtue ethicist. He criticises them for turning what is no more than helpful rules of thumb into strict moral laws. He warns people against blindly following rules and calls upon them to focus instead on reforming their characters. And he shows a willingness to make exceptions to some rules when it is better to do so.

One of the most curious of Jesus's parables also makes more sense in the light of virtue ethics. The eponymous protagonist in the Parable of the Unjust Steward (7:40–50) is given notice by his boss. Unable to think of how else he might earn a living after this disgrace, he curries favour with the debtors by getting them to write their debt down so that 'they may receive me into their houses'. Far from being angry at this devaluation of his balance sheet, the boss actually praises the steward. Why would Jesus commend this?

The Gospel offers two explanations. The first seems cynically instrumental: 'Make to yourselves friends of the mammon of unrighteousness; that, when ye fail, they may receive you into everlasting habitations.' The New International Version translation makes this a little clearer, if not totally pellucid: 'Use worldly wealth to gain friends for yourselves, so that when it is gone, you will be welcomed into eternal dwellings.' It is not clear whether this means you should use money to make friends and influence people so that when the chips are down they will be there to help you; or whether using money in this way helps to gain entry to the afterlife. The former seems more likely, but neither interpretation sounds laudable or chimes with much else of what Jesus says about avoiding worldly goods and reputation.

The second reason for praising the steward, however, makes more sense. Jesus says, 'He that is faithful in that which is least is faithful also in much: and he that is unjust in the least is unjust also in much. If therefore ye have not been faithful in the unrighteous mammon, who will commit to your trust the

true riches?' (7:47–48). The idea here is one of the main principles of classical virtue ethics: if you do the right thing in all
small, everyday matters, you cultivate the habits to do the right
thing in rarer, more important situations. Hence the steward is
praised because he shows himself to be acting in such a way that
reflects a virtuous character: generous to the debtors and pru-
dent regarding his own interests. This is laudable even though
it actually means he breaks the rules. He is more faithful to
the virtues necessary to live well than he is to his strict duties.

The idea that we reveal our moral selves in all our actions
agrees with our intuitive judgements about which people are
truly good. Whenever we see someone behaving badly in one
respect, even a small one, we tend to doubt their character.
When we see an important person treating people in lower-
status jobs badly, we mistrust their bonhomie with their peers.
We tend to despise jobsworths who insist on sticking to the
precise letter of the rules when it is obvious that an exception
would be helpful and harmless. We also take seriously the
testimony of character witnesses, since we believe that there
is at least some general consistency in people's behaviour. If
someone is widely respected and taken to be trustworthy, that
is in itself a reason to respect and trust them (but not an infal-
lible one).

If we agree that character is the key to goodness, moral
teaching is not about the transfer of knowledge but about helping people with their own moral development. Aristotle, for
instance, emphasises the need for *phronesis*, usually translated
as 'practical wisdom'. This is the ability to make good moral
judgements – swiftly if necessary, carefully if not – on a case
by case basis.

If we acknowledge the need to attend to the specifics
of each situation we will always be wary of universal laws.

This means that when two people act differently, it doesn't necessarily follow that one is wrong. Take Jesus's complaint that when 'John the Baptist came neither eating bread nor drinking wine' people said, 'He hath a devil', but when Jesus came eating and drinking they said, 'Behold a gluttonous man, and a winebibber, a friend of publicans and sinners!' (11:37). On one level this is a simple attack on the hypocrisy of those who condemn some for fasting too much and then move the goalposts to criticise others for not fasting enough. But given that Jesus was baptised by his cousin John and never criticised him, it can't be that Jesus thought they ought to choose which of the two of them was fasting in the right way. Rather he is suggesting that there is more than one way to behave that is consistent with goodness. John wasn't wrong to fast as much as he did and Jesus was not wrong to fast less. Both manifested their goodness in different ways. It would be speculative to specify what that difference is, but it could be something along the lines that Jesus's mission required him to work among the people more than John and therefore he had to adopt a less austere lifestyle.

The ability to be sensitive to contextual differences requires acute moral judgement. This is a skill and so moral education has to be seen as a kind of training. This conception of moral training has been very common in many traditions across history and the globe. Early Buddhism used the language of skilful and unskilful actions rather than good and bad ones, emphasising the need to learn the art of acting ethically. Confucianism stresses the need to cultivate virtue. Xunzi says, 'When you observe goodness in others, then inspect yourself, desirous of studying it. When you observe badness in others, then examine yourself, fearful of discovering it. If you find goodness in your person, then approve of yourself, desirous of holding firm to it. If you find badness in your person, then reproach yourself, regarding it as calamity.'[1]

But how do you teach ethical mastery? Parables are one very effective tool. Take the most famous parable of all, the story of the Good Samaritan (9:14–24). Jesus tells a legal scholar to follow the commandment that 'Thou shalt love thy neighbour as thyself.'[2] The scholar replies, 'And who is my neighbour?' Jesus answers with the story of a man who was attacked and left half dead by thieves. A priest and a Levite (an assistant to a priest) both passed by the man without helping. He was eventually saved by a Samaritan, someone from a distant tribe. 'Which now of these three, thinkest thou, was neighbour unto him that fell among the thieves?' asks Jesus. 'He that shewed mercy on him,' replies the scholar, drawing out the conclusion for himself. Jesus confirms he is correct by saying, 'Go, and do thou likewise.'

At no point in this exchange does Jesus clearly articulate a moral principle. That is not because it is too obvious to state. Jesus is deliberately opaque. Although it is commonly believed that Jesus taught in parables to make his ideas easily understandable to all, the Gospel makes it clear that the intention was the exact opposite (7:10). Jesus tells his disciples that he teaches in parables because the masses 'seeing see not; and hearing they hear not, neither do they understand. For this people's heart is waxed gross, and their ears are dull of hearing, and their eyes they have closed; lest at any time they should see with their eyes and hear with their ears, and should understand with their heart, and should be converted.' Jesus explains the meaning of the parables only in private to a select group: 'But when they were alone, he expounded all things to his disciples' (7:27).

Jesus teaches in parables because they require the listener or reader to complete the argument for themselves. If someone is not able to do this, they are not ready for the message the parable contains. It is like Confucius's principle: 'When I have presented one corner of a subject to any one, and he cannot from it learn the other three, I do not repeat my lesson.'³ If you require everything to be spelled out you haven't yet learned enough.

Merely stating moral principles is no use for moral development because to be good you need something other than knowledge of facts, and doing the right thing requires more than having correct information. Moral wisdom is more a kind of *know-how* than *know-that*. To be good, it is never enough to have good theories about what is right. It is not even necessary to have a moral theory. Indeed, one characteristic of many morally admirable people is that when asked why they act as they do they can give no theoretical answer at all. Like Mamadou Gassama, they feel they can't but help respond with kindness and they just don't understand callousness and cruelty. A good person doesn't need moral rules to be spelled out for them. 'Those who don't steal don't need precepts against theft,' said the Zen master Bankei Yōtaku.⁴ The flipside of this is that a bad person cannot be taught how to be good simply by being given moral precepts, no matter how sound they are.

Parables were not the only means Jesus used to present his moral teaching. Perhaps even more importantly, throughout his life Jesus is presented as an example for others to follow. When he washes his disciples' feet he states plainly, 'For I have given you an example, that ye should do as I have done to you' (5:29). He also explicitly tells his followers that one of the most important ways in which they can spread the word is to be examples themselves. 'Let your light so shine before men, that they may see your good works,' he says (2:19). This idea is captured in one of his most famous images: 'Ye are the light of the world.

A city that is set on an hill cannot be hid. Neither do men light a candle, and put it under a bushel, but on a candlestick; and it giveth light unto all that are in the house' (2:16).

Jesus is perhaps at his most exemplary during his trial and execution. He endures mockery and mistreatment without reaction, showing no malice towards those who abuse and kill him. He remains dignified and calm, refusing to sink to the level of his executors. This example is even more powerful without a resurrection. To maintain one's virtue with no prospect of reward is more admirable than to do so temporarily knowing that you'll be paid back in time, as will those who abuse you.

Brian Mountford agrees that the crucifixion's power is somewhat lessened by the resurrection: 'The spiritual and moral heart of the Gospel is expressed not so much in Easter Day as in all that goes before. If you haven't got the message by the time Jesus is nailed to the cross, you're never going to. In telling the story, our contemporary culture has concentrated on everything being lovely on Easter Day, and decorated it with kitsch – eggs and bunnies – whereas the power of the story is in Jesus's resilience and integrity as he walks through the valley of the shadow of death.'

This might be a more authentically Christian view than you'd think. The earliest of the four Gospels, Mark, didn't pay much attention to the resurrection. It originally ended at chapter 16 verse 8, without any sightings of the risen Christ. Mary Magdalene, Mary the mother of James (not Jesus) and Salome go to Jesus's tomb and see 'a young man sitting on the right side, clothed in a long white garment'. He told them, 'Be not affrighted: Ye seek Jesus of Nazareth, which was crucified: he is risen; he is not here: behold the place where they laid him. But go your way, tell his disciples and Peter that he goeth before

you into Galilee: there shall ye see him, as he said unto you.'
What follows was added later.

Of course, this passage still proclaims that Christ is risen
and that people will encounter him, but it leaves mysterious
the nature of that resurrection and the encounters to come.
The last sentence is not one of reassurance but of fear: 'And
they went out quickly, and fled from the sepulchre; for they
trembled and were amazed: neither said they any thing to any
man; for they were afraid.' This more enigmatic ending makes
Jesus's death on the cross more real than the one in which he
miraculously springs back to life.

Experience confirms that the absence of resurrection is
precisely what makes the example of self-sacrifice so powerful. War memorials in particular bring this home to me. Take
Mark Wallinger's *Folk Stones*, which consists of 19,240 pebbles
set into the ground in a square formation, each numbered to
represent the men killed on the first day of the Battle of the
Somme in 1916. I've seen it several times in Folkestone, the
town where I grew up. I find it profoundly moving because it
captures the immense loss and waste of life. The battle made
each of those soldiers as lifeless as the stone that represents
them. That's why we feel the need to honour and remember
their ultimate sacrifice and are humbled by their example.
Such monuments bring home the seriousness of Jesus's words
'Greater love hath no man than this, that a man lay down his
life for his friends' (2:44).

Memorials and monuments are not the only manifesta-
tion of the importance of great moral exemplars. In 2019,
for instance, people around the world expressed admiration
for how the New Zealand prime minister, Jacinda Ardern,
responded with compassion and dignity to the killing of
fifty-one people in and around a Christchurch mosque. She

understood the importance of showing by example how a society can refuse to take the bait of hatred and can instead come together to resist those who would divide it. We also appreciate quotidian moral exemplars. I am frequently shamed by how kind, non-judgemental and generous other people are in daily life compared to myself.

The importance of moral exemplars is reflected in society's focus on 'role models'. We have an intuitive sense that the behavior of the people we look up to affects the behaviour of others. Think of how significant it was when celebrities like Angelina Jolie took a stand against 'blood diamonds' extracted by slave labour. When even someone associated with bling says no to a rock, people take notice. Conversely, influential people can legitimise bad behaviour. The way in which Donald Trump modelled racism and misogyny during his presidential campaign and in office is deplorable.

The idea that a good person acts as an exemplary beacon for others is found time and again in the world's great moral traditions. Akeel Bilgrami has argued that Mahatma Gandhi implicitly endorses the principle that 'When one chooses for oneself, one sets an example to everyone.'[5] In the *Bhagavad-Gītā*, it is written, 'Whatsoever a great man does, the same is done by others as well. Whatever standard he sets, the world follows.'[6] The *Bhagavad-Gītā* is part of the fifth to second-century-BCE Indian epic the *Mahābhārata*, which also says, 'If the king regards it, righteousness becomes regarded everywhere.'[7] Confucius advised rulers that if they guide the people with virtue, 'the people will have a sense of shame and will rectify themselves'.[8] Buddhism also has a strong tradition of seeing the enlightened bodhisattva and the Buddha himself as someone who transmits and spreads virtue by example. 'The fragrance of virtue o'ersweeps the wind, all pervasive is virtue of the good,' says the *Dhammapāda*.[9] And the Qur'ān describes the prophet Muhammad as 'an excellent model'.[10]

Jesus himself is portrayed as having a confident and charismatic presence which impresses everyone who comes into contact with him, even his enemies, who are frightened by his power. When he calls his disciples they follow without question. The manner of his speech and behaviour exudes a kind of authority. Early in his mission he is reported to have 'taught them as one that had authority, and not as the scribes'. (3:32).

In the Gospels, Jesus's authority came not just from his example but from his performance of numerous miracles. But in many ways this flaunting of a divine mandate jars with the central message we have in his teachings. In one key passage he scolds the people for wanting miraculous signs, telling them they do not need them because all the signs they need are around them. He goes so far as to call them 'an evil generation' because they seek a sign (10:45–47). That is one reason why many prefer to see the miracle stories as allegorical tales of spiritual healing rather than historical records of physical cures.

If being good is a kind of skill, then it makes sense that we can develop it by emulating others. This is after all how we acquire most skills. Musicians copy their teachers, actors study other actors, craftspeople usually learn by apprenticeship. In each case it is never enough simply to be *told* what to do, you have to *see* how it is done and practise yourself. This emulation cannot simply be copying, since part of what we are trying to emulate is having a sensitivity to the needs of every specific person and situation. As the theologian Richard Burridge put it, what matters is not impersonating Jesus but imitating him, which is unavoidable today because we face many situations that Jesus of Nazareth never had to.[11]

No matter how differently Christians conceive the divine status of Jesus, all take him as some kind of example to be followed. You see this in the popularity of the acronym WWJD (What would Jesus do?), which many sport on wristbands, belts and even tattoos. Nonetheless, Jesus is perhaps most attractive to the non-religious as an example to others. 'The idea that Jesus is someone be imitated belongs to the part of Christianity that focuses on the human Jesus,' says Clare Carlisle, a philosopher who is not a Christian herself but has a religious sensibility. 'Obviously there's the idea that Jesus brings salvation, and the claim that Jesus is divine. But seeing Jesus as a model to imitate is the ethical side of Christianity.'

The view of Jesus as a model to imitate was reinforced in a dialogue between the Benedictine monk Fr Laurence Freeman and the 14th Dalai Lama. 'Jesus is a model for how to live my life,' said Freeman. 'I consider him a universal teacher, a person of integrity with natural authority who embodies the truth.' It is significant that when Freeman thinks of Jesus in this way, the question of his divinity becomes irrelevant. 'I think of Jesus as a human being, a historical person later understood as the Son of God,' he said. 'I relate to him as a natural Jesus, an extraordinary human being, one of the few who have become universal teachers.' This human Jesus has the potential to become a moral teacher for all. When Freeman made these remarks, his Buddhist interlocutor was able to reply enthusiastically, 'Wonderful, wonderful, that's really my own understanding of Jesus.'[12]

One neglected feature of Jesus's example is that he models the need for work on the self. The supposed divinity of Christ tends to make us think of his goodness as being inherent, but this is not how he is portrayed in the Gospels. For sure he had a precocious wisdom, as demonstrated by his discussions with learned doctors in the temple at the age of twelve: 'all that heard him were astonished at his understanding and answers. And Jesus increased in wisdom and stature' (1:9). And yet he did not begin his ministry until he was thirty. Even someone as morally gifted as Jesus needed time for his wisdom to grow, and that wisdom needed constant nurturing. Jesus often goes away alone to pray, which we might understand in secular terms as a kind of meditation. Jesus models the idea that goodness is not simply a quality we do or do not have but one that needs to be developed.

Jesus also shows that this work on the self is never completed, that no one can ever claim to be truly good. 'Why callest thou me good?' Jesus asked someone who addressed him as 'Good Master'. In the original Gospels Jesus says, 'there is none good but one, that is, God.' In *The Godless Gospel* this becomes the plainer 'there is none good' (6:13). Jesus here echoes Socrates, who claimed to know nothing. The fact that he knew this is what made him the wisest man in Athens, according to the Oracle at Delphi. Similarly, the suggestion in the Gospel is that in order to be as good as we can be we have to know that we can never be fully good. If even that great moral exemplar Jesus does not merit the accolade of good, no one does. Understanding that makes the need to work on improving our characters even more important, much more so than memorising rules and following them.

3

A REVOLUTION OF THE LAW

During my early teens I was a committed Christian. I had been brought up to believe in God and I found it odd that the older I got, the less people around me appeared to give even a moment's thought to their ultimate purpose or destiny. However, my existential seriousness was to be my faith's undoing. The Christian story seemed increasingly implausible, its theology incredible. Gradually my assumption that there was a god was replaced by an equally strong conviction that there wasn't. Now, having been a convinced (but not dogmatic) atheist for all of my adult life, I am sometimes surprised to be reminded of the seriousness of my religious youth. Remembering how things that once seemed obvious to me now seem just as obviously absurd is a good reminder not to be too quick to dismiss those whose views appear ridiculous.

For a while at least I attended Christian Union meetings at

my school. I only know this because I remember one occasion when an earnest evangelical boy shared a dilemma with the group. He was torn about taking a weekend job that required him to work on Sundays, Christianity's sabbath. He didn't want the wages to buy frivolous things. His single mother was struggling and he would have liked to help contribute to the family budget. But at the time everyone seemed to think it was a difficult choice. Since I had a weekend job myself, the debate made me question my own piety. It seems obvious to me now that the spirit of Jesus's teaching would have approved of the boy's sacrificial act of love. All the hand-wringing was a sign of how many Christians have failed to take on board their founder's teachings about all religious laws, not only those governing the sabbath.

Jesus's repeated calls to follow the spirit rather than the letter of the old laws is intimately connected to his ideas about moral self-development. A person of good moral character never blindly follows rules but is sensitive to the needs of every situation. For example, on one occasion his hungry disciples pluck ears of corn, thresh them with their bare hands and eat them. This is on the sabbath, when work is forbidden. When challenged by the Pharisees, Jesus says, 'The sabbath was made for man, and not man for the sabbath' (10:17–26). The purpose of religious laws is to help human beings to be their best selves. Once these laws become fixed, people tend to forget this and think of the laws in purely mechanistic terms, as though all that matters is that we follow them.

That is precisely what the Pharisees do. Such is the inflexible strictness of their interpretation of the law that they even object to the healing of the sick on the sabbath. Jesus calls them hypocrites, saying that none of them would hesitate to 'loose his ox or his ass from the stall, and lead him away to watering' or pull a sheep out from a hole. The double standard is clear enough. But there is a deeper sense of hypocrisy at work. To uphold the law with literal rigidity creates a contradiction between the moral purpose of the law and its actual consequences. If moral laws cease to guide us towards our highest selves they cease to have their proper function and so actually undermine their own purpose. For instance, when we preach the morality of compassion and forbid the practice of it by our moral laws, we become hypocrites.

The way the story continues underscores this message. Jesus is said to be angry at the Pharisees, 'being grieved for the hardness of their hearts'. Their major failing is a lack of sympathy, allowing rules to trump the heart and fellow feeling. The fact that the Pharisees are shown to plot against Jesus in reaction to his teaching only emphasises how those who most rigidly follow the law are on the side of evil, not good.

We need to be careful not to overstate Jesus's opposition to rules. *Metanoia* is a change of heart, not of laws or principles. Jesus's attack on excessive rigidity occurred in a very particular historical context. 'First-century Palestine was a post-exilic, post-Maccabean revolution society,' says Elizabeth Oldfield, director of Theos. Oldfield was been a reliably interesting interlocutor over the years, equally committed to her deeply held beliefs, rational debate and giving others a sympathetic hearing. 'The Jews were desperately trying to hold their minority identity together in a very pluralistic, syncretistic pagan context. One of the ways they're doing that, in a way minority groups often do, is to double down on identity signifiers: food laws, no intermarriage, hand-washing rituals. One way of reading the Gospels is Jesus going around almost impishly turning that upside down, challenging those very understandable ways that identity hardens under pressure.'

In this interpretation, Jesus is to a certain extent exaggerating his rejection of the letter of the law as a necessary corrective to the disproportionate importance that the old laws came to have at the time. He's not so much rejecting the law as correcting it. Jesus is clear that his interpretations of the old laws are in full accordance with their true meaning and purpose. 'I am not come to destroy, but to fulfil' the law, he says. '... one jot or one tittle shall in no wise pass from the law, till all be fulfilled' (2:21).

To many this sounds disingenuous. How can you both turn a tradition upside down and claim to be continuing it at the same time? Actually, most revolutions of thought occur within traditions. Shankaracharya, Kapila and other key thinkers of the orthodox schools of Indian philosophy, for instance, have all been people who claimed to be doing nothing more than upholding the truth revealed in the ancient *Vedas*. Yet their interpretations have been so diverse and often original that in practice they brought about huge changes.

Likewise, Jesus transformed the moral teachings of Judaism, but he did not transform it into something else. Take as an analogy the kinds of radical innovations of the great jazz musicians. The likes of Charlie Parker completely changed jazz when they developed bebop. But they did not change jazz *into something else*, something that was not jazz, like heavy metal or baroque chamber music. In contrast, in recent years the Chinese Communist Party has transformed communism into a form of state-controlled capitalism that only they believe (or claim) is still communism at all. Jesus clearly saw himself as *transforming the law* rather than *transforming the law into something else*.

Several passages reinforce this interpretation. One of the more enigmatic is 'every scribe which is instructed unto the Kingdom of Heaven is like unto a man that is an householder, which bringeth forth out of his treasure things new and old'

(9:12). The idea here is that to follow Jesus's teachings, the best of both old and new are required. The old law is an antique treasure which must be cherished and valued. The new jewel is the insight that the best way to honour the law is to follow its spirit and not be trapped in dogmatic adherence to ritual practices.

It is in part because Jesus takes the law for granted that we struggle to find a clear and complete moral system in his teachings. 'He's not saying, "Here's how to be a good person,"' says Karen Kilby. Kilby was president of the Society for the Study of Theology when it made the remarkably ecumenical decision to invite me to address its annual conference. The occasion provided yet more evidence that respectful and intelligent dialogue is possible across the atheist/believer divide, if only people have the right attitude.

'I think he assumes that his audience already has the law to live by and so already has a pattern of life,' continues Kilby. 'Within that pattern there are certain things he's radicalising and challenging. To me he's more of a disrupter than a presenter.' It's certainly striking how on several occasions when Jesus is asked what people should do, he simply refers them back to the law. 'What is written in the law? how readest thou?' (9:15) and 'have ye not read in the law?' (10:20).

It is not therefore a matter of whether the law is to be followed or not – Jesus is clear that it must be. The question is what following the law means. For Jesus it is about respecting its spirit, and also respecting the humanity of those it was designed for. This more humane approach to the law is illustrated towards the end of Jesus's life when some of John the Baptist's disciples asked Jesus why his disciples didn't fast as often as the Pharisees. Jesus replied, 'Can the children of the bridechamber mourn, as long as the bridegroom is with them?

but the days will come, when the bridegroom shall be taken from them, and then shall they fast in those days' (10:40–41). To fast in accordance with the law when Jesus had so little time with them would not respect Jesus as valuable in himself, to be treasured while he was still alive. To put the laws on fasting first would put ritual over humanity.

What is remarkable about Jesus's transformation of the law is that while it might superficially appear to make it less rigorous, it actually makes it more demanding. It is easy enough to avoid murdering someone, but Jesus says that rage is itself sinful, even when not murderous: 'whosoever is angry with his brother without a cause shall be in danger of the judgment' (2:24). Adultery remains forbidden but it is not enough to refrain from fornication: 'whosoever looketh on a woman to lust after her hath committed adultery with her already in his heart' (2:27). Little wonder, then, that Jesus says, 'your righteousness must exceed the righteousness of the scribes and Pharisees' (2:23). The requirement is to be better than those who go through the motions of following the rules and to instead nurture true purity and virtue of intent. That is how deep *metanoia* must go.

The context of Jesus's teaching is therefore clearly a religious one. He was a Jew advocating reform of Jewish law, not someone trying to establish an alternative to it. Nonetheless, his message about going beyond the law has secular resonance. It's not a matter of taking on excessive religious guilt or feeling dreadful because we have the odd lustful or violent thought. It's about appreciating the difference between those who keep their noses clean out of purely prudential self-interest and those who are motivated to behave well. Only the latter inspire real respect and affection.

Jesus's knowledge, understanding and respect for the Hebrew law is most evident when the Pharisees and scribes chastise his disciples for eating without washing their hands, on religious rather than hygiene grounds (10:27–33). Jesus's sophisticated response draws their attention to the fact that this is merely a tradition and not prescribed by the moral law at all. He then criticises them for upholding other principles on the basis of traditions that he says go against the moral law to honour thy mother and father. 'Ye hypocrites, This people draweth nigh unto me with their mouth, and honoureth me with their lips; but their heart is far from me, For laying aside the commandment, ye hold the tradition of men, as the washing of pots and cups: and many other such like things ye do ... Full well ye reject the commandment, that ye may keep your own tradition.' He thus damns them as hypocrites.

This is a passage which the Christian churches would do well to attend to more. So much religious practice is mere tradition and not mandated by the Bible. Indeed, much of Christian practice actually goes against the Gospels. Jesus clearly condemned riches yet there are churches around the world full of ornate and expensive adornments, furnishings, vessels and objects. It is easy to imagine Jesus seeing all this today and saying, 'For laying aside the commandment, ye hold the tradition of men'.

The second key message in his response to the Pharisees is that once again they are prioritising outward show and performance over the more important holistic reality. 'Now do ye Pharisees make clean the outside of the cup and the platter; but your inward part is full of ravening and wickedness.' Jesus goes further and insists that it is what takes place inside that matters and that if this is right, nothing external can tarnish us. 'There is nothing from without a man, that entering into him can defile him: Because it entereth not into his heart, but into the belly'. We are made morally unclean by the bad things that we do, things that issue from a corrupted mind. 'The things which come out of him, those are they that defile the man' (10:34).

To ensure that we do not become too concerned with the outward show of goodness, it is best not to make any unnecessary outward show at all. In the Sermon on the Mount Jesus lists three things that you should do as discreetly as possible: giving alms, praying and fasting (3:1–3). If you fast, for example, don't go around looking grim and pale, telling people how hard it is. Try to look normal and don't even mention you're fasting.

Jesus's teaching here is unequivocally critical of those who give money to charity in order for their name to be emblazoned on buildings, or even listed in programmes or put on the backs of seats. The usual defence for this kind of egotism is practical: recognising benefactors makes them more likely to give and making a show of philanthropy puts more pressure on others to do the same. That's the rationale behind Bill Gates and Warren Buffett's initiative 'The Giving Pledge', which is 'a commitment by the world's wealthiest individuals and families to dedicate the majority of their wealth to giving back'. Its aim is 'to help shift the social norms of philanthropy … and inspire people to give more, establish their giving plans sooner, and give in smarter ways'.

If your goal is creating as much 'social value' as possible through philanthropy this seems entirely reasonable. But Jesus of Nazareth was no utilitarian, someone who believes we ought to do whatever it takes to increase the number of lives saved or decrease the amount of suffering in the world. He commends these as important goals but puts the duty to act with integrity and a good will first. So even if it could be proved that following his injunction to give discreetly would lead to less giving overall, we have no reason to think he would have changed his advice. As John Cottingham writes,

'The overriding imperatives enjoined by God in the Judaeo-Christian Scriptures are not utilitarian ones but moral ones, in the strong sense of duties, summed up in the paramount duty to love one's neighbour as oneself.'[1]

Jesus is primarily concerned neither with following strict laws nor with doing whatever it takes to produce the best outcomes. His focus is on our becoming the best versions of ourselves that we can be. How far we have succeeded is demonstrated not by declarations of piety but by what we do. Many of Jesus's stories ram home the message that actions speak louder than words. In the Parable of the Two Sons (9:3–7), a man asks his sons to go to work in his vineyard. The first says he won't 'but afterward he repented, and went', while the second says he will 'and went not'. Jesus asked, 'Whether of them twain did the will of his father?' The answer is, of course, the first.

Jesus often criticises those whose actions do not match their words more than he praises those who live by their beliefs. It is as though the good need no praise as they are already thriving. It is the lost sheep who need attention, not the saved. The story of the Good Samaritan, for instance, condemns two people – the priest and the Levite – and praises only one (9:14–24). Note how the story ends with Jesus saying, 'Go, and do thou likewise.' The injunction is always to *do*.

His most angry denunciation of hypocrites comes in one of his long rants against the scribes and Pharisees (11:39–53). It is full of invective against those who preach one thing and do another, who have the outer appearance of goodness and 'for a pretence make long prayer' but lack true goodness. His words are full of vivid, memorable images and phrases. He calls them 'blind guides, which strain at a gnat, and swallow a camel', people who 'make clean the outside of the cup and of the platter, but within they are full of extortion and excess'.

He compares them to 'whited sepulchres, which indeed appear beautiful outward, but are within full of dead men's bones, and of all uncleanness'.

Actions matter not because what we do is more important than who we are but because what we do reveals and expresses who we are – an echo of virtue ethics, which says that if you become good you do good, and being good is about how you are. Jesus says that if you truly listen to him and follow his teaching, you will be like 'a wise man, which built an house, and digged deep, and laid the foundation on a rock: and the flood arose, the winds blew, and the stream beat vehemently upon that house, and could not shake it: for it was founded upon a rock' (3:30). Your integrity will be unshakeable and you will act accordingly. If not, you will be like 'a foolish man, which built his house upon the sand: And the rain descended, and the floods came, and the winds blew, and beat upon that house; and it fell: and great was the fall of it.' (3:31) A similar idea is expressed when Jesus draws out the moral of the Second Parable of the Fig Tree: 'A good man out of the good treasure of the heart bringeth forth good things: and an evil man out of the evil treasure bringeth forth evil things' (9:31).

Jesus's repeated criticism of people who follow rituals but lack compassion and true goodness is part and parcel of prioritising the link between pure heart and pure action. Religious rituals break this connection, introducing formal requirements that end up becoming more important than either the motivation to do good or the actual doing of it. That is partly why he prohibits taking any oaths (another clear teaching most Christians have ignored), saying, 'Swear not at all; neither by heaven Nor by the earth: neither by Jerusalem. Neither shalt thou swear by thy head.' Rather 'let your communication be, Yea, yea; Nay, nay: for whatsoever is more than these cometh of evil' (2:33–34). The message here is that for a good person their word is enough; for a bad one, adding an oath does nothing to make them stay true to their word.

The essence of this teaching can be captured in the slogan 'deeds not words'. It is not what we say that proves our goodness but what we do. Jesus expresses this most memorably in an image used more than once: 'Know them by their fruits' (3:25). The Second Parable of the Fig Tree extends the metaphor (9:27–30). A man has a fig tree planted but after three years it still hasn't produced fruit. He asks 'the dresser of his vineyard', as the King James Bible beautifully calls him, to cut it down 'for the tree is known by his fruit'. But the dresser asks to give it another year, 'till I shall dig about it, and dung it: And if it bear fruit, well: and if not, then after that thou shalt cut it down'. Here, the idea that we are what we do comes with the threat that some kind of judgement will befall us if we don't prove ourselves by our deeds.

'Deeds not words' has the corollary 'deeds not creeds'. This message is often lost by later followers who emphasised doctrinal orthodoxy over moral practice. They would do well to remember a slogan (falsely) attributed to St Francis of Assisi: 'Preach the Gospel at all times. Use words if necessary.' For the church to become more relevant to people today it could do worse than preach less and focus more on offering an example of a higher, more selfless life.

There are a few complications to the simple 'deeds not words' message. One is that our words are among our fruits. Hence Jesus also says, 'every idle word that men shall speak, they shall give account thereof. For by thy words thou shalt be justified, and by thy words thou shalt be condemned' (9:32). Words are not irrelevant. Speech can be hateful, inciteful, spiteful, malicious. Certain forms of speech are deeds as well as words, because there are things we do with words: we embarrass, we slander, we silence, we humiliate.

Another complication is the baffling story about the fig tree Jesus comes across on the way back from Bethany when he is hungry (9:25–26). When he examines the tree he finds it to be without fruit, which should not be surprising since we are told 'the time of figs was not yet'. Nonetheless, Jesus curses the tree, saying, 'No man eat fruit of thee hereafter for ever.' This has always been a difficult passage to make sense of. It would seem to suggest that though we are to be judged by our fruits, that judgement could be grossly unfair. It could be a hyperbolic way of showing us that time is not on our side and the promise of fruit to come is not enough. Perhaps, however, it is simply a rare glimpse of Jesus's human frailty. It is not often I can say that Jesus reminds me of myself, but an outburst of unjustified petulant impatience when hungry seems to me to be a very human reaction.

Although Jesus's moral teachings are firmly located within the Jewish tradition, it is once again striking how well they translate into the purely secular. His approach to rules and principles helps illuminate and possibly improve one of the most famous secular moral theories: the deontological system of the eighteenth-century Prussian Immanuel Kant. Kant's ethics focuses on duty, which is the meaning of the Greek root word *deon*. Although Christian ethics is often categorised as deontological, Kantian ethics is often associated with precisely the kind of rigidity of rule that Jesus criticised – in large part due to the claim made by one of Kant's contemporaries, Benjamin Constant, that he believed 'it would be a crime to lie to a murderer who asked us whether a friend of ours whom he is pursuing has taken refuge in our house'. In reply Kant maintained, 'To be truthful (honest) in all declarations is therefore a sacred command of reason prescribing unconditionally, one not to be restricted by any conveniences.'[2]

Scholars contest whether Kant's response effectively confirmed Constant's charge. Whatever we make of that, it would be wrong to see Kant's deontological approach purely as an advocacy of universal, exceptionless laws. One of his key ideas has nothing to do with rigid rules and is consistent with Jesus's teaching. 'It is impossible to think of anything in the world, or indeed even beyond it, that could be considered good without limitation except a good will,' he wrote. Even if a person were unable to achieve anything good, if they were sincerely intent on doing the right thing, 'like a jewel' their good will 'would still sparkle all by itself'.[3] His idea is reminiscent of the story that Jesus tells of the widow who gives two mites to the synagogue treasury, a tiny amount compared to the gifts of the rich (6:8–9). She is praised for giving more than those who have more, for 'she of her penury hath cast in all the living that she had, even all her living'. Her sincere good will counts for more than the actual money itself.

For Kant, 'a will unconditionally good' would always follow the 'supreme law: act always on that maxim whose universality as a law you can at the same time will'.[4] In other words, do as you would have others do. This sounds very much like the golden rule of Jesus: 'as ye would that men should do to you, do ye also to them likewise' (2:38). While Kant thought that this meant following universal laws, Jesus explicitly rejected following laws to the letter rather than to the spirit. But if we take seriously Jesus's claim that he came not to destroy but to fulfil the law this difference becomes less significant. Indeed, it could be argued that it is precisely an attention to the 'spirit of the law' that Kant needs to save his system from absurdity. A person who has Kant's treasured good will would never follow a law blindly, like the Pharisees, but would pay attention to the purpose and motivation behind the law.

A second aspect of Kant's deontological ethics echoes the teachings of Jesus. A person, said Kant, 'is not a thing, and hence not something that can be used *merely* as a means, but must in all his actions always be regarded as an end in itself'.[5] To use another human being as a mere tool is always wrong. We must always respect the humanity of others.

Jesus never explicitly advocates a principle like this, but the way in which he prioritises the spirit of the law over the letter fits this way of thinking. Jesus puts human well-being above rule-following. When the Pharisees put the letter of the law above the needs of human beings they are guilty of precisely the crime Kant described: they are treating humans as a means to fulfil the law, not respecting their value as ends in themselves.

Jesus is clearest on this when he attacks the experts on religious law which the King James Bible misleadingly calls 'lawyers'. He says they 'lade men with burdens grievous to be borne'. When they instruct in the law they are not interested in making people understand what their moral purpose is, they merely want them to obey. Hence they 'have taken away the key of knowledge'. At the same time, these lawyers 'touch not the burdens with one of your fingers'. For them, following the law requires no sacrifice, as their work and status make it easy. And because they do not concern themselves with the inner meaning of the law, it is enough for them to go through the motions without worrying about the deeper demands of the law to serve and respect others. Jesus's criticism of these lawyers could not be more fierce: 'Ye serpents, ye generation of vipers, how can ye escape damnation?' (11:54–56).

Jesus was fully justified in his anger. Think about how doctrinal orthodoxy has been used as a reason to torture and even kill people over the years. It is shocking that the Christian church has so often been guilty of just the kind of rules-first dogmatism without compassion that Jesus so clearly detested.

The simple slogans 'deeds not words' and 'follow the spirit of the law rather than its letter' fail to capture how nuanced and radical his revolution of the law is. At the root of Jesus's moral teaching is the need to cultivate a good will. Such thinking generates law-like principles because it requires a degree of consistency in how we behave, so we don't hold others to rules we do not ourselves follow. These rules should never be absolute, because compassion and sensitivity to human need require more sensitivity than rigid laws can provide. This seemingly flexible approach to moral law is actually more demanding than a rigid one as it requires more than just ticking the boxes of 'right' actions. It demands instead a continual effort to act out of good will, in good faith and in good heart. True Christian morality is not a long list of dos and don'ts. It's a challenge to respond with love to the specific needs of every individual situation.

4

THE RENUNCIATION
OF THE WORLD

Once Jorge Mario Bergoglio had been elected head of the Roman Catholic Church in 2013, he swiftly became known for his solidarity with the poor. He chose to live not in the papal apartments of the Apostolic Palace but in the Vatican's guesthouse, where visiting clerics live communally. He declared a Jubilee Year from December 2015 dedicated to the theme of God's mercy, which he considers to be Jesus's most powerful message, and which was part of a wider attempt to encourage the church to focus more on issues of social justice and poverty.

Pope Francis's predecessor, Joseph Ratzinger, chose Benedict as his papal name. St Benedict founded the Benedictine order of monks, which was committed to simple living. The brothers were prohibited from owning private possessions and shared all the daily tasks of cooking, cleaning, cultivating food and tending to animals. It was only when Pope Benedict retired, however, that truly Benedictine winds blew though the corridors of the Vatican again.

To anyone who knew only the Gospels and nothing of church history, the idea that the head of the church would be anything other than ascetic might seem bizarre. It is very clear that Jesus profoundly renounced both worldly goods and power. The nature of his path was clear from the start of his mission, when we are told: 'He returned from Jordan, and went into the wilderness, And in those days he did eat nothing: and when they were ended, he afterward hungered. And when had ended all the temptation, Jesus returned into Galilee' (1:11–12).

This short passage frames Jesus as an archetype that everyone at the time would have recognised: the ascetic renunciant who turns away from the material comforts of the world in search of a higher good and purpose. Across the ancient Mediterranean, sages and philosophers almost universally agreed that the good life required placing no value on worldly possessions or concerns. They differed only in the extremes of their austerity. The Roman Stoic Seneca, for example, taught that we should not be attached to worldly possessions although he was very wealthy himself. He did not consider this hypocritical because he thought that as long as you relate to your possessions with indifference it doesn't matter whether you have them or not.

The ancient Greek Cynic Diogenes would not have been impressed by Seneca's flexibility. 'It is the privilege of the gods to want nothing, and of godlike men to want little,' he wrote. His namesake Diogenes Laertius tells a wonderful story of how Plato spotted Diogenes washing lettuces and said to him, 'If you courted Dionysus [the God of wine and revelry], you would not be washing lettuces.' His reply was, 'And if you washed lettuces, you wouldn't have courted Dionysus.'¹ In other words, if you practise simple living, you will not feel the need to pursue fleeting physical pleasures.

Several passages in the Gospel tell us that Jesus was not as much of an ascetic as John the Baptist. But even though he was indulgent by the standards of John, he was most certainly a renunciant by the standards of today, something that modern followers of his moral teaching find all too convenient to overlook. The nature of his asceticism seems close to the precepts laid out in *The Rule of Benedict*, which was strict without being excessively austere. The monks ate only two meals a day, except when fasting, and were allowed a choice of two dishes at each meal. They were also allowed half a pint of wine a day but not to get drunk, which would have been difficult anyway given the comparative weakness of the wine at that time. St Benedict wrote that he hoped 'to establish nothing harsh, nothing burdensome' but warned that some things would be 'set forth somewhat strictly for the correction of vice or the preservation of charity' and that prospective monks should not 'in fear and terror flee back from the way of salvation of which the beginning cannot but be a narrow entrance'.²

Monastic vows of poverty chime with Jesus's unambiguous teaching that wealth is incompatible with goodness. 'But woe unto you that are rich! for ye have received your consolation,' he says. 'Woe unto you that are full! for ye shall hunger (2:12). Jesus applies this principle to the rich young man who asks him how he can 'inherit life' (6:12–18). Jesus first tells him he has to obey the commandments, one of many reminders that he had not abandoned his tradition. When the man confirms that he has done this since he was a child, Jesus says, 'go thy way, sell whatsoever thou hast, and give to the poor: and come, take up the cross, and follow me.' The young man was 'sorrowful:

for he had great possessions' and walked away. Jesus was quick to make an example of him: 'How hardly shall they that have riches enter into the Kingdom of Heaven!'

The moral of the story is unequivocal: 'it is easier for a camel to go through the eye of a needle, than for a rich man to enter into the Kingdom of Heaven' (6:19). The fact that he was not pointing a finger only at the *very* rich is made clear by the reaction of the apostles. They were 'astonished out of measure' and asked, 'Who then can be saved?' Jesus's reply, 'all things are possible', provides some hope but it certainly doesn't imply that entry to the Kingdom of Heaven will be for all (6:20–21). If we took Jesus's moral teaching seriously we could never be morally comfortable with being materially comfortable.

I find it extraordinary how many Christians try to dilute this message. One particularly desperate manoeuvre is to quibble with the translations of texts that seem crystal clear. For example, one hypothesis is that the word *kamêlos* (camel) was a mistranscription of *kamilos* (rope). Even if this is true, the central message remains clearly and undeniably the same, since getting a rope through a needle's eye is nigh on impossible. One of my favourites is that the 'eye of the needle' was actually the name of a narrow gate into Jerusalem through which camels could pass only when unladen. This encourages people to believe that it is not nearly impossible for the rich to enter heaven, merely difficult. But if the gate was what Jesus was referring to, it only makes the message clearer. The image here is of the camel needing to be completely unloaded before it can pass, which fits Jesus's instruction to the man to give away everything.

There can be no serious doubt that Jesus saw wealth as a problem. But why? It is not simply that 'a man's life consisteth not in the abundance of the things which he possesseth' (6:23).

Almost everyone agrees that the size of your bank account is not the measure of your life's worth and that there are many things that money can't buy. Jesus goes further than this, insisting that money and worldly possessions are incompatible with living a good life. This needs explaining.

The laden camel is a useful place to begin. It's an image that helps make sense of Jesus's otherwise puzzling claim that 'my yoke is easy, and my burden is light' (8:13). Given how often Jesus states that the path to goodness is extremely difficult, this statement would appear to be plain inconsistency. Yet if we understand it in the light of the camel, it becomes more comprehensible. His way requires us to unburden ourselves of material and worldly concerns, like the camel getting ready to pass through the gate. A lightness and liberation await for us if we can do this, but, as Jesus's teaching makes clear, we find this renunciation very difficult.

This reminds me of a remark the philosopher Bertrand Russell made in a letter to Lady Ottoline Morrell about the philosopher Ludwig Wittgenstein, who came from a very wealthy family. 'He gave all his money to his brothers and sisters,' wrote Russell, 'because he found earthly possessions a burden.'[3] According to Russell, Wittgenstein had even thought of being a monk, although Russell sceptically dismissed this as 'an idea, not an intention'. Nonetheless, Wittgenstein pursued his philosophical vocation with high moral seriousness and found the distractions of money too much to bear. He would have understood Jesus's idea that giving up wealth is a kind of relief – but he would also have appreciated how difficult it is to do. Wittgenstein never really 'gave away' all his money. His family had his share and there was no doubt that it would be his whenever he asked for it.

The idea that giving up our attachment to wealth is a

liberation makes good secular sense, and is a more credible reading than the more obviously religious explanation of why Jesus denounced worldly possessions: if we are essentially spirit and destined for a life in heaven, then shedding our attachments to material things could be an essential preparation. For secularists who don't believe in an afterlife, fixing your eyes on a distant heaven is not only a mistake, it is a very dangerous one. Even those who believe in a life to come would agree that an excessive focus on the heavens can foster a lack of concern for those who dwell on earth. The most shocking example I have come across is of a woman who was allowed to babysit for her relatives even though they knew she was a drug addict. It was only when they found out she was an atheist that the babysitting stopped. The idea that an atheist poses more risk to a baby than an addict would strike most of us as absurd. But, of course, if you are convinced that only believers go to heaven, then the comparative risk shifts decisively. The worst a drug addict can do is kill the baby; the worst an atheist can do is send her to hell.

While an extreme example, the same disturbing prioritising of the eternal is evident in many religious believers. One of the most serious charges against the Roman Catholic missionary Mother Teresa, for instance, is precisely that her concern for the poor of Calcutta was more for their spiritual salvation than for their terrestrial well-being. When Robin Fox, editor of the British medical journal the *Lancet*, visited her Calcutta homes in 1991 he found that the sisters had poor medical knowledge and did not make enough use of analgesics and that the order was unable to distinguish between curable and incurable patients.[4] A review of almost all the literature on Mother Teresa by a group of Université de Montréal academics in 2013 concluded, 'In the eyes of Mother Teresa, poverty, suffering and death are great opportunities to unite with God and to share the passion of Christ ... For Teresa, the optimal care that can be offered is prayer ... What's more, when the bell rings to announce the prayer, the sisters must, according to the testimony of one of them, immediately stop caring for the sick and go to the chapel.'[5]

Those who think that it is wrong to be concerned about the life to come have Jesus on their side. Even in the Gospels it is not at all clear that it was the promise of the afterlife that underpinned Jesus's unworldliness. Jesus never offers a clear promise of an other-worldly heaven to come. The Kingdom of Heaven is never explicitly extraterrestrial and is often explicitly here and now – in tune with Judaism's relative lack of concern with an afterlife.

Even if you do believe in heaven, it does not automatically follow that it is a place where worldly things have no value. For our afterlife to be recognisably human there would have to be a kind of embodiment, a sense of the passage of time, and sensory experience. In other words, heaven, as many imagine it, is a life of plenty in which sickness, poverty and misery are eradicated but the good things of human life are in abundance, more reliable and without downside. To completely reject worldly goods would mean rejecting our human nature. An afterlife in which we are transformed into pure spirit (whatever that might mean) is not really a continuation of our life at all, but some kind of radically different outgrowth from it.

The case for rejecting worldly concerns is better built on the idea of poverty as an unburdening. Elements from the Sermon on the Mount underpin this argument. This is the only lengthy set-piece sermon Jesus delivers in the Gospels, one which launches his ministry. Here Jesus tells his followers plainly, 'Take no thought for your life, what ye shall eat, or what ye shall drink; nor yet for your body, what ye shall put on' (3:4–10). Two of the reasons he gives for this justify indifference to wealth and possessions but not outright rejection of them. The first is the familiar and uncontroversial idea that there is more to life than these material things: 'Is not the life more than meat, and the body than raiment?' (3:6).

The second is that concern for wealth is pointless. The lilies of the field do more than well enough even though they neither toil nor spin, as do the birds who don't sow, reap or gather into barns. The pedant could reply that human beings have for better or for worse evolved to be the kinds of creatures who cannot survive on instinct alone. We actually do need to work and clothe ourselves. But the point is not that we should literally become animal-like. 'Are ye not much better than they?' Jesus asks rhetorically. It's simply that when it comes to matters of survival, worrying doesn't help. 'Which of you by taking thought can add one cubit unto his stature?' (3:7).

Jesus goes further, giving two more reasons why we should actually spurn worldly goods. The first is that earthly goods are corruptible: 'Lay not up for yourselves treasures upon earth, where moth and rust doth corrupt, and where thieves break through and steal' (3:4). Such goods are a fragile locus for value and a flimsy basis on which to construct a life. This is an idea shared by many sages and philosophers. As it says in Proverbs 27:24, 'For riches are not for ever: and doth the crown endure to every generation?'

Both Buddhism and Stoicism emphasise the impermanence of material things and the need to focus on our own virtue. This also seems to me the main message in Jesus's words about the temple in Jerusalem (11:11–15): 'Seest thou these great buildings? There shall not be left one stone upon another, that shall not be thrown down.' Standardly read as a prophecy about the temple's destruction, this statement should be taken with a pinch of salt for various reasons, not least that it was written down after the temple had been destroyed by the Romans in 70 CE. More importantly, the message Jesus conveys requires no prophetic content. It doesn't take a seer to know that in time even the greatest buildings will be reduced to rubble. The point he is making is that matter is perishable but truth and goodness are in a sense eternal: 'Heaven and earth shall pass away, but my words shall not pass away.'

Both this line of thought and the comparisons with birds and lilies suggest more than simply a rejection of the value of material possessions. They suggest we should not give thought to our future at all. Karen Kilby wonders if this is Jesus's most profound challenge to middle-class values: 'I sometimes think that what makes me middle class is the number of layers of protection I have – through family, through education, through making sure I have a career and savings. Jesus is definitely not promoting layers of security.'

The desire for security and the illusion we can have it are peculiarly middle-class afflictions. We would do well to remember that the world is fickle and unpredictable and that it is therefore foolish to rely on a comfortable future. But for Jesus the fundamental problem is not that nothing is entirely dependable. It's that worldly prosperity is simply the wrong kind of thing on which to place value. He explains this in the fourth and most important reason he gives in the Sermon on the Mount for rejecting worldly concerns: 'For where your treasure is, there will your heart be also' (3:4). He might equally have said, 'For where your heart is, there will your treasure be also.' We should seek to transform and enrich our hearts not our wallets, seek inner transformation not the betterment of external circumstances. If you accumulate wealth you almost inevitably end up placing value on it and that means that your heart becomes set on the wrong things.

We see how this works all around us. The more we have, the more we tend to become attached to what we have and believe that we can't do without it. Even things that at first seem like miraculous luxuries can soon become things we can barely imagine living without. That is partly why so few people in prosperous countries count themselves as wealthy: they get used to their level of income and can't imagine surviving on less. Money and material security become traps rather than comforts. As Jesus put it elsewhere, 'No servant can serve two masters: for either he will hate the one, and love the other; or else he will hold to the one, and despise the other. Ye cannot serve the good and mammon' (7:49). This would be true even if our health and wealth were secure and incorruptible.

We once again come back to the idea that what matters above all else is to make yourself a better person: 'seek ye first righteousness' (3:9). This task is all-consuming and is incompatible with worrying about what may or may not happen in the future. 'Take therefore no thought for the morrow: for the morrow shall take thought for the things of itself. Sufficient unto the day is the evil thereof' (3:10). That last sentence is critical. We have enough to worry about struggling to keep our worst selves in check.

This teaching is striking but it is not especially original or religious in character. In fact, none of Jesus's moral teachings are unique or completely original. 'A lot of what Jesus did say isn't that distinctive,' suggests Lucy Winkett. 'Some New Testament scholars say you can find two moral teachings that were new or unusual in Jesus,' says Keith Ward. 'One was no divorce and the other one is never take an oath. I don't actually believe either of those.' The biblical scholar

Runar M. Thorsteinsson catalogues the innumerable ways in which Jesus's ideas are similar to others prevalent in the Graeco-Roman world in his meticulous and fascinating *Jesus as Philosopher: The Moral Sage in the Synoptic Gospels.*[6]

Even by Jesus's time, many philosophers had advocated a lack of concern for the future and the rejection of illusions of security. For example, the Stoics believed that the only thing truly good or bad was your moral character, your virtue. Everything else we ought to consider as 'indifferents', simply not worth our concern. A life of virtue for them was one lived according to the principles of reason and of nature.

Jesus goes further than the Stoics because he believes we ought to be more than merely indifferent to the concerns of the world; we should be actively hostile to them. In this respect his teachings are closer to those of the Buddhists. In the Buddhist tradition, the renunciation of the world can be remarkably severe. There are Buddhist death meditations that are supposed to be undertaken at charnel grounds, the corpses reminding us of how disgusting bodies are. We are even encouraged to nurture disgust for our own flesh. In one text a nun says, 'I am repelled and humiliated by this foul, putrid body, subject to break up, fragile: I've uprooted sensual craving.'[7]

Although Jesus tells us to reject the things of the world, nothing he says is as extreme as this. So how hostile does he think we should be to worldly goods? Some, like theologian Elizabeth Oldfield, see the world-denying aspects of his teaching 'as a continuation of the Old Testament obsession with idolatry. Don't deny the world just don't worship it'. But often Jesus sounds much harsher than this. In a long passage in which he issues instructions to the apostles (5:30–42), the divide between higher and worldly concerns is put in the strong language of hatred: 'If the world hate you, ye know that it hated me before it hated you.' Those who pursue righteousness have to expect that the world will reject them. But the disdain is mutual. 'Ye are not of the world, but I have chosen you out of the world,' Jesus tells the apostles. The message is plain: to follow the way of Jesus is to turn your back on the world, even to despise your earthly existence. 'He that hateth his life in this world shall keep it.'

The world is portrayed as full of wolves and vipers. The apostles are sent to teach Jesus's message but when they find that message is not heeded, which they will, they are told to respond with gestures that openly show scorn for those who remain attached to the world: 'shake off the very dust from your feet for a testimony against them,' he says. He talks with contempt of those who don't accept his philosophy: 'Cast not ye your pearls before swine, lest they trample them under their feet, and turn again and rend you.' This somewhat jars with the image of a Jesus who is kind and charitable to all.

The most challenging aspect of the rejection of the earthly is acceptance that even your body is nothing. As Jesus says, 'Be not afraid of them that kill the body, and after that have no more that they can do' (11:35). If a human being is taken to be a soul temporarily housed in a physical body, this is easy enough to understand. For example, in the *Phaedo*, an account of the last days of Socrates, Plato argues that we should have no fear of physical death. Death is nothing but 'the separation of soul and body'. This is to be desired because 'while we are in the body, and while the soul is mingled with this mass of evil, our desire will not be satisfied'.[8]

In a gospel without faith, this lack of concern for the body makes no sense. But even in the original Gospels, it's not clear that Jesus believed in anything like the Platonic idea of a complete separation of body and soul, or even of a life after death of any kind. Scholars generally agree that the Platonic conception of body and soul as two discrete entities was absent from early Christianity. The Jesuit philosopher Roland Teske wrote that there was no idea of spirit as non-corporeal substance until the time of Augustine in the fourth century.[9] That is why accounts of both Christ's resurrection and the promise of the resurrection of the dead at the last judgement were both fully corporeal. In John 20:27, Jesus tells doubting Thomas to 'Reach hither thy finger, and behold my hands; and reach hither thy hand, and thrust it into my side.' It mattered that he had risen body and all, not merely as a spirit. That is true even in John, widely agreed to be the most Greek-influenced of the Gospels and also the most dualistic.

Whatever Jesus's original intent, it is possible to make sense of his teachings about our bodies without requiring a belief in immaterial souls. If, as Jesus argued, what matters above all else is our virtue, then it can be argued that this is what has to have the highest value, above even life itself. Even if your life is taken from you, your virtue is untouched. True goodness is invulnerable, not because it will live on without the body but because it is not a property of bodies at all.

Think about what we say about good people who are killed serving a good cause. Take the British Member of Parliament Jo Cox, killed by a white supremacist in 2016. Cox was a tireless campaigner for human rights and many of the tributes to her focused on how the murder did not extinguish her goodness. Her widowed husband, Brendan Cox, later wrote, 'Jo would have maintained her optimism despite all that has happened. Not out of blind faith, but because she believed that what we hold in common is more significant than our differences. It is our job to realize her vision.'[10] We have a strong conviction that the good people do survives them. Even when you undo the good work someone has done you can't make it untrue that it was good work. Virtue is in that sense immortal.

Although we can make some sense of the invulnerability of goodness, we are on shakier ground regarding the invulnerability of good people. In a wholly secular world view, the fact that our virtue is in a sense untouchable is a consolation but it shouldn't make us indifferent to suffering and death. Aristotle clearly had Plato in mind when he said, 'Those who maintain that, provided he is good, a man is happy on the rack or surrounded by great disasters, are talking nonsense.' Nor did Aristotle believe that the good person should be less concerned about death. On the contrary, the better a person is 'the more pain he will feel at the thought of death. For life is especially worth living for a person like this, and he knows that he is losing the greatest of goods – and this is painful.'[11]

The case for the almost complete rejection of worldly goods and fortune is very hard to make if we believe that this life is the only one we have. Some sense can be made of Jesus's claims that death cannot touch what most matters in our lives. But unless there is life in the first place, and one that is free from extreme suffering, nothing of value exists to be touched.

The world-renouncing teaching of Jesus is hard to swallow for anyone remotely attached to their mortal existence. Perhaps that is why there are many who claim that Jesus is not as unworldly as some of his pronouncements suggest. How much he says we should turn our backs on the world seems to depend on the context. When he first sends out his apostles to preach, for example, he tells them, 'Take nothing for thy journey, save a staff only; no scrip, no bread, no money in your purse: But be shod with sandals; and not put on two coats' (5:36). However, on the Mount of Olives, anticipating their mission after his death, he says, 'he that hath a purse, let him take it, and likewise his scrip' (12:23). This is not inconsistent because Jesus prefixes these instructions with a reminder that he 'sent you without purse, and scrip, and shoes' and that they lacked nothing as a result. His instruction had changed because circumstances had changed.

Other examples show Jesus tinkering with the severity of his message. We've already seen how he told the rich young man to sell everything he had. But we have also seen that he was not as ascetic as John the Baptist. He praises Zacchaeus the tax collector for giving away only half his wealth (8:6–13) and is happy to have his feet anointed with expensive ointments (10:11).

It is, however, somewhat desperate to point to these examples as evidence that Jesus did not commend simplicity and poverty. The moral teaching of the Gospel is not a systematic treatise. It would be perverse to deny that Jesus had a very strong anti-materialist, world-renouncing message on the basis of a few instances where he accepted worldly goods. Taken as a whole, Jesus utterly rejects the value of wealth and calls upon all who follow him to take something like a vow of poverty. Accept hospitality and fine things in passing if they came your way, but you should not covet, seek or grasp hold of them.

It is not surprising that contemporary Western Christians find this a hard teaching to fully embrace. Indeed, the most comparably demanding version of this message in contemporary moral thought is from the strict secular utilitarianism associated with Peter Singer. Singer argues that we 'ought to give as much as possible, that is, at least up to the point at which by giving more one would begin to cause serious suffering for oneself and one's dependants'.[12]

The Christian thinkers I spoke to admitted to an unease in enjoying their comfortable lifestyles while ostensibly following Jesus. They could offer a few explanations as to why they weren't less materialistic but admitted they fell short of good justifications.

Brian Mountford, for example, said, 'It's difficult to choose an ascetic life in modern Britain without being thought something of a misfit, and there's a related sense in which it's helpful for a religious leader to live in the same social category as those he or she serves.' He mentioned a fellow vicar who lived in a poor parish outside Liverpool where everyone was equally badly off. He lived simply by modern standards, and empathetically with the community he served, despite living in the biggest house in Kirby – but the vicarage was still frequently broken in to. Before retirement, Mountford lived in North Oxford, 'where some houses are £6 million a shot', and admits that rubbed off on him. He remembers when he first moved there, 'We'd be entertained by people with very big spiritual questions to discuss, which we did over the finest claret. I sometimes felt guilty about living in this bubble, and wondered what it would be like to live on a run-down housing estate, but I absolutely believed there was a gospel for the rich as well as a gospel for the poor.'

One other way for people to reassure themselves that living the comfortable or even wealthy life of a modern Westerner is compatible with Jesus's teaching is to argue that although Jesus told us not to try to amass wealth and make money our master, he strongly suggested that if you did the right thing you would receive all these rewards anyway. This idea has become known as the 'prosperity gospel' or 'prosperity theology'. Many churches have become rich preaching it. The message is that in order to receive you first have to give, so congregations tithe a lot of their money. One of the most famous prosperity pastors is Joel Osteen of Lakewood Church, Texas. He is not embarrassed by his wealth, estimated at the time of writing as $60 million, or of the $10.7-million mansion he calls home. 'If you do your part, God will do His,' he writes. 'He will promote you; He'll give you increase.' Another prosperity gospel pastor, Paula White, gave a blessing at President Trump's 2017 inauguration, prayed at the launch of his re-election campaign and was given an official White House role in the Office of Public Liaison in 2019. White resists the prosperity gospel label but she believes in financial miracles and a typical tweet is 'I declare mind blowing blessings are going to overtake you & your family! You will be blessed in your health, wealth, & relationships!'

Advocates of the prosperity gospel often quote Jesus saying, 'I am come that they might have life, and that they might have it more abundantly' (3:28). Evidence that this means material abundance comes from passages such as that in the Sermon on the Mount, when Jesus says, 'Therefore take no thought, saying, What shall we eat? or, What shall we drink? or, Wherewithal shall we be clothed?' but immediately follows this by saying, 'But seek ye first righteousness; and all these things shall be added unto you' (3:9).

Other lines in the sermon echo this promise of material reward for virtue. 'Give, and it shall be given unto you,' he says. 'For with the same measure that ye mete withal it shall be measured to you again' (3:16). A few lines later he seems to offer a version of the so-called 'law of attraction' made notorious by various bestselling books over the last century, most recently *The Secret* by Rhonda Byrne, which sold 30 million copies. This principle says that positive thoughts bring positive experiences into a person's life. Jesus's version is: 'Ask, and it shall be given you; seek, and ye shall find; knock, and it shall be opened unto you. If thou canst believe, all things are possible to him that believeth. Therefore I say unto you, What things soever ye desire, when ye pray, believe that ye receive them, and ye shall have them' (3:19–21).

However, in all these verses only the phrase 'all these things shall be added unto you' explicitly refers to material benefits and these are no more than the basics of food, drink and clothing. Once again we must be careful not to allow the divergent sayings to cancel out the more dominant ones. The most natural reading of most of these verses is that the rewards of being good are not the same as the rewards of wealth. Even the idea that you will receive 'What things soever ye desire' if you pray and believe is in a context in which Jesus repeatedly told people not to desire or to ask for plentiful worldly goods. Obviously Jesus didn't mean that faith, for want of a better word, guaranteed that any desire would be fulfilled. Given what he says elsewhere, it would make no sense for him to say that faithfulness will give you the malicious revenge or adulterous affair you want. To pretend he is promising material wealth in these verses is to wilfully ignore the powerful world-renouncing message that beats through his teaching and to make too much of a couple of ambiguous notes.

The promise of the Sermon on the Mount is simply that goodness will be repaid with goodness, not with cash. The poor will receive 'the Kingdom of Heaven', but it is generally agreed that the Greek word traditionally translated as 'kingdom', *basileia*, is better understood as 'reign' or 'rule'. Whenever he talks of the *basileia* of God or heaven he seems to be referring to a state of mind or being rather than a state to be ruled. So when Jesus tells Pilate, 'My kingdom is not of this world' (13:18), he is not saying that it is a literal place beyond the clouds. He is saying that it is not the same kind of kingdom at all. The *basileia* of material things and the *basileia* of the spirit are not two different places, but two ways of living here on earth. Understood in this way, Jesus is not suggesting that we should put the world to come over the here and now. Rather, he is saying we should put the world of the heart above the world of material goods. Hence when Jesus promises the meek that they shall inherit the earth, he was not making a prophecy about temporal power. To 'inherit the earth' is to become at home in the world rather than to struggle in it.

In my view, the Beatitudes, which open the Sermon on the Mount, suggest a too simplistic relationship between doing good and being done well by. We know that the merciful are not always shown mercy, that those who weep or mourn do not always find laughter or comfort, and that the hungry are not always filled, literally or metaphorically. It could be that Jesus believed in a kind of karmic law. It could also be that these teachings really do require a transcendent God to set things right in the long run in another life, since he all too clearly doesn't do so in this one. However, it is not much of a stretch to read these words as hyperbolic, in keeping with the prophetic mode of discourse Jesus adopted. Read in that way we can agree that peacemakers are generally praised, that we achieve deep satisfaction in life only if we hunger and thirst after righteousness, that if we are living in the right way we may not be happy now but we have more chance of being content in the long run. If the Beatitudes describe where virtue *tends* to lead rather than where it inevitably takes us, they make some sense.

Jesus's renunciation of worldly goods does not therefore require an embrace of other-worldly ones. There is certainly a great deal of wisdom in focusing less on acquiring things and more on how we develop our character. We should also be aware that there is no ultimate security in material things, since they all decay and perish. Jesus's emphasis on inner transformation is a useful corrective in a world where we too often seek salvation though increased wealth and social status. As Brian Mountford puts it, Jesus offers 'an ideal to hold up as an antidote before the spectre of acquisitiveness, consumerism and self-aggrandisement'.[13]

Jesus does, however, go further than most of us think desirable. If we can avoid being too acquisitive and obsessive about wealth, why not use material resources to improve our chances of a comfortable and long life? We can distance ourselves too much from the material world in which we live and die. We cannot live a full human life if we deny our essential corporeality. Rather than try to make ourselves invulnerable to the fragility of earthly delights, we could accept that the price of the miraculous opportunity to live a good life is that nothing in it lasts or is guaranteed. To fully appreciate the joy of living is at the same time to appreciate the sadness of its finitude.

5

THE RENUNCIATION
OF POLITICS

In the autumn of 2011, activists supporting the anti-capitalist group Occupy pitched camp outside St Paul's Cathedral in London. It was to prove a tough test for those running the church. They had to decide whether to evict the protesters or welcome them with open arms. Most in Occupy were not Christians, but they knew enough about Jesus's teachings to make the decision very uncomfortable for the church authorities. They unfurled a banner saying 'Throw the money changers out of the temple', a reference to Jesus's cleansing of the temple. In a statement referring to their alleged rough treatment by the police, they repeatedly quoted the Sermon on the Mount: 'Blessed are those who are persecuted because of righteousness, for theirs is the kingdom of heaven ... Blessed are those who hunger and thirst after righteousness, for they will be filled' (Matthew 5:6 and 10).

Many within the church expressed sympathy with their cause without going so far as to take their side. The Archbishop of Canterbury, Rowan Williams, accepted that 'a marker had been put down', saying 'something must be done'. However, he added that 'the demands of the protesters have been vague' and that it was easy to be 'wise after the event and to pour scorn on the Cathedral in particular and the Church of England in general for failing to know how to square the circle of public interest and protest'.[1]

A year after the protests, David Ison, Dean of St Paul's Cathedral, was similarly equivocal. He agreed there was a 'need to reform financial structures and to engage everyone in building a society more focused on sustainability, in order to work for the common good of all'. But 'the other side of the coin is that we still depend on financial institutions for much of our national income and pensions as well as day by day functioning of the economy'.[2]

Yet the cathedral supported the protestors' eviction. The canon chancellor of the cathedral, Giles Fraser, resigned after failing to persuade his colleagues that the church should not cooperate with the eviction. 'St Paul's, designed by a scientist, speaks vividly of the cosmological God, the omnipotent God of the stars and the heavens,' wrote Fraser. 'But it finds it much harder to speak convincingly of the poor, incarnate, vulnerable God of Bethlehem. That God was, to my mind at least, much more clearly articulated within the camp itself.'[3]

Several months later, Fraser asked the man who would soon become the next archbishop of Canterbury, Justin Welby, whether he thought the Occupy protesters were right. 'Of course they were right,' he replied. 'Absolutely. And everything we are hearing now says that.'[4]

The Occupy episode goes to the heart of one of the most

controversial aspects of Jesus's teaching. Was he a proto-socialist, advocating radical reform of the structures of society to benefit the poor, the weak and the oppressed? Or was he apolitical, only concerned with personal transformation, believing we should 'render therefore unto Caesar the things which are Caesar's' (11:20)?

No one could deny that Jesus shows great concern for the poor and sick in the here and now. Service to others is a recurrent theme: 'Whosoever will be chief among you, let him be your servant' (5:20). One of the most famous Gospel sayings is 'He that hath two coats, let him impart to him that hath none; and he that hath meat, let him do likewise' (Luke 3:11). Although this was actually said by John the Baptist, it's often attributed to Jesus because it sounds so much like what he would have said.

Such teachings have inspired Christian socialism and other movements for radical political change. They have often argued that Christianity is incompatible with a political conservatism that does not make increasing material equality a high priority. Over the centuries, many have been more inspired by Jesus's social teachings than by his promise of salvation in a life to come. As fewer people believe in heaven and hell, this has understandably become more of a focus. The charity Christian Aid, for example, has used the striking advertising slogan 'We believe in life before death'.

However, if you look closely at Jesus's words, there is little evidence that he believed in pursuing his social goals by political means. For Jesus, political change is at most a low priority, at worst a distraction from the more important task of changing yourself. He would have been somewhat inconsistent if he placed a lot of emphasis on creating a more materially equal society when the anti-worldly thrust of this teachings suggests that no one should have any concern for their worldly, material condition at all.

Jesus urged his followers to give up their wealth, but he always asked people to do this voluntarily. He did not, for instance, instruct people to seize the second coat of a person who has two and redistribute it to someone who has none. Second, and more importantly, giving up wealth was primarily good for the person who did it, not for whoever that wealth was then passed to. Jesus says, 'When thou makest a dinner or a supper, call not thy friends, nor thy brethren, neither thy kinsmen, nor thy rich neighbours; lest they also bid thee again, and a recompence be made thee. But when thou makest a feast, call the poor, the maimed, the lame, the blind: And thou shalt be blessed; for they cannot recompense thee' (4:16–17). Notice here that the feast-giver is blessed by this apparent act of generosity, not the poor. And the reason given for inviting the poor is not to help them, but because they cannot offer recompense.

Similarly, when Jesus instructs the rich man to sell his goods and give to the poor, it is only because the gate to the Kingdom of God is narrow and no one burdened by wealth can go through it (6:19). Giving away money is necessary for our own salvation, not for that of those we give to. Giving too much to the poor might even make them too wealthy to be saved themselves.

The most striking indication that the alleviation of poverty is not a prime concern for Jesus comes when a woman anoints his feet and head with expensive ointment and oil (10:1–12). Those around Jesus were indignant, saying, 'Why was this waste of the ointment made? For it might have been sold for more than three hundred pence, and have been given to the poor.' But for Jesus, the woman's acts were a sign of love, which he saw as more important than helping the poor.

In perhaps Jesus's most notorious lines, he said, 'For ye have the poor with you always, and whensoever ye will ye may do them good: but me ye have not always.' This suggests a certain fatalism about the possibility of political change and a focus instead on the goodness and kindness we can do one to one. Helping the poor is good to do when you can, but it is not the highest priority.

We should not be surprised that Jesus is less concerned with improving the lot of the poor than we might have liked. A disturbing corollary of any ethics of renunciation is that it involves downgrading not only your own worldly concerns but also those of others. This is often the trade-off when a moral system puts self-cultivation first. For instance, Buddhism advocates compassion as a central virtue. But its emphasis on self-discipline and inner training often leads devotees to retreat from the concerns of daily life, even those of life and death. I have always found it odd that in many Buddhist cultures even the poor are expected to give food to the monks, not the other way around.

Jesus's lack of concern for temporal power extends far beyond a relaxed attitude to structural economic injustice. No form of secular justice seems to matter to him. His behaviour at his own trial is surely intended to be exemplary in this regard (12:42–54). He refuses to defend himself, often saying nothing. His only defence is essentially that he doesn't need one: 'I spake openly to the world; I ever taught in the synagogue, and in the temple, whither the Jews always resort; and in secret have I said nothing. Why askest thou me? ask them which heard me, what I have said unto them.' He treats the trial as a sham and refuses to take part in it. It is as though he does not want to dignify the structures of political power.

One of the most cited passages used to support the apolitical interpretation of Jesus comes when he asks the Pharisees whose image and superscription (inscription) is on their coins. When they reply, 'Caesar's', he says, 'Render therefore unto Caesar the things which are Caesar's' (11:20). This is often quoted to justify keeping religion out of secular politics. However, we have to be careful not to read too much into this one comment. It is made in response to a trap set by the Pharisees, who try to lure Jesus into making seditious remarks by asking whether it is 'lawful to give tribute unto Caesar'. Karen Kilby suggests that Jesus's answer can be read as a specific ploy to avoid the trick rather than a general comment about accepting the status quo.

Kilby is right to highlight the significance of the context of the remark. Nonetheless, it is reasonable to assume that the teachings of Jesus that were passed down were the ones that had a general application and were not specific to a particular situation. If Jesus's words were not seen as a comment about political power, then the only purpose of telling this story would be to show how clever Jesus was in avoiding the snares set for him. And there is no evidence that Jesus sought to reform the political structures of his society. He told Pilate, 'My kingdom is not of this world' (13:18) and his followers 'the Kingdom of Heaven is within you' (11:15). We also saw earlier how, in the Parable of the Unjust Steward (7:40–50), Jesus commended fulfilling our secular duties, even to mammon.

We're often told that Jesus's followers were frustrated and even angered by his refusal to engage politically and lead an uprising against the Romans. In reply, he constantly stressed how the kinds of justice and goodness he promoted had nothing to do with politics. 'And ye shall know the truth, and the truth shall make you free' (4:6). The people protested, saying they were not slaves and so didn't need setting free. Jesus then explained, 'Whosoever committeth sin is the servant of sin' (4:7). The freedom he says truth brings is personal and moral, not political. Liberation is not a political struggle but an individual one.

Jesus's most radical rejection of worldly power and the most difficult to embrace is his pacifism. Jesus's teaching always leaves room for interpretation but there is little wiggle room to avoid the conclusion that he rejected the use of all lethal violence. Kilby is surely right to say, 'If you're going to derive your military ethic from the teachings of Jesus alone, I think you'd have to go for pacifism.' Few of his followers over the centuries have followed him, and too many have gone the other way, killing and even torturing in his name. It was the issue that raised visible discomfort in most of my interviewees. 'It is very hard to see how you can derive an ethic which legitimises the use of compulsion or force from what Jesus says,' Nick Spencer acknowledged. Yet all the Christians I interviewed attempted in one way or another to dilute the pure pacifist message.

The case for Jesus's pacifism is clear enough. In the Sermon on the Mount he says, 'whosoever shall smite thee on thy right cheek, turn to him the other also' (2:35). He adds later, 'love ye your enemies, and do good, and lend, hoping for nothing again; and your reward shall be great, and ye shall be the children of the Highest' (2:41). His actions speak even more clearly than his words. He refuses to be a revolutionary leader and allows himself to be executed by the Romans. In the Garden of Gethsemane he rebukes the disciple who attempts to defend him by cutting off the ear of the servant with a sword. Jesus tells him, 'Put up again thy sword into his place: for all they that take the sword shall perish with the sword' (12:39). This radical refusal to fight back was not so novel or shocking that we have any reason to doubt its plain sincerity. Socrates, for instance, says, 'We ought neither to requite wrong with wrong nor to do evil to anyone, no matter what he may have done to us.'[5]

Those who argue that it's more complicated than that point to a couple of passages that seem to muddy the waters. In one, Jesus is preparing his disciples for life after his death. Having previously instructed them not to carry swords, he tells them, 'he that hath no sword, let him sell his garment, and buy one' (12:23). They reply, 'here are two swords', to which he replies, 'It is enough' (12:24). Why would Jesus tell his disciples to go out into the world armed when he had previously been so clearly against the use of violence? Christian non-pacifists argue that this is clear evidence that Jesus allowed the use of violence in self-defence. But this jars with his instruction to turn the other cheek.

To understand this apparent contradiction and the way out of it, we have to look more closely at what turning the other cheek actually means. The passage in question gives three instructions that to the modern ear sound submissive. First, 'whosoever shall smite thee on thy right cheek, turn to him the other also.' Second, 'if any man will sue thee at the law, and take away thy coat, let him have thy cloak also.' Finally, 'whosoever shall compel thee to go a mile, go with him twain' (2:35–36).

The theologian Walter Wink points out that to understand these injunctions you have to understand the specific context of Palestine under Roman occupation. Jews would routinely be hit across the face with the back of a Roman's hand as a means of humiliating them, since any resistance would lead to their arrest. Debt collectors could seize clothes if the poor were unable to pay, leaving them with only their undergarments. And Roman soldiers were legally allowed to compel civilians to carry their often heavy packs but only for up to a mile, to avoid sowing too much resentment.[6]

Wink argues that what Jesus was telling his followers to do in response was not a sign of weak submission. Rather, he was telling them to act according to principles of non-violent resistance similar to those advocated by Gandhi, an admirer of Jesus. By turning the other cheek you were saying, 'See, you haven't humiliated me, and no matter how many times you hit me I won't be humiliated.' By giving your cloak as well as your coat you would be leaving yourself naked, causing more shame to the person forced to see you than to yourself. And by walking more than a mile you were forcing the solider who made you walk one to break the law, causing him more problems than yourself.

Whether Wink has this exactly right or not (I'm not entirely convinced by the cloak and coat explanation), his general point seems to be correct. Jesus is teaching defiance. You resist evil not by violence but by demonstrably not showing evil back, even if that appears to be to your cost. In fact, it will be to your benefit because in Jesus's ethics the highest reward is becoming your best, most moral self, one of the 'children of the highest'.

Wink shows how turning the other cheek is an act of strength, not weakness. But this interpretation only underscores the point that the resistance Jesus preached was resolutely non-violent. In this light, the instruction to go out into the world with a sword makes some sense. Jesus did not believe it was good to be bullied or beaten. He didn't want his disciples to leave themselves more open to physical danger than they had to. Carrying a sword, they would be less likely to be attacked. But if they were, can we be in any doubt that he would not have wanted them to actually use their weapon? His rebuke of the sword-wielding disciple in the Garden of Gethsemane should make the answer to that plain.

There are a few other straws some Christians clutch at to save their faith from pacifism. One is that Jesus ran amok at the temple with a whip, cleansing it of its moneylenders. But there is nothing in the account that suggests Jesus caused harm to any person. The other is that Jesus said, 'I came not to send peace, but a sword' (10:51). In context, however, this is clearly a piece of metaphorical hyperbole to make the point that he was bringing division.

Yet with few exceptions, notably the Quakers, Christianity has not been a pacifist religion. Its position on armed conflict is best captured in the just war theory, first developed by the Roman African theologian and bishop Augustine in the fifth century. This specifies the moral requirements for both going to war and conduct within it. Although demanding, it is clearly no pacifist charter. How, therefore, did Christianity get from Jesus's pacifism to the complex legitimisation of violence in the just war theory?

It was not possible for the early church to avoid the issue of the ethics of killing for long. As Nick Spencer says, 'There's not a single record of any Christians serving in the Roman military until the end of the second century. From that point onwards, what do they do? On the one hand they've got to abjure violence, on the other hand they've got to use it.' One early attempt at squaring the circle is so lame as to be comical: 'Apparently you get these stories of Christians being baptised holding their swords above the waters.'

The early church soon learned the usefulness of distinguishing between the legitimacy of state and personal violence. A good Christian could, it seems, reluctantly support a nation's army while privately refraining from waging war. This is a vivid example of the kind of moral self-indulgence pacifism always risks, where you keep yourself 'pure' at the price of either having other people do your dirty work for you or standing by while innocents are massacred.

The only defence of Christian non-pacifism I find remotely persuasive is the idea that Jesus's messages were directed at his followers at the time, not for millennia to come. We just don't know what Jesus would have thought we should do in the face of the Third Reich, for example. Rather than comb the Gospels for the answer, we should accept that we have to use our own judgement. We have to ask what would be most consonant with his message of love and support for the weak. For many that would mean defending them even to the death. Jesus would not just have sat back and wept at Belsen, he would have fought to liberate it.

Although I can see this argument, I remain unconvinced. Jesus never argued that the ends justify the means and he is clearly opposed to violence as a means. He also thinks that it is worse to be a bad person than it is to suffer or even die. So I can see him sincerely believing that it is better to let the innocent be killed than to lose your own soul by sinking to the level of a killer yourself. It's not an argument I find compelling but it is the one that seems closest to the Gospels' teaching.

There is one final sense in which Jesus was opposed to temporal power, one which should make many of his followers today uncomfortable. It seems very clear that Jesus had no time for ecclesiastical power. Organised religion is only ever criticised and Jesus neither modelled nor promoted a new kind of formal clerical structure. His words about the destruction of the temple are clearly intended to indicate how the true site of holiness is the heart, not any building. As the Sikhs teach, 'The mind is the temple, and the body is the fence built around it.'[7]

The cleansing of the temple also helps reinforce this teaching (11:7–10). Jesus drives out the money changers and traders, saying, 'Is it not written, My house shall be called of all nations the house of prayer? but ye have made it a den of thieves.' Part of the message is that mammon and goodness are incompatible. But it's not just about money. He was not driving out market traders who just happened to be using the temple as a place to do business. The people he chastised were selling religious goods and services, such as animals for slaughter or changing money into the only currency accepted in the temple. Jesus was protesting about the transformation of religion into a kind of industry selling rituals people must pay to perform. The temple had become a site of sacralised capitalism. Add to that the frequent instances in which Jesus was seen as being in opposition to all forms of clerical authority – scribes, lawyers, Pharisees, Sadducees – and it seems undeniable that Jesus was against organised religion.

Although Jesus did not make political change his goal, we should be careful not to jump to the conclusion that he didn't care at all about political and social structures. 'The clearest single piece of historical information about Jesus is that he died as a political provocateur,' wrote the Marxist biblical scholar Norman Gottwald.[8] Kilby picked up on the same idea. 'In Latin American liberation theology, as I read it, they don't so much claim that Jesus is a political thinker as that the church has overly depoliticised him.' Jesus's challenge to political structures is real but indirect. 'He's putting himself at odds with the political order and disrupting how society works, which surely has to do with why he ends up crucified. Can you really say that's non-political? Later political movements could draw their inspiration from that even though he didn't lay out a plan for reorganising society.'

Keith Ward made a similar point. Ward is an eminent Oxford theologian with a rare ability to make his ideas clear and relevant. We've crossed paths on many occasions at events for schools. As Ward says, 'Jesus gave no recommendations for how the state should be run, whether you should have slaves, whether women should be treated the same.' At the same time, 'The notion of a Kingdom of God was a social concept, so it does look as though there's some social or community interest.' Jesus taught and modelled what we now call bottom-up social reform rather than top-down political change. Our challenge to the status quo is made not by manning the barricades but by humbly defying the hierarchies of power and wealth in what we do. When churches open up their doors to refused asylum seekers, for example, they are challenging the systems which deny them the right to work for a living. This may or may not lead to structural reform, but the fact that people do it anyway is a symbol of defiance to the dominant order.

Jesus's teachings were of their time. To put aside thought of politics and material goods made more sense then than it does today. Many may have assumed that the existing political structures were natural. Even if they weren't, seeking liberation from Rome was not a realistic goal, and life in Palestine was even more fragile than it is now.

But in the modern world, the political domain provides opportunities to improve the lot of the poor. Food banks and soup kitchens, which are so often run by religious organisations, are social sticking plasters for problems that governments can solve, and in a democratic society they can be mandated to do so. We do not need to choose between changing ourselves and changing society, loving the poor and increasing their prosperity.

The fact that most Christians agree shows how wise they are not to swallow the whole of Jesus's teaching uncritically. The idea that Jesus sought radical political reform appears to be completely unfounded. The important changes to be made are within our hearts, not within our societies. Care for the poor matters, of course. But for Jesus it is a profound mistake to see the political structures of society or the material well-being of anyone as being of prime importance.

6

MAKING YOURSELF HUMBLE

Jean Vanier was universally praised as an extraordinary and admirable man. He had served in the British and Canadian navies during the Second World War and had gone on to become a professor of philosophy at the University of Toronto. There he taught his students about Aristotle's ideal of a flourishing life, in which we are able to exercise all human capacities, free from poverty or sickness. In his late thirties he had everything he needed to live such a life. But he was so disturbed by the miserable plight of the young men he saw in a mental institution in Trosly-Breuil, north of Paris, that he felt moved to do something about it. In 1964 he bought a small wreck of a stone house in the village and invited two of the young men from the institution to live there with him. Both had been physically and mentally broken by their years in so-called 'care'. Nonetheless they shared the chores and their meals.

The house was named L'Arche, the Ark. By the time Vanier died in 2019, it had grown into a worldwide network of nearly 150 similar communities where people with and without learning disabilities live together. His obituaries were glowing. Secularists such as myself who admired him could not avoid noting that, in his eyes at least, the story of his goodness was not a purely human one. He believed that Jesus was behind everything he did. It's not just that he responded with compassion, as so many of Jesus's commendable parable characters did. Vanier, like Jesus, put the last first. He turned Aristotle on his head, seeing the highest value in those who had come last in the game of life.

In choosing to live alongside life's apparent losers, Vanier appeared to make himself their equal and profoundly humble. Sadly, he ultimately turned out to demonstrate just how difficult it is to truly achieve this. A report published in 2020 by L'Arche International revealed that Vanier had 'manipulative and emotionally abusive' sexual relationships with six women between 1970 and 2005, for which he offered 'spiritual and mystical justifications'. Like so many of Jesus's ethical aspirations, genuine humility is so very hard to achieve.

We are accustomed to thinking of humility as a virtue, but for most of human history there was nothing good about it. When Uriah Heep described himself as an ''umble man' in Dickens's *David Copperfield* he was not boasting. He was rather referring to his lowly status. We still talk about victors 'humbling' those they crush in defeat. In Jesus's morality, however, humility is not a curse of the weak and powerless but a blessing. The vanquished are transformed into the virtuous. The pitiful humiliated are turned into the exalted humbled.

Nietzsche famously disparaged the Christian and Jewish admiration of humility as a symptom of their degenerate 'slave morality'. If we see human life clearly, Nietzsche argues, it is obvious what distinguishes good and bad. Health, strength, prosperity and power are all good. Sickness, weakness, poverty and powerlessness are evidently bad. This is not a moral judgement, simply a description of the facts which no honest person would disagree with. When a person is sick it is natural to want to become well. When people are poor it is normal to want that poverty alleviated. If we didn't think that we wouldn't admire people who help the sick and the poor.

But what happens if your position in the world makes the attainment of the good almost impossible? What if your entire tribe is enslaved, or if you belong to a downtrodden social class? You could seek to rebel, to overthrow the powerful and to claim your share of the riches. But this is difficult and has no guarantee of success. The genius of the Jews, thought Nietzsche, and the Christians after them, was to channel their resentment of the thriving in another way. Rather than seek to *become* good, in the sense of having a good life, they inverted and changed the very *meaning* of good. To be poor, downtrodden and enslaved was now good, not bad. To be rich and powerful was no longer good but worse than bad: it was *evil*. The factual descriptors 'good' and 'bad' were transformed into moral judgements 'good' and 'evil'. One consequence of this is that, paradoxically, humility becomes a matter of pride. Nor is there any shame in being among the poor or hungry, for they are the most blessed.

Jesus's Parable of the Feast (4:16–29) fits Nietzsche's image of a Christian morality rooted in resentment of the wealthy. A king arranges a marriage feast for his son, but despite repeated invitations, people keep making their excuses for not coming. Some even slay the servants sent with the invitations. The king is angry and vengeful, and 'sent forth his armies, and destroyed those murderers, and burned up their city'. When he invites the poor, the maimed, the halt (physically disabled) and the blind instead, it is simply because he is angry with the people he really wanted to come in the first place, whom he now deems to be 'not worthy'. This fits Nietzsche's resentment thesis. Had the king been a genuine friend of the poor surely they would have been on the initial guest list, not the ones seemingly used to spite those who turned him down. Indeed, they are not so much invited as forcibly rounded up: 'Go out into the highways and hedges, and compel them to come in, that my house may be filled.' When one turns up wearing the wrong clothes, he tells his servants, 'Bind him hand and foot, and take him away, and cast him into outer darkness, there shall be weeping and gnashing of teeth.' The motivation seems to be to ensure the first come last, with the last coming first simply an inevitable consequence.

Whether or not we buy into Nietzsche's argument about resentment, it is clear that in Jesus's teachings the downtrodden end up being elevated, shaping the moral imagination of Christendom in which the poor are often idealised. Bertrand Russell described how the better-off can come to believe in 'the superior virtue of the oppressed', a self-serving notion which tends to emerge when oppressors begin to have a bad conscience. 'The idealizing of the victim is useful for a time,' says Russell. 'If virtue is the greatest of goods, and if subjection makes people virtuous, it is kind to refuse them power, since it would destroy their virtue.' There is something of this comforting logic in the idea many well-intentioned Westerners have that the global poor are really happier and better off in their purity than those of us in the decadent materialist developed world. Few, however, believe this sincerely enough to give up all they have and go and live in a Mumbai slum or rural Bihar.

Belief in the superior virtue of the oppressed is surprisingly common among those who actually seek to end their oppression. For example, Russell says, 'many Socialist and Communist intellectuals consider it *de rigueur* to pretend to find the proletariat more amiable than other people, while professing a desire to abolish the conditions which, according to them, alone produce good human beings.'[1]

Jesus looks to be guilty of this self-contradiction when he says that the weak will become strong and the poor rich. This would imply that all the while they remain in poverty the poor aren't really blessed after all. That seems to be the moral of the parable in which Jesus tells his followers not to 'sit not down in the highest room' at a wedding, in case someone with a higher rank comes along and they are then forced to 'begin with shame to take the lowest room'. Better to start in the lower room and be invited to move up. 'For whosoever exalteth himself shall be abased; and he that humbleth himself shall be exalted.' (5:7–14). Humility is presented here not as good in itself but as a means to an end, a rather cynical strategy to enjoy greater rewards in the long run. It also sends a message that although it's bad to enjoy high rank and riches, it won't be in the future when the poor get their rewards. But if being rich and healthy would be good in the future, why should it be bad in the present?

We seem to hit an interpretative dilemma here. If we think the poor and the weak will be rewarded with riches and strength, there is nothing genuinely good about being poor and weak at all. Nor is there anything bad about being rich and strong. But to consider the unfortunate fortunate is as contradictory as it sounds and makes no sense from a purely secular point of view.

There is, however, a way of making better sense of Jesus's praise of humility and those who have been humbled. This requires some interpretative subtlety that some might think is mere sophistry. 'Blessed are the poor' doesn't mean 'all the poor are blessed' or that 'poverty is the greatest blessing'. Rather, poverty provides the opportunity to see the hollowness of worldly goods and success, opening the door to a truly good life. To put it another way, all the poor are 'blessed' with an easier opportunity to reject shallow material rewards than the rich, but not all will take it.

There is a powerful example of this in Viktor Frankl's *Man's Search for Meaning*. Frankl describes talking to a woman in a concentration camp who knew she was going to die the next day. Nonetheless, she was cheerful, telling Frankl, 'I am grateful that fate has hit me so hard. In my former life I was spoiled and did not take spiritual accomplishments seriously.'[2] Frankl does not tell this story to make the obscene suggestion that the people sent to the concentration camps were fortunate. Rather, for all the undeniable horror they had to suffer there was at least one blessing, in the form of an opportunity for a spiritual awakening.

Here is a humane way to interpret Jesus's sayings about the blessedness of the wretched of the earth. Although it would be better not to suffer, there are some important lessons only suffering can teach us. Misfortune both curses and blesses us. That does not mean that the blessings justify the pains, or that everyone who suffers benefits. Jesus's teaching is a comfort to the unfortunate, not a denial of their misfortune.

This interpretative shift from 'all the poor are blessed' to 'some of the poor are blessed in some ways' has strong scriptural support. Jesus says, 'there are last which shall be first, and there are first which shall be last' (4:5) and also 'many that are first shall be last; and the last first' (4:29). Both these formulations are very clear that not all the last will be first and vice versa.

When he does make more sweeping statements, we can see these as being hyperbolic or as meaning something a little different. For instance, we can read, 'Whosoever exalteth himself shall be abased; and he that humbleth himself shall be exalted' not as a prediction about future pay-offs but as a more profound revaluation of values. To exalt yourself is actually to debase yourself, as you turn yourself into a vain egotist. To be humble, in contrast, is to elevate yourself to a higher, more ethical mode of being.

On this reading, the most praiseworthy are not those who simply happen to be poor or persecuted but those who suffer because they are good. These are indeed the people Jesus most explicitly praises: 'Blessed are they which are persecuted for righteousness' sake. Blessed are ye, when men shall revile you, and persecute you, and shall say all manner of evil against you falsely' (2:14). We need not take Jesus to mean that it is better to be reviled or persecuted than not. But when those misfortunes arise as a result of your own goodness, that is in itself a sign that you are living well and therefore in a deep sense are living a truly great life. That's why we admire people like aid workers who die helping others. We do not think them blessed because they died but something in us recognises that they achieved a higher level of being than the rest of us. In one sense they were more 'blessed' than those of us who chose the comfortable path instead.

It seems to me that Jesus is challenging us to understand that there is a higher form of flourishing than superficial enjoyment and doing well in the conventional sense. 'A worthwhile life, is not just one of happiness,' says Keith Ward. 'It is feeling that you are worthwhile and there's something worthwhile that you can do, that it's not just one meaningless thing after another. That's a very rare feeling in our culture. The sense that young people have that they're not worthwhile, comparing themselves with other people on the internet and saying, I'm not good.'

Many believe that this kind of higher calling is nigh on impossible without God. 'Jesus's teaching of love is so absolute, so final,' says Nick Spencer. 'Your willingness to empty yourself, to give of yourself, has to be greater than your willingness to hold on to your own self. The problem with fully secularising it is that, bluntly, why the hell would you? If this is all that there is, if there's no resurrection of the dead, no final restoration, whatever it is, why would you love to the point of death?'

Vanier would seem to bear testimony to this. Anyone can admire him, but without his faith in God would he have been as willing to give up so much to serve others? Of course, we cannot know. Yet a negative answer conflicts with Jesus's teachings about compassion rather than belief being the root of service to others. Around the world there are plenty of people who are outstandingly self-giving without any religious belief. Plenty of doctors who risk their lives in conflict zones with Médecins Sans Frontières, for example, are atheists.

Take the French Catholic priest Jean Meslier (1664–1729), who completely lost his faith, in part through disgust at the corruption of the church. He 'held in contempt those who laughed at the simplicity of the blinded people, who piously furnished large sums for the purchase of prayers'. He kept his atheism a secret during his lifetime but left a posthumous *Testament* which is the first avowedly atheist text in Christian Europe. One reason why Meslier did not leave the priesthood is that the role enabled him to serve his poor parishioners. Addressing them, he wrote, 'My brothers, you will no doubt render me the justice that is my due. The sensitivity that I have shown for your sufferings protects me against your suspicions ... Have I not always proven that I received more pleasure from giving than receiving?' Here is a man whose commitment to supreme self-denying love required him to *give up* his faith, not cling to it.[3]

Spencer himself says that the idea of self-giving love 'reso-nates with people irrespective of whether they have a religious belief'. Many people know what it is like to face a hard choice between being the kind of person they can look at in the mirror and taking an easier way out. Even without the promise of God setting things right, people sometimes choose death over a form of life they feel is one of moral degeneracy rather than flourishing.

Mulling over this, I found myself thinking of Paolo Sorrentino's film *The Consequences of Love*. Both its mood and its denouement have stayed with me. The central character is a man whose life has become an empty one of effective slavery to the Cosa Nostra, albeit with a very large expense budget. Eventually, he defies his masters, stealing their money, because, he says, they 'stole my life'. He is given a chance to save himself by telling them where the money is but he refuses. In a long final scene, he stands impassively while he is slowly buried alive in concrete. His defiance seems to be an answer to Jesus's ques-tion, 'For what shall it profit a man, if he shall gain the whole world, and lose himself or be cast away? What shall a man give in exchange for his soul?' (4:15). Sometimes, paradoxically, we flourish more by dying than by saving our life, in that being willing to die we fulfil our potential for goodness more than we do by staying alive but compromised. We want to know that our lives have added up to something, and the way for them to do so does not always involve comfort, pleasure or happiness.

Jesus not only spoke well of weakness, he spoke very badly about the apparent signs of success. That does not necessarily mean he thought it wrong to laugh or to be spoken well of.

Rather, as a matter of fact, those who had the most cause for laughter in his time were generally the oppressors. Those who enjoyed the highest reputations were not well regarded for genuine virtue but for more shallow reasons, like the regard in which the rich and celebrities are often held.

If we take his teachings as a whole and assume he is no fool, Jesus cannot really be saying: poverty good, wealth bad; sickness good, health bad. Rather, he is saying that these simply aren't the most important sources of value. What matters most is becoming the best person you can be. So, for example, he tells his disciples, 'If any man desire to be first, the same shall be last of all, and servant of all' (6:31). This is not a way of saying that servitude is the slow but sure way to mastery, but that to serve others is part of what makes for a good life. Service is a way of becoming first in a different sense from that in which the master is first: first in spirit, not in status and power.

Similarly we should not underestimate the apparently humble. The Parables of the Mustard Seed and the Yeast (7:22–27) tell us that the tiniest seed can become the greatest herb of all and that a little yeast can cause a whole loaf to rise. These are metaphors that suggest humility has its own power to enlarge our souls and make us spiritually great, not that it's the smart way to worldly greatness.

Humility of the best kind is not about self-abasement or celebrating misfortune. It is about acknowledging our own weakness and fallibility. When Jesus says, 'Can the blind lead the blind? shall they not both fall into the ditch?' (3:11), he seems to be talking about all humanity. No one is qualified to make themselves master over others because we are all lacking perfect moral vision.

On more than one occasion Jesus reserves special praise for those who seem to acknowledge their weakness and imperfection. On one occasion a centurion was hoping to have his servant cured. But the centurion did not consider himself good enough to face Jesus in person to ask for his help. Although he was 'a man set under authority' who says to his soldiers, 'Come, and he cometh', and to his servant, 'Do this, and he doeth it', he said, 'I am not worthy that thou shouldest enter under my roof: Wherefore neither thought I myself worthy to come unto thee' (5:2–6).

Jesus's reply is curious. He says, 'I have not found so great faith, no, not in Israel.' Faith seems to be the wrong word. Why does it show faith to acknowledge one's own inferiority? But this is not the only occasion when Jesus responds to humility with this word. On another occasion a woman comes to Jesus to seek help with her daughter (6:1–5). Despite his reputation for kindness, Jesus ignores her the first time she pleads with him. It is only when his disciples complain she is bothering them that he starts to properly engage, perhaps not just to teach them a lesson but in belated recognition that he had not been exemplary himself.

What he then says is a little cryptic: 'It is not meet to take the children's bread, and to cast it to dogs.' She replies, 'Truth, Lord: yet the dogs eat of the crumbs which fall from their masters' table.' This is the remark that finally persuades Jesus that she deserves credit. 'O woman, great is thy faith: be it unto thee even as thou wilt.' Like the centurion, her faith is said to be great when she says something that puts herself in a humble position, like a dog taking crumbs from the master's table.

Why would either the centurion's or the woman's humility be described as faith? The word 'faith' derives from the Latin *fides*, meaning 'trust'. Humility is linked to trust because when we accept that we are flawed and imperfect, we accept that we are not self-sufficient and so we have to trust in others. Faith is born not of certainty and conviction but of an opening up that springs from an acceptance of our own inadequacy.

Jesus's teaching here loses something when stripped of its divine attributes. It is a common religious trope to believe that human beings lack the capacity to save themselves, that we need to give ourselves over to some higher power. Islam itself means 'submission', not because God is a tyrant who wants to dominate us but because only by submitting to him can we achieve what we cannot achieve alone. Pure Land Buddhism teaches that enlightenment is reached by reciting the phrase '*Namu Amida Butsu*' ('I take refuge in Amitābha Buddha'). The Kyoto School philosopher Tanabe Hajime describes this as an act of giving oneself over to 'other-power'. Without a belief in any such higher power, the deep acknowledgement of our inadequacy commended by Jesus would seem to become a source of despair rather than a route to salvation.

That problem runs deep, since the fundamental moral wretchedness of humanity is baked into Jesus's vision. Its roots are in the Hebrew Bible's account of the fall, when Eve ate the fruit from the tree of knowledge of good and evil and humanity was banished from Eden. The idea that all humanity inherits this 'original sin' was developed in early Christian thought. The orthodoxy became that this sin could not be removed without the sacrifice of God's only son on the cross. But you don't need to believe in Adam and Eve or original sin to see the story as an allegorical statement of human moral inadequacy. Perhaps this is why Keith Ward finds that 'Jesus's moral teaching is very ambiguous but very challenging at the same time. You never know specifically what you're supposed to do but you do know that you're failing whatever you're doing.'

The inability of fallen humanity to save itself was one reason why several of the Christian thinkers I spoke to doubted that the Gospels could be made fully secular. For instance, Ward believes that Jesus advocated 'a change of attitude rather than a change of principle' in which you 'become not arrogant and proud but humble, loving and caring'. That sounds as though it is entirely translatable to secular terms. But a key element of Jesus's teachings would be missing, namely that 'having that kind of love is said by Jesus to be due to a power of God within human lives. It's not from your own resources, it's something you feel as coming from outside. Without a sense of some power other than myself which could overcome my worst inclinations I wouldn't overcome them.' The slogan Ward likes here is, 'Let go and let God. You let go of trying to do it on your own and you just give yourself to some higher power.' Although he accepts that 'you don't have to call it God', it has to in some sense be transcendent, beyond the human.

Most Christians share a sense that without a transcendent dimension, represented by the resurrected Christ, we are left helpless. Taken as a whole, that is the message of the New Testament. Paul wrote to the Corinthians, 'But if there be no resurrection of the dead, then is Christ not risen: And if Christ be not risen, then is our preaching vain, and your faith is also vain' (I Corinthians 15:13–14). Lucy Winkett quotes her favourite line from *The West Wing*, 'A leader without followers is just a guy taking a walk', then says, 'I sometimes think about Jesus in that way. Ultimately, he ends up as a guy taking a walk to crucifixion, because they've all gone. If you stop there, there's an arc of colossal failure about his earthly ministry. That's why the transcendent aspect of his nature is really vital from a Christian perspective. If you just leave Jesus as a moral teacher long ago, he's someone we know hardly anything about and from whom we have a few sayings, not many of which are very original. You can admire his remarkable life, his incredible energy and a passion that leads him to be crucified for what he believes in. But will it make you change your life? What Christians would say is that we can live that life not just by copying Jesus but by accompanying Jesus today. So the resurrection, however you understand that, is incredibly important. It's not a happy ending to a sad story. It changes everything. It means that there's a kind of assurance underneath, a promise of God of eternal life. And if life is actually eternal it's started already. So we're living in a reality that is both imminent and transcendent now.'

The impossibility of humanity saving itself is a strong theme in Kierkegaard's thought. As Clare Carlisle explains, Kierkegaard 'says that to be a Christian is to imitate Christ, and then he also says this is impossible to do, but that's OK because you'll be saved by Christ. There's this double aspect of setting up an ethical ideal that on the one hand is so strict, demanding and rigorous that it's impossible to attain, but on the other hand is infinitely lenient because Jesus in his mercy and grace forgives everything. Kierkegaard emphasizes these two extremes of rigour and leniency.'

However, it seems to me that we can deal with the intractability of our own imperfection without divine aid, as hinted at by something Elizabeth Oldfield said: 'We know we're not good enough, we know we don't live up to it, that's the point of the cross. Christians don't read the New Testament as pure ethical teaching which we either pass or fail. It's are you moving towards or moving away?' It's true that for Christians there is also a sense that 'because you're known and loved by God, God himself closes that gap'. Nonetheless, the godless can share the same aspiration to do our best to move in the direction of goodness without any faith that God will make up for our failure to reach it.

Such a position would not have satisfied Kierkegaard. Carlisle says Kierkegaard thought you needed both the rigour and the leniency of Christianity: 'He's critical of people who only accept the leniency. On the other hand, if you only have the rigour you'd be left in despair, you'd just feel terrible about yourself for falling short of this impossible ideal.' Oldfield and Spencer take Kierkegaard's side. Without divine grace, the imperative to try to overcome our frailty is, as Oldfield puts it, 'just another yoke on someone's neck', to which Spencer adds, 'a bloody enormous one which will crush you with guilt'.

I don't think that's inevitable. There is a way to make sense of the profound humility taught by Jesus in secular terms. By accepting our own weakness, we come to accept our dependency on others and to become more modest about ourselves and how good we can be. For sure, this gives life a tragic edge, like in Albert Camus's 'The Myth of Sisyphus'. The eponymous protagonist is condemned for eternity to push a rock to the top of a hill, only for it to roll back to the bottom for him to start again. Sisyphus, we are told, must embrace his fate. If he does so 'one must imagine Sisyphus happy'.[4] We can work on becoming the best person we can be, knowing that we will always fall short and that death will cut our endeavour short too.

We can see the importance of acknowledging our dependency on others and our own weakness in Jesus's repeated rejection of hierarchy. His own humble origins bear witness to this. When Jesus began his mission, the people in the synagogue could not believe his wisdom, asking, 'Is not this the carpenter's son, the son of Mary, the brother of James, and Joses, and of Juda, and Simon? And his sisters, are they not all with us? Whence then hath this man all these things?' (1:16). Jesus's very person evidenced the need to overthrow old hierarchies of blood and nobility. Your social status has nothing to do with your moral status, which matters a lot more.

Does that mean that there are no hierarchies at all in Jesus's moral vision? Some of his sayings do suggest an absolute egalitarianism, such as 'The disciple is not above his master: but every one that is perfect shall be as his master' (3:12). Jesus says something very similar when he washes his disciples' feet, telling them, 'The servant is not greater than his lord; neither he that is sent greater than he that sent him' (5:29).

One of the most striking anti-hierarchical passages comes when he says, 'But be not ye called Rabbi; and all ye are brethren. Neither be ye called masters. But he that is greatest among you shall be your servant. And whosoever shall exalt himself shall be abased; and he that shall humble himself shall be exalted' (11:42–43). There should be no ecclesiastical hierarchies: no priests, only brethren. It seem extraordinary how flagrantly almost all Christian churches have ignored this clear instruction and have created arcane layers of clerics.

Jesus's final word on hierarchy comes at the Last Supper, when the disciples fight over who among them is the greatest. It is not the only time they come across as a rather slow-witted bunch who have failed to take in the essence of their master's teaching. Jesus tells them, 'He that is greatest among you, let him be as the younger; and he that is chief, as he that doth serve. For whether is greater, he that sitteth at meat, or he that serveth? is not he that sitteth at meat? but I am among you as he that serveth' (12:7).

The message is more complicated than the simple elimination of all hierarchy. Look more closely at the story of Jesus washing his disciples' feet. It begins with him telling them that no master praises his servants simply for doing what they are supposed to do, so when he sends them to act as his servants in the world they should expect to be treated as nothing more than servants: 'say, We are unprofitable servants: we have done that which was our duty to do' (5:18).

But then he washes their feet to show that the master must also be a servant to those he rules. The point is not that there is no difference between master and servant. It is rather that both servant and master have to serve. They must not be like the Gentile princes who 'exercise dominion' over their subjects. Instead, 'whosoever will be great among you, let him be your minister; And whosoever will be chief among you, let him be your servant' (5:20). Hierarchy is not so much abolished as changed. Masters too must serve but they do not stop being masters.

This chimes with Keith Ward's understanding of what he sees as Jesus's main teaching: the Kingdom of God or the Kingdom of Heaven. Like many theologians he thinks this best translates as the rule of God. 'The kingdom is of a peculiar sort because those who lead ought to be the ones who serve, so it's not a hierarchical kingdom but one of mutual service.' At the same time, 'It's implied in the Gospels that Jesus is the king in the kingdom.'

Whether or not Jesus sought to abolish hierarchy or to radically alter its meaning, he clearly did believe that in order to be great we have to serve, and to serve we need to become humble. His own example, however, sends a mixed message. Yes, he serves others and refuses all elevating descriptions. For instance, he corrects the man who calls him 'Good Master', saying none deserved that description. At his trial he refuses to say he was the King of Jews, pointing out that Pilate said that (13:5, 19 and 23).

But he is far from always humble. He has a deep self-assuredness and a strong sense of vocation. He seems utterly certain in his declarations and appears to be free of self-doubt on all but a few brief occasions. When he arrives in Jerusalem he allows himself to be paraded in by a huge crowd and tells the Pharisees that if the people 'should hold their peace, the stones would immediately cry out' (11:5). Like many moral teachers of the time, not just in Judaea but across the Graeco-Roman world, he claims to have a divine mission. 'I must preach the Kingdom of Heaven to other cities also,' he said, 'for therefore am I sent' (1:22). There is no reason to think that this claim by itself entailed a belief in his own divine status. It does, however, show a self-belief that is somewhat in tension with Jesus's other displays of humility. This is not a man unsure of his own importance.

Jesus did believe, however, that even he should not elevate himself too high and should always be willing to serve others. If he is portrayed as being knowingly superior by those who described his life and teachings, this was perhaps justified. There are people who are better than almost all others. To embrace the ethic of humility is not to pretend that none are better or worse than others. Humility in Jesus's teaching has nothing to do with what we would today call self-esteem. It is simply a matter of seeing the poor, the sick and the weak not as people to be pitied but as challenges to our value system. They show us that serving others is a higher calling than simply serving ourselves and that not only is material comfort less important than our goodness but it can distract us from fully developing it. That is a call for humility that still deserves to be heard today.

7

NON-JUDGEMENT

On 13 November 2015, a coordinated series of terrorist attacks in Paris left 130 people dead. Every victim and their relatives had their own heartbreaking story, many of which we heard in the weeks that followed. One of the most powerful was an open letter to the attackers written by Antoine Leiris on Facebook. His wife was one of ninety people massacred at an Eagles of Death Metal concert at the Bataclan theatre. Headed 'you won't have my hate', Leiris's letter brought tears to my eyes then and still does now.

It began, 'Friday night you stole the life of an exceptional being, the love of my life, the mother of my son, but you will not have my hatred. I don't know who you are and I don't want to know, you're dead souls. If this God for whom you kill blindly made us in his image, every bullet in the body of my wife is a wound in his heart.'

He continued, 'I won't make you this gift to hate you. You have been looking for it, but responding to hatred with anger would be to yield to the same ignorance that has made you what you are.'

Leiris's dignity was not for lack of grief or anger. In his letter, he did not spare anyone the depths of his sorrow. 'I saw her this morning. Finally, after nights and days of waiting. She was as beautiful as when she left this Friday night, as beautiful as when I fell madly in love more than 12 years ago. Of course I am devastated by sorrow, I concede this little victory, but it will be short. I know that she will accompany us every day and that we will meet in this paradise of free souls to which you will never have access.'

The letter is extraordinary. It states in earnest, unpretentious prose how neither death nor hate can defeat love. To many, this 'refusal of hate' seemed exactly the right response. It might seem to fall short of the Christian injunction to forgive and not to judge others, but to me it expresses all that is best in Jesus's teachings while avoiding all that is potentially wrong about a forgiveness that is too easy and a refusal to judge that is too absolute.

Jesus's teachings about forgiveness and non-judgement are of a piece. They are best approached through one of the most famous Gospel stories, of the woman taken in adultery (8:56–63). The scribes and Pharisees take her to Jesus to ask whether they should stone her, according to the law of Moses. It is one of their typical traps. Jesus has claimed to be upholding the law, but clearly many of his teachings go against common practice. He is also evidently against any violent justice. The idea was to force him to contradict himself or the law and so expose him as a seditious force.

Jesus's answer is cleverer than their question. He stoops

down and writes in the sand with his finger, initially silent 'as though he heard them not'. Eventually he answers them, saying, 'He that is without sin among you, let him first cast a stone at her.' None are able to do so: 'being convicted by their own conscience,' the Gospel says, they 'went out one by one'.

Jesus then turns to the woman and says, 'where are those thine accusers? hath no man condemned thee?' She replies, 'No man, Lord.' Jesus then says, 'Neither do I condemn thee: go, and do wrong no more.'

This short episode captures a great deal of what non-judgement means in Jesus's morality and why it is so important. One detail is particularly interesting: his initial silence. For me it points to Jesus's thoughtfulness, which is modelling a refusal to rush to judgement. Being judgemental in the wrong way is often a matter of being too quick to judge.

One of the most notable points the story makes clear is that Jesus does not reserve judgement completely. He is unequivocal that adultery is a sin and the woman has done wrong. This is entirely in keeping with his other pronouncements. Jesus constantly makes judgements in the Gospel, often very harsh ones. The scribes and Pharisees are denounced as hypocrites and many actions are condemned as wrong. If non-judgement requires refusing to say whether anything is right or wrong, Jesus certainly never practised it.

So what does he mean when he says, 'Neither do I condemn thee'? In one sense, he has very clearly done exactly that, as by saying, 'do wrong no more', he judges her action to have been wrong. There is, however, a distinction between *judging a person's actions* and *condemning the person* themselves. This is often summed up in the words 'Love the sinner, hate the sin.' It is thought that we owe the origins of this phrase to St Augustine. In a letter to a convent he advised the nuns to punish those of their number who repeatedly gave 'wanton looks' with 'due love for the persons and hatred of the sin'.[1] Although Jesus never said the exact words, it does seem to capture something important in his message.

The mantra is not without its critics. Many whose sexuality does not conform to neat heterosexual norms complain that it is a principle that allows people to hide their hatred of them behind a professed hatred of something more abstract. Another criticism is that in practice people just aren't good at keeping the two apart. Many have argued that despising Islam should not be called Islamophobia because it does not mean despising Muslims. While that is technically true, all too often we see that when we allow a belief to be viciously attacked, the demonisation of believers often soon follows.

The common elision of hatred of sins and sinners made Gandhi wary of the call to keep them apart. He agreed that 'Man and his deed are two distinct things' and that while 'a good deed should call forth approbation and a wicked deed disapprobation, the doer of the deed, whether good or wicked, always deserves respect or pity as the case may be'. Nonetheless, it is sadly true that '"Hate the sin and not the sinner" is a precept which, though easy enough to understand, is rarely practised, and that is why the poison of hatred spreads in the world.'[2]

Despite being aware of this difficulty, Gandhi saw the sin/sinner distinction as essential to his principle of non-violence (*ahimsa*), especially his advocacy of non-violent resistance or 'fighting with peace' (*satyagraha*), a connection potentially illuminating for Jesus's teaching. For Gandhi, to fight serious wrongdoing effectively you need to have no hostility to the wrongdoer. That is the only way to bring about the right kind of change. Hatred only breeds hatred. So *judgement of injustice* requires *non-judgement of the unjust*. It is only because you judge the injustice to be so serious and wrong that you are in the position of having to refrain from judging the perpetrators themselves. This kind of reasoning explains Jesus's attitude towards the woman caught in adultery. The need not to judge her only arises out of the need to judge the sinfulness of her act.

But why not judge the person? There are several reasons. Augustine suggests one in his instructions to the nuns. He tells them not to feel bad when they inform on their sisters' misdemeanours. Reporting wrongdoing is not malevolent but kind, since it would be wrong to 'allow sisters to perish, whom you may correct by giving information of their faults. For if your sister had a wound on her person which she wished to conceal through fear of the surgeon's lance, would it not be cruel if you kept silence about it, and true compassion if you made it known? How much more, then, are you bound to make known her sin, that she may not suffer more fatally from a neglected spiritual wound.'

If we love someone, we want the best for them. The best for anyone is not to live immorally and therefore suboptimally. So it is because we love rather than hate people that we always need to help them to see when they are doing wrong. Non-judgement is therefore more than simply refraining from something. It is tied in with active care for them. That is why Jesus did not just refuse to judge sinners, he actively sought their company.

Take, for instance, the story of Jesus eating with Levi the tax collector and his equally iniquitous friends (8:1–5). The scribes and Pharisees were outraged, but Jesus said, 'They that are whole have no need of the physician; but they that are sick.' He provokes the same reaction when he accepts an invitation into the house of Zacchaeus the tax collector (8:6–13). 'For I am come to seek and to save that which was lost,' he says.

Jesus's message is very simple and has a self-evident truth

to it. If you care about helping people to become good, you need to focus most energy on those who fall most short. This is the message of Jesus's repeated sheep and shepherd analogies (8:14–23). 'What man of you, having an hundred sheep, if he lose one of them, doth not leave the ninety and nine in the wilderness, and go after that which is lost, until he find it?' And he who finds that lost beast 'rejoiceth more of that sheep, than of the ninety and nine which went not astray.'

Historically, societies have always been quick to write off their most renegade members. Jesus was unusual to emphasise helping to virtue those whom others have discounted. The belief that anyone could in principle become a sage was widespread in Greek and Roman philosophy, but it was understood that very few, if any, could actually succeed. So the idea that the apparently irredeemable were actually redeemable would have seemed very strange. Jesus holds out the hope and promise that no matter how low we have fallen, there is still the possibility of *metanoia*, a change of heart.

His willingness to consort with the sinful also challenges a widespread idea especially prevalent in virtue ethics: that virtue and vice are both contagious. As Confucius said, 'Virtue is never solitary; it always has neighbours.'[3] Aristotle was typical in advising people who wanted to be good to seek the company of the good and avoid that of the wicked. In the virtue ethics tradition, being good is a matter of habit and so it is natural that to cultivate the right habits you should be surrounded by people who help you to do so. 'A sort of training in virtue may result from associating with good people,' wrote Aristotle, endorsing the view of Theognis.[4] Jesus's defiance of this could be a sign that he is such an exemplary person that he is incorruptible, or that all good people have a duty to serve as examples to others, especially those who most need it.

If we accept that the most important thing is to become the best versions of ourselves, we have another reason to refrain from judging other people. If we realise how truly difficult it is to become 'perfect', as Jesus commands his followers to do, we also know we are in no position to judge the imperfections of others. 'Can the blind lead the blind? shall they not both fall into the ditch?' asked Jesus in the Sermon on the Mount (3:11). All of us have flawed moral vision, so none of us should claim to be able to see clearly what others should do. As Clare Carlisle puts it, the impossible demand of perfection 'counters moralism because no one can do it. So you learn that you must let go of the moralistic idea that we're doing it right and you're not. There's something quite levelling about the impossibility of this high ideal. And you never really know if you're doing it right anyway.'

That is the power behind Jesus's command 'He that is without sin among you, let him first cast a stone at her.' Note that Jesus himself does not throw a stone, implying either that he rejects the law or that he does not consider himself without sin. The latter is more in keeping with the overall tenor of the Gospel story than the former.

Jesus's refusal to judge individuals is a recurrent feature of his life and teaching. When one man asked him to resolve a dispute with his brother, Jesus said, 'Man, who made me a judge or a divider over you?' (6:23). One good reason to refrain from judging others is that it is a distraction from the more important task of improving yourself. 'And how canst thou say to thy brother, Brother, let me pull out the mote that is in thine eye, when thou thyself beholdest not the beam that is in thine own eye?' asks Jesus. 'Thou hypocrite, cast out first the beam out of thine own eye, and then shalt thou see clearly to pull out the mote that is in thy brother's eye' (3:13). The unstated caveat here is that no human being is capable of becoming so pure as to have an unsullied moral eye, and so no one is ever in a position to see the mote in another's.

There is one important way in which Jesus repeatedly does judge sinners as well as sins. He is critical of many *classes* of people, especially the scribes and Pharisees. Is he breaking his own rules? It might look like it. If I say, 'All bankers are greedy,' and you are a banker, what I have said entails that you are greedy. To protest that I was not talking about *you* is disingenuous, since I was in fact talking about you and all your peers.

One way to erase the inconsistency is to deny that Jesus's general criticism of groups strictly entails judgement of every member of the group. In everyday speech, generalisations are not always assumed to be universal statements. 'Men are taller than women' is understood to mean that men are on *average* taller than women. 'Philosophers are odd' means that philosophers *tend to be* odd. When Jesus talks about scribes and Pharisees, it is more in keeping with natural language to assume that he is talking of how they generally are and not how they literally all are. So when he denounces the group he is not judging any individual member of it.

Even if he is talking about all scribes and Pharisees, there is an important way in which addressing a group is different from addressing an individual. When we talk of a person or an object as an instance of something, we are not saying that it cannot be an instance of one or more other things. For example, I can treat *The Thinker* as a sculpture, as part of the oeuvre of Rodin, as a lump of rock, as an investment, as a representation of a philosopher and so on. None of these captures all that it is. What I say of *The Thinker* as a sculpture is very different from what I'd say of it as a mineral.

When Jesus criticises Pharisees, he is indeed attacking

individuals *as* Pharisees. But a Pharisee is never *just* a Pharisee. So there is a legitimate sense in which Jesus can say that attacking a Pharisee as a Pharisee is not the same as attacking a Pharisee as an individual, a whole human being. He is in effect saying: I do not know whether you are a good or a bad person, but *as a Pharisee* your behaviour is reprehensible. It's similar to when we remonstrate with a bureaucrat or an employee without believing it is anything personal.

It would be a very good thing for public life and civility if we were more careful to distinguish between whole people and their many specific roles and identities. In recent years this has become rarer and harder. For example, in the USA Democrats have always disagreed with Republicans and vice versa, but it didn't generally get in the way of friendship. It was taken for granted that a person could be good or bad irrespective of their political views. When, in 1958, Gallup asked a representative sample of Americans whether they wanted their daughter to marry a Democrat or a Republican, 18 per cent said Democrat, 10 per cent Republican and 72 per cent didn't mind. This has changed. In 2016 an almost identical question, generalised to all children, found that 28 per cent wanted a Democrat, 27 per cent a Republican and only 45 per cent didn't care. Gandhi was right. It's very difficult to keep our judgements of what is a sin and who is a sinner apart, and society is poisoned when we don't.

Although Jesus makes a good case for the virtue of non-judgement, there are also several suggestions of a more self-interested, karmic motivation: 'Judge not, that ye be not judged: condemn not, that ye be condemned: forgive, that ye be forgiven: For with what judgment ye judge, ye shall be judged: and with what measure ye mete, it shall be measured to you again' (3:14–15). Jesus follows this warning about negative karma with a promise of the positive variety: 'Give, and it shall be given unto you; good measure, pressed down, and shaken together, and running over, shall men give into your bosom. For with the same measure that ye mete withal it shall be measured to you again' (3:16).

There are so many similar karmic expressions in Jesus's teaching that it seems likely he did believe in some kind of law of moral cause and effect. The Beatitudes which open the Sermon on the Mount read almost as a catalogue of the various ways in which the universe will redress unjust imbalances: those who hunger shall be filled, those who mourn will be comforted, those who weep will laugh. At the same time, those who are full will hunger, those who laugh will soon be crying, while those who are praised will have their true nature revealed.

However, when it comes to judgement we don't need to believe in any karmic or supernatural forces of justice to make sense of the not judging so as not to be judged. We could instead see it as a simplified attempt to articulate an idea central to many moral theories: the principle of universalisability.

A notable example of this is Kant's 'categorical imperative', which states, 'Act only according to that maxim whereby you can, at the same time, will that it should become a universal law.' In other words, do only what you can and would permit others to do and don't do yourself what you are not able or willing to permit others to do. Don't steal if you are not prepared to have others steal from you, don't lie if you don't want to be lied to. That is not because being good karmically causes others to be good to you. It is rather that if you don't follow this categorical imperative you are being a hypocrite, giving yourself more moral slack than you are willing to give others.

In practice, this rule is very similar to Jesus's instruction 'as ye would that men should do to you, do ye also to them likewise' (2:38). Jesus is not a systematic moral philosopher and he does not derive from this a strict rule of rational consistency, as Kant does. But within Jesus's teachings we can find both key components of the categorical imperative: the instruction to do as you would be done by and the observation that you are a hypocrite if you do not.

Both Jesus and Kant are offering a version of the golden rule, which recurs in many moral traditions. Confucius said, 'Do not impose on others what you do not wish for yourself.' Like Kant, this places limits on what we allow ourselves to do to others. It is therefore essentially negative, telling us what not to do. But for Jesus the golden rule is a positive obligation to treat others well: 'And as ye would that men should do to you, do ye also to them likewise' (2:38). Only the Jains are more demanding, broadening the principle to cover all life: 'A man should wander about treating all creatures as he himself would be treated.'[5] There is a radical impartiality in this teaching. Everyone should be treated the same, regardless of their goodness.

Although I have argued the 'do as you would be done by' ethic need not be rooted in any idea of karma, there is a weaker sense in which we can say wrongness does often come back to bite the wrongdoer. The mechanism for this is conscience, dramatised in the Gospel by the story of Judas Iscariot. Judas betrays Jesus for thirty pieces of silver. No one in the Gospel ever judges or punishes him for this. Even Jesus, who is shown to know Judas will betray him, simply tells him, 'That thou doest, do quickly' (12:14). But ultimately Judas sees he has done wrong and condemns himself. He goes to the chief priests and elders to return the silver, saying, 'I have sinned in that I have betrayed the innocent blood.' Then he hangs himself (13:2–3). The price of 'sin' is not that you will be sent to hell by a divine judge or that karmic forces will ensure you're paid back. The price of being bad is that you have to live with being the person who did wrong.

This story provides a secular surrogate for the divine judgement which is usually assumed to be an essential part of Jesus's teaching. But is the judgement of ourselves strict enough to do the work required of it? Conscience is often easily appeased, or not even pricked. One disturbing fictional treatment of this theme is Woody Allen's film *Crimes and Misdemeanours*. The plot concerns a man, Judah, who has his ex-mistress killed in order to stop her revelations ruining his life. For a long time he is racked with guilt. But at the film's end, under the pretence of describing a fictional story, he says of himself, 'Maybe once in a while he has a bad moment, but it passes. And, with time, it all fades.'

His interlocutor, a film-maker called Cliff, is sceptical: 'Here's what I would do. I would have him turn himself in. Cos then, you see, your story assumes tragic proportions because, in the absence of a God, he is forced to assume that responsibility himself.'

Cliff's case for self-judgement as a secular alternative for the divine kind is exactly the same as mine. That is bad news for me. Cliff is a fool who doesn't understand human nature. Judah tells him, 'That's fiction. That's movies.'

Allen's story provides a dose of realism for those who think Jesus's moral teaching will lose nothing when separated from the divine. The disturbing truth is that the bad will not always be judged, even by themselves. Jesus's words have power only for those who are already committed to seeking a good life. If you are so committed, knowing others will not be is no reason to give in to our baser instincts and join them.

Nor should we simply accept that some people don't care about living a morally good life. Jesus's teachings suggest that we should all think carefully about living with the consequences of our actions. You might reject morality and simply seek pleasure or worldly goods. But before you go down that path, Jesus suggests you think seriously about what it means to embrace amorality. As we have seen, it may look like the easy path but ultimately it becomes a life devoted to transient, shallow and fragile goods. The challenge is to find the courage to judge the weight of our own lives while we still have time to change.

The most demanding requirement of Jesus's ethic of non-judgement is that you do not merely have to refrain from judging; sometimes you also have to forgive. For many this is what makes Christian ethics special. Although it's certainly not the only moral system to advocate forgiveness, it does seem to give the value a distinctively central place. The forgiveness Jesus asks for stretches the bounds of generosity. When Peter asks him how many times he should forgive his brother, suggesting seven, Jesus says, 'Until seventy times seven.' Nor should we limit the number of sins we are willing to forgive. If your brother 'trespass against thee seven times in a day, and seven times in a day turn again to thee, saying, I repent; thou shalt forgive him' (8:31).

Yet understanding what exactly Jesus asks us to do when we forgive is not straightforward. It is not unconditional. When describing how forgiveness of the brother should be carried out, Jesus gives very specific instructions: 'go and tell him his fault between thee and him alone: if he shall hear thee, thou hast gained thy brother. But if he will not hear thee, then take with thee one or two more, that in the mouth of two or three witnesses every word may be established. And if he shall neglect to hear them, tell it unto the church' (8:32–34).

This makes no sense if forgiveness can be unilateral. Jesus

is making it clear that forgiveness requires some acknowledgement of the wrongdoing from the one forgiven. They have to be willing to do what is necessary to restore the relationship their actions have broken. This teaching is confirmed by the Parable of the Unforgiving Servant (8:35–43), in which a king resolves to have his servant sell his wife, his children and all that he has to meet a debt. When the servant throws himself on the king's mercy he is moved by compassion and forgives the debt. This man, though, goes on to try violently to extract from others the debts they owe him. When the king finds out he revokes his earlier forgiveness. Forgiveness is conditional: when it is offered it has to be properly taken. If it is not we have a right to annul it. In both this parable and in his answer to Peter, Jesus makes it plain that forgiveness is meant to have an effect on the forgiven and if it does not do so, then there is no longer any obligation to forgive.

Forgiveness is an interaction between two people with a social function, not a divine prerogative to magically erase sins. As Nick Spencer puts it, 'The point of forgiveness is that you're focusing on getting the relationship back on track. You forgive someone so that the relationship is restored with them.' This is perhaps why Jesus denies that it is blasphemous for him to forgive sins. His statement 'Ye may know that the Son of man hath power on earth to forgive sins' (8:28) may make it sound as though he has divine absolutory powers. But this cannot be the case since he tells others to forgive too. Forgiveness is something any person can do in an attempt to change people and the relations between them.

This relational aspect of forgiveness could be a way of understanding a major part of the source Gospels which I eventually decided to leave out of *The Godless Gospel*. Jesus is reported to have performed many healings in the four Gospels. Although these look miraculous and are often described as such, many have argued that they can be understood in more naturalistic terms. One such way is to believe that Jesus was some kind of doctor. More interesting is the idea that 'healing' was not a matter of curing physical disease but restoring people's social standing, or sense of dignity and well-being. People with deformities and skin diseases ('leper' is arguably a mistranslation) were often deemed unclean and were outcasts. It could be that Jesus 'healed' these people by telling them that they were clean, returning them to society. Like forgiveness, healing was a matter of restoring relationships.

Although I find this interpretation attractive, I do not think it fits the actual descriptions of healing in the source Gospels. These often read as very literal and miraculous. If Jesus's healings were more social and psychological, they seem to have already been transformed into something more fantastical by the time they were recorded.

The second limit Jesus places on forgiveness is that he says there is a point at which we should give up. He concludes his instructions on pursuing forgiveness with your brother by saying, 'but if he neglect to hear the church, let him be unto thee as an heathen man and a tax collector' (8:34). (Notice also here that he speaks ill of heathens and tax collectors. As we say earlier, Jesus judges groups of people harshly even as he judges individuals with leniency.)

Forgiveness is therefore in one sense limitless and in another conditional. 'There's one level on which you never stop forgiving,' says Karen Kilby. 'There was somebody in a village I used to live in whose partner was somewhat abusive. In one way I think she was right to try to forgive him, including by reflecting on the hardships of his own childhood and how he might have been doing the best he could. But when it comes to whether one stays living with a person, it seems to me there's a process to go through, maybe of trying to talk to them, and then trying in a different way, and at a certain point the right thing to do is to leave. So in terms of how you try to interact with them you ought to give up at a certain point; in terms of whether you judge them as an individual you might go on forever seeking to forgive.'

The limits of forgiveness were brought home to me when I met Julie Nicholson, whose daughter had been murdered in the London bombings of 2005. Nicholson was a vicar in the Church of England and she ended up resigning because she was unable to forgive her daughter's killers. I think a compassionate Jesus would not have asked her to go so far. So long as she didn't seek vengeance or allow her grief and anger to blind her to her own need to live well, that would have been enough.

One other aspect of forgiveness relates to Jesus's emphasis on the importance of self-transformation. Saying 'I forgive you' is not so much an act of charity and kindness as a way of keeping the focus on our own goodness and our relationships. When we harbour resentments we remain focused on the failings of others, which it is not in our power to change. When we forgive we relieve ourselves of a burden of grievance and can return to focus on our own virtue. In Shakespeare's *The Merchant of Venice* Portia captures this link between self-cultivation and forgiveness in her line, 'We do pray for mercy, and that same prayer doth teach us all to render the deeds of mercy' (Act 4, Scene 1).[6] This is part and parcel of the ethic of non-judgement: to refuse to forgive is to remain in a position of judgement over others, whereas to forgive is to refrain from judging.

Forgiveness therefore has two dimensions, an other- and a self-facing one. The other-directed aspect of forgiveness is a form of compassion. It is telling that in Jesus's stories of forgiveness, compassion is at its root. The father of the prod-igal son and the master of the indebted servant both forgive, not as the result of deliberations on justice, but out of pure human sympathy. The self-facing aspect is the need to focus on our own virtue and vice, not on that of others. The self- and other-facing elements meet in the capacity of forgiveness to restore relationships, to fix bonds that were broken. Forgiveness requires that we do not judge others but that we judge what is right and what is wrong, with some severity. Without that, there isn't anything to forgive.

There is nothing about this model which requires a 'vertical' connection to the divine. 'Forgiveness is Jesus's key distinctive ethic and you can do that horizontally,' says Lucy Winkett. 'You don't need him to be the son of God to make that work.' What you need is 'a conviction of what you've done that's fallen short, followed by confession, followed by absolution, forgive-ness. So you can do something or say something to me that hurts me and offends me, you realise it, you confess it, you are forgiven by me and on we go.'

Believing Christians also have another, vertical dimension, a belief that 'we live in a constant state of post-resurrection forgiveness, so when I do something wrong – as I will every moment of every hour of every day – that doesn't lead me to despair'. Without this, forgiveness is limited and incomplete: 'Forgiveness for me is both a deeply spiritual and practical mechanism to handle the past which we are powerless to change. Confession and forgiveness give me a way of living with all the risks I've taken that didn't pay off, all the things I didn't say and didn't do.'

Once again we can see how a religious interpretation of Jesus's teaching offers us a sense of completeness, of ultimate resolution and salvation. No secular ethic can promise this, certainly not the secularised version of Jesus's morality. We are left instead with the imperfect, the incomplete and the ultimately unresolved. Justice is never fully done and salvation is not always found. There is no divine assistance to bridge the gap between our weakness and fallibility and the ideal people we would like to be, or the ideal world in which we'd like to live.

For the atheist these are cold, hard truths that must be faced. When many believers themselves say they couldn't bear to live in such a meaningless universe, it is easy to assume that believers are simply too weak to confront the truth. But some believers retort that atheists are too proud to admit there is a power greater than themselves to whom they are accountable. It profits no one to speculate about our deep psychological needs. The important difference is that believers find themselves convinced for intellectual and/or spiritual reasons that there is a transcendent reality in the universe, while atheists are equally convinced that the immanent world is all that there is, and agnostics can't see compelling reasons to take either side. The case for non-judgement and forgiveness does not entirely rest on which of these views you take, even though it might be an easier teaching to accept if you believe in ultimate divine justice.

From what he wrote after the Bataclan attackers murdered his wife, Antoine Leiris did believe in some kind of life after death. If so, he may have been reassured that ultimately justice would be done. But the core sentiments of his letter resonated with everyone, atheist or believer. He didn't practise pure non-judgement as he clearly condemned the killings. Nor did he offer forgiveness, which is surely too much for most of us to do in such situations. He was angry and heartbroken. But he managed to do two of the most important things Jesus commended. First, he didn't return hate for hate and that defied the killers in the way that most mattered. Second, he focused instead on himself, those he loved and wider society. There was no relationship to be restored with the dead killers but there were relationships to be strengthened in response to their actions.

We have already seen how Jesus urges us to look for the spirit and intent of his teachings rather than their letter. I do not see in the Gospel absolute rules about not judging and forgiving. Sometimes we need to judge. What matters is how we do it. Clare Carlisle offered as an example the judgement of parents on their children's behaviour. Any parent has to judge and discipline a young child, but a good parent will do so kindly, out of love, not harshly. For me, the core of Jesus's teaching on judgement is an encouragement to focus more on our own goodness than on the badness of others, to heal relationships rather than to further break them, and to refuse hate and say yes to love. For those reasons, Antoine Leiris is as good an illustration of what is true and good in Jesus's message as any of his parables.

8

AGAINST FAMILY VALUES

It is a source of much despair for many Christians that when their churches are in the news, it is very often because of disputes about sex and sexuality. As I write this, closer ties between the Church of England and the Methodist Church were put in jeopardy by the latter's proposals to allow same-sex marriage within the church, which the Anglicans prohibit.[1] A few years ago, a global summit of thirty-eight primates from the Worldwide Anglican Community almost split over the issue of gay marriage. Gafcon, an alliance of conservative Anglican churches opposed to same-sex marriage and increased gay rights, called on the church 'to stand for the truth', saying, 'The power of God is at work.'[2]

Reading the Gospel, it is somewhat bizarre to think that modern Christianity is consumed by debates about sexual morality when Jesus himself said so little about it. The churches are fiercely divided between conservatives, who insist that homosexual and extramarital sex are wrong, and liberals, who think these are theological non-issues. Sex and sexuality remain decisive issues in almost all Christian denominations. The two camps are also divided on gender equality, with a remarkable number of churches still either opposed to female ordination or with limits on the opportunities for female clergy that are not placed on men.

On the issue of extramarital sex, most official teaching remains fairly stringent. In Christianity, sex only within marriage is generally held up as the ideal and remains an absolute requirement in some denominations. The Archbishop of Canterbury at the time of writing, Justin Welby, has said 'regardless of whether it's gay or straight, sex outside marriage is wrong' and that 'to abandon the ideal simply because it's difficult to achieve is ridiculous'.[3] The divorced are still prohibited from taking communion in the Roman Catholic Church.

Within the church, conservatives may have the upper hand doctrinally but they are out of kilter with permissive Western social mores. Even in the USA, the most religious of the developed Western nations, around 95 per cent of people have premarital sex and the median number of past sexual partners for those aged between twenty-five and forty-four is nearly four for women and over six for men. At the time of writing, gay marriage has been legalised in twenty-eight countries. Many countries have sexual discrimination laws that would lead churches to be prosecuted for barring women from certain offices, were it not for religious exemptions.

However, morality is not a popularity contest and the disagreement between liberals and conservatives needs to be settled on the basis of Jesus's teachings, not social consensus. The problem is that Jesus supports neither camp. Liberals are right to say that Jesus talks relatively little about sex, but the bad news for them is that when he does, he is extremely conservative. In some ways, his sexual morality was even more demanding than that of his time. He endorses the old commandment 'Thou shalt not commit adultery' but adds, 'whosoever looketh on a woman to lust after her hath committed adultery with her already in his heart' (2:27). He also explicitly prohibits divorce, except when the wife has been unfaithful: 'whosoever shall put away his wife, saving for the cause of fornication, causeth her to commit adultery: and whosoever shall marry her that is divorced committeth adultery.' His views contradict the more liberal orthodoxy of the time, which was 'Whosoever shall put away his wife, let him give her a writing of divorcement' (2:32). Note also that Jesus's words don't challenge the idea that only a husband can divorce his wife and never the other way around.

These teachings only concern what it is right to do once married. Jesus says literally nothing about premarital sex or about homosexuality. There is therefore wiggle room for liberals to argue that Jesus's teaching is consistent with a relaxed attitude to sex outside marriage and is only strict about the commitment marriage entails. The Gospel is sufficiently sketchy about sexual morality to make this position consistent. However, it would seem extremely unlikely that someone who held marriage to be sacrosanct would have been laissez-faire about sex outside it. Given that Jesus claimed to uphold the law, it is improbable that he thought anything other than that marriage and marriage alone provided the right context for sex.

Although we have no reason to believe that Jesus was anything other than a sexual conservative, there are good reasons to think that the spirit of his teachings points to a more accommodating position today. The key is to ask why someone like Jesus would have judged extramarital sex to be wrong. Could it be because, as many religious conservatives argue, Jesus believed in God and God created man, woman and sex in order to have families and for nothing else? Theologically that is an extremely shaky argument. If God designed sex in that way he was quite simply a shoddy craftsman. Not only did he make it possible for people to have sex when they were infertile or post-menopause, but he also made some people sexually desire people of their own sex who they can't reproduce with. Anyone who studied human sexuality and knew nothing about the designer's purpose would conclude that its most likely purpose was to encourage anything but lifelong, purely heterosexual monogamy. If Jesus was a great moral teacher, he surely would not have been persuaded by this logic.

He could, however, have had a good secular reason for being opposed to divorce. For most of human history, sex and procreation went almost inevitably together and people did not live until they were very old. What's more, scraping a living was difficult. Financial security was the preserve of an elite few. Divorce would almost always mean separating the parents of children and potentially depriving them, and their mother, of a livelihood.

The hardship for divorcees would also explain why Jesus did not challenge the idea that the only possible way to have a divorce was for a man to divorce his wife and not vice versa. 'Divorce at the time could be unilateral and absolute,' says Nick Spencer. 'There was no problem at all for a Jewish man simply to divorce his wife for no reason whatsoever. Women weren't allowed to provide a bill of divorce for their husbands so there was no reason to tell them not to do it.' It wasn't sexism that underpinned Jesus's teaching that men should not divorce women but a recognition that only men *could* divorce in his society. Furthermore, women were almost always the ones to be disadvantaged by divorce and so needed to be protected against it, not given the right to initiate it.

Although Jesus said nothing about homosexuality, it is also easy enough to see why his society would not have approved. Survival of the tribe depends on families producing children to look after older generations. Put brutally, in such societies homosexuality would have seemed like an indulgence. When people point to Greece and Rome as proof of how attitudes to sexuality were more liberal they forget that these permissive attitudes were promoted by aristocratic elites served by slaves.

Today, however, those old reasons to promote family above all else simply don't apply. We have plentiful and easy contraception and we don't need children to provide for us. In fact, the world needs far fewer children. Those of us who don't reproduce are doing society a favour, not letting it down.

While it cannot be denied that Jesus was a sexual conservative in his time, given he offered no rationale at all for this stance, let alone a compelling one, it is open for people who embrace his moral teaching to diverge from him. Sexual morality is a peripheral part of his system and so can be adapted to the times without contradicting any of its basic principles. In fact, the general thrust of Jesus's moral philosophy makes it hard to believe he would be too concerned about what specific sexual acts people got up to. His main concerns would surely be that people tend to place too much importance on sex and neglect their own moral development. But that would not mean that sex was itself immoral.

Although it is obviously speculative to bring Jesus's sexual morality up to date in this way, the general idea that old moral systems need revising for changing times should not be controversial. Whenever we try to apply moral teachings from centuries ago we always have to undertake some updating.

Contemporary virtue ethicists leave behind Aristotle's acceptance of slavery, the successors of David Hume ignore his racism and Confucians excise their founder's misogyny. All these elements can be removed from their teachings without contradicting their basic principles. Indeed, many believe that to be, say, against slavery today is to be much more Aristotelian than to be for it. If Aristotle were to follow his own arguments knowing what we know today, free from the prejudices of his age, he would never condone slavery. Similarly, it is hard to see how Jesus would be sexually conservative in a world in which the most powerful reasons for keeping sex within marriage have weakened.

The sparsity of Jesus's teachings on sex strongly suggests that he did not count sexual sin as among the most serious and that it is not the business of civic law to police. The story of the woman taken in adultery, which we looked at in the previous chapter, is often taken as evidence that Jesus did not condemn adultery, but even a cursory read shows this cannot be true. Not only does he tell the woman to 'sin no more', but the story begins with Jesus saying to the crowd, 'Whosoever putteth away his wife, and marrieth another, committeth adultery: and whosoever marrieth her that is put away from her husband committeth adultery' (8:57). There can be no doubt that Jesus believed the woman had done wrong.

Still, he does refuse to condemn her. As I suggested earlier, this is at least in part a refusal to extend the judgement that she did wrong to a judgement on her as a person. But that can't be the whole story. When asked 'hath no man condemned thee?' she replied, 'No man, Lord' (8:62–63). Yet her accusers clearly had judged not just her action but the woman herself. What can it therefore mean to say no man had *condemned* her? The only explanation that makes sense is that no man had condemned her *to punishment*, and nor should anyone do so. Sexual immorality just isn't something society should punish anyone for. If that's right, then no follower of Christ should support legal restrictions on how people express their sexuality in consenting relationships. The law should set rules for divorce but should not punish people for extramarital sex.

Before we interpret Jesus too liberally, we ought to consider that there are more reasons for being against adultery than moralistic conservative ones. Elizabeth Oldfield believes that 'underlying the political and social theology of the Bible is a whole story about healthy relationships between God and human beings and healthy relationships between humans and other humans. There is a particular focus on a form of idolatry that treats other humans as objects and that plays out most clearly in sexual ethics. That is why I, as a twenty-first-century some-days-reasonably-liberal progressive-leaning woman, still think the Christian sexual ethic at its base is a beautiful thing, because it's about avoiding treating other people as objects, avoiding consumerist and self-pleasure-seeking ways of using our bodies. It's about the dignity and worth of every human being and particularly those to whom you have covenanted. Adultery is often about looking for the next good thing and something about saying, "No, this person with all their failings and faults is who I am committed to and I'm staying with them," is a very powerful thing to be applauded.'

Lucy Winkett, who says she 'would be given the liberal label', also says she doesn't mind the adultery teaching: 'If it's a teaching about being faithful, then good. I don't think it's not undoable or unforgivable. But adultery unravels people. The pain that's caused by adultery in its broadest sense – betrayal of a vow or a broken promise – is immense. There's an ethical fierceness that I think we need. It's really easy, especially today, to take a promise absolutely assuming that you're going to break it.'

To the modern secular mind, Jesus's sexual teachings are somewhat problematic and not entirely convincing. Much as we might applaud his desire for society to refrain from punishing fornication, his insistence that divorce is a form of adultery places unjustified emphasis on the requirement of marriage for sex. Nor is it progressive to refuse to accept the legitimacy of consenting divorce or subsequent marriages. Jesus is tolerant of people's sexual sins, but has a very conservative conception of what a sexual sin is. The only way to avoid having to simply disown Jesus's moral teachings about sex would be to argue that following the spirit of his teaching today would require a major revision of his stated views in the Gospels.

On balance, Jesus's teachings on sexual ethics give more support to conservative values than liberal ones. But there is another aspect to his teaching which leans the other way. As Karen Kilby puts it, 'When people say, "I'm a Christian, I believe in family values," I always think there are very few family values, as these are usually understood, in the New Testament.' One or two passages show that he thought if people married they had to honour the commitment. But many more show beyond reasonable doubt that he didn't much rate the institution of the family in the first place and it was better to avoid it altogether.

Marriage was not especially valued by Jesus or the early church. It was not until the thirteenth century that the Catholic Church made marriage a sacrament and even then it did not enforce strict observance of it. The gap between its contemporary importance and its initial unimportance is evident if you pay attention to the Anglican marriage service. In the liturgy nothing can be cited as evidence that Jesus valued marriage, except for the rather desperate lines which assert 'Marriage is a way of life made holy by God, and blessed by the presence of our Lord Jesus Christ with those celebrating a wedding at Cana in Galilee.' Since Jesus was also present at the homes of tax collectors and prostitutes, the idea that his mere attendance at a wedding constitutes a blessing seems absurd.

Brian Mountford suggested to me that one reason why marriage held so little interest was that Jesus's followers, particularly St Paul writing to the Corinthians on marriage, believed that the *parousia* – the second coming of Jesus – was going to happen in their lifetime. All thought of starting any long-term worldly commitment would have seemed foolish. Better to concentrate on heaven. Although there is probably something to this, I find it difficult to believe that this fully accounts for all his negative teachings about marriage.

One of the milder expressions of this hostility to marriage comes after his condemnation of adultery, when his disciples draw the conclusion 'it is not good to marry'. Jesus essentially agrees but acknowledges this is difficult: 'All men cannot receive this saying, save they to whom it is given.' It requires a man to be made a 'eunuch'. Some are born this way, some are mutilated to become so, but there are others 'which have made themselves eunuchs for the Kingdom of Heaven's sake'. Those who can do this should: 'He that is able to receive it, let him receive it' (11:28–29).

I find it interesting that none of the Christians I spoke to thought of this passage when considering Jesus's views on marriage. When I suggested that he had indicated it was better not to marry, they all initially protested that I was referring to Paul, not Jesus. In his first letter to the Corinthians, Paul famously wrote, 'I say therefore to the unmarried and widows, it is good for them if they abide even as I. But if they cannot

contain, let them marry: for it is better to marry than to burn'
(I Corinthians 7:8–9). It seems to me pretty clear, however, that
this same sentiment is expressed by Jesus in his comments that
those who can make themselves eunuchs should. Given this
and other passages, how marriage ever became a sacrament,
one of the most important rites in Christianity, is something
of a mystery.

There is an interesting exchange straight after this when
the Sadducees, who did not believe in an afterlife, tried to
trick Jesus into showing the absurdity of heaven. They asked
him who would be a man's wife in paradise if he had married
more than once due to widowhood. Jesus's answer is startling:
'The good is not the good of the dead, but of the living. The
children of this world marry, and are given in marriage: For
he is not a God of the dead, but of the living: for all live unto
him' (11:32). We can take this in two ways. One is that marriage
is something purely of this world and has no place in heaven.
The other is that there is no afterlife at all. Given how often
the 'Kingdom of God' appears to refer to this world, such an
interpretation is not outlandish.

Some other passages are so clear and strong in their rejection
of family that they leave little room for alternative interpretations. (Although we know that many people in defence of a
religious ideology are not short of interpretative ingenuity.) For
instance, the first time Jesus dismisses family loyalty is when he
calls a man to follow him. The man requests, 'suffer me first to
go and bury my father.' Jesus refuses, saying, 'Let the dead bury
their dead: but go thou and preach the Kingdom of Heaven.'
What follows hardens the message even further: 'If any man
come to me, and hate not his father, and mother, and wife, and
children, and brethren, and sisters, yea, and his own life also,
he cannot be my disciple' (4:9–10).

Were this a one-off we could possibly try to dismiss it as dramatic hyperbole. But he repeats the message with similar extremism on another occasion when people tell him that his mother and brothers are there. Rather than being delighted and going to see them, he says that his followers are his true brethren (10:48–50). That is not the only time he distances himself from his family, denying it the central role most people give it. On one occasion, the Gospel reports that a woman 'lifted up her voice, and said unto [Jesus], Blessed is the womb that bare thee, and the paps which thou hast sucked. But he said, Yea rather, blessed are they that hear the word, and keep it (6:10–11). The 'rather' and the 'but' the Gospel writer inserts indicates that Jesus is not adding to but contradicting the statement. We see here a startlingly explicit indication that Jesus would not have approved of the words of the Hail Mary, which say of his mother 'Blessed art thou'.

Jesus has very few kind words for blood families. Dying on the cross, he sees his mother and one of his disciples and says, 'Woman, behold thy son!' and to the disciple, 'Behold thy mother!' We are told that 'from that hour that disciple took her unto his own home' (13:48). But that's pretty much it. Nor is this an especially filial act. It is not too harsh to say that, having pretty much ignored his mother all his adult life, Jesus leaves it to someone else to be the son he never was.

While acknowledging that Jesus is no supporter of what we now call family values, the Christian thinkers I spoke to toned down the antipathy to family that I think is all too evident. They argued in different ways that he wasn't against family per se but against placing too much importance on the nuclear family, as we are today so wont to do. 'Love of family can be idolatry,' said John Cottingham. 'People get so wrapped up in their ego and how that ego is reflected in their children or the trophy wife or whatever it might be, or nepotism when they put family before public duty. So I think what he's saying is that the demands of the good – of morality, of justice, of righteousness – override mere partiality to family.'

Similarly, Elizabeth Oldfield said, 'I don't think he has a problem with family. He has a problem with family as primary. He's essentially saying that your primary identity is as a child of God, as inheritor of the kingdom, and follow me. Don't let the obligations of life stand in the way of that.'

Another way to soften Jesus's message about family is to argue that Jesus is, as Nick Spencer puts it, 'extending rather than abandoning the family. It's striking that the metaphor of brothers and sisters is picked up almost immediately by the New Testament church to refer to fellow believers. You don't do that with something that is completely insignificant. The problem with some contemporary Christianity is the way in which it deifies the family and then treats it as an exclusive unit at the expense of the other social bonds.' Lucy Winkett backs this up: 'One of the strongest strands that I get from his ethical teachings is that blood ties are not as important as the family you create. That's really clear to me. So the focus on the nuclear family makes no sense.'

Although I can agree with much in these attempts to turn down the volume on Jesus's opposition to family, I don't think we can entirely remove the hard edge of Jesus's teaching. In one passage Jesus talks about followers becoming his brethren, but he presents this as an alternative to loyalty to their blood families, not as a mere addition to it: 'For from henceforth there shall be five in one house divided, three against two, and two against three. The father shall be divided against the son, and the son against the father; the mother against the daughter, and the daughter against the mother; the mother in law against her daughter in law, and the daughter in law against her mother in law. And a man's foes shall be they of his own household' (10:52).

What I find extraordinary about these passages is that were anyone to use such rhetoric today they would be accused of leading a cult. It is a characteristic feature of cults that they seek to separate followers from their families, demanding exclusive devotion. And yet it is precisely these cults which, in this respect at least, most faithfully follow Jesus's teaching.

Jesus's strict teachings on adultery and his dismissal of the importance of family might seem to be strange ethical bedfellows. On the one hand the marital bond must not be broken in almost any circumstance, but on the other family is better avoided altogether. Yet there is a logic to this. Jesus treats family bonds as distractions from the more noble goal of making ourselves pure. If we do marry, we have to make sure we contain the passions we have unleashed, not least for the sake of the children. But it is much better not to marry at all and avoid the intimate and consuming ties of wedlock and family.

For modern secularists, here is yet another example of the world-denying nature of Jesus's teaching. The good life for most who live without God involves a deep appreciation of the things of this world, especially close relationships. Jesus advocates something much more detached and rarefied. But that does not mean his vision makes no secular sense. It is simply that the ideal of the good life Jesus advocates is austere and ascetic, focused on cultivating virtue rather than worldly comfort. Once again, we can see how the moral teaching of Jesus is deeply challenging, whether you are religious or not.

9

SOWING THE SEEDS
OF DIVISION

The history of the Christian church is one of schism after schism. The first major break was when the Eastern Orthodox Church broke from the Catholic Church in Rome in 1054. Theologically, the key dispute was over the doctrine of the trinity: the divine triumvirate of God, Jesus and the Holy Spirit. Rome inserted the 'Filioque' clause into the Nicene Creed, asserting that the Holy Spirt proceeded from the Father *and* the Son, whereas the Orthodox Church insisted it proceeded solely from the Father. The real causes of the break were probably more political than theological, but it would be foolish to deny dogma didn't matter at all. The second major split came in 1517, when Martin Luther gave birth to a nascent Protestantism by publishing his Ninety-five Theses, challenging the authority of Rome.

Christians often lament these and other countless divisions, but anyone who reads the Gospels with a modicum of attention would realise that Jesus foresaw anything but unity. Jesus's promise to divide families is part of a wider rhetoric in which division rather than unity is legion. Without even attending to his words, it is clear that by his example he presents a divisive figure, one who creates dispute and conflict. The pattern is set when he begins his mission in Galilee, Nazareth and Capernaum (1:10–22). One minute people are 'astonished', asking, 'Whence hath this man this wisdom?' The next they are 'filled with wrath' and 'thrust him out of the city', ready to throw him off a cliff edge.

Jesus repeatedly tells his followers that they too can expect to divide people. 'He that heareth you heareth me; and he that despiseth you despiseth me' (10:56). What is most striking is that he tells people not only to expect this but to accept it. The peacemakers may be blessed but on no occasion is his warning about the divisions ahead followed by an encouragement to heal them. His notorious line 'I came not to send peace, but a sword' (10:51) is a hyperbolic and proud statement that division is part of his mission, not a side effect of it.

Another unequivocal statement of division is Jesus's claim 'He that is not with me is against me' (10:44). At first sight this seems not only illogical but designed to stoke unnecessary conflict. It uses the same logic as President George W Bush did after 9/11 when he announced, 'Every nation, in every region, now has a decision to make. Either you are with us, or you are with the terrorists.' At the time Bush was widely criticised for making enemies of anyone who maintained neutrality. To see Jesus the 'prince of peace' using the same tactic is somewhat shocking.

To try to understand what he meant, we need to attend to

both the meaning of the phrase and its context. Sometimes such statements are merely descriptive: as a matter of fact everyone not for us happens to be against us. This would not seem to be the case for Jesus (or Bush). Certainly Jesus was a divisive figure, but it is simply implausible that there wasn't at least some indifference to him and his followers.

On other occasions, the purpose of stating the division is actually to create it. Bush, for example, was telling other nations that he demanded their support and the price of not giving it would be to become an enemy. In Jesus's case, it seems there is a similar intent. He may not be creating the division but he is cementing it. In the preceding words Jesus says, 'Every kingdom divided against itself is brought to desolation; and a house divided against a house falleth' (10:42). This warning against division might seem like a strange prelude to a statement encouraging it. But the metaphor is clearly not about the world or society as a whole. Kingdoms and households need to be united in order to protect themselves against *other* kingdoms and households. The implication is that Jesus's followers need to stick together with fierce loyalty or they will crumble in the face of attacks from others. They must be clear whose side they are on and shouldn't imagine that they can carry the torch for Jesus by being anything other than his followers. Anything else will undermine the cause: not being for it will have the same effect as being actively against it.

Interpreting Jesus's position in this way makes sense of his apparently contradictory statement just a few lines later when he says, 'He that is not against us is for us' (10:58). The context of this utterance is very specific. The disciples had seen someone acting in Jesus's name. (In the source Gospels he is casting out demons.) They forbade him from doing so because he wasn't one of Jesus's followers. But Jesus says they were wrong to do so. This incident adds an important qualifier to Jesus's previous teaching about knowing which side you're on. Anyone who acts in his name belongs on his side. Here he is warning against factionalism: don't reject people who preach the same as we do just because they do not choose to join our gang.

This squares what would otherwise be a four-cornered circle. In 'He that is not with me is against me' the people 'not with me' are working for another cause. In 'He that is not against us is for us' the people 'not against us' are working for the same cause. The contradiction is removed but the upshot is still a world divided between those who can be placed on one side and those who can be placed on the other.

Why would Jesus glorify his capacity to tear people apart? One answer is that he never did. The Gospels were written many years after Jesus died by members of a fledgling sect who were already often persecuted. It seems very likely that Jesus was portrayed foreseeing division to give these early Christians encouragement and confidence. The message is: don't lose heart because people have turned against you, since this is exactly what Jesus said would happen. To put it another way, the early church fathers found themselves persecuted and made a virtue out of necessity. They portrayed the world's rejection of them as evidence of the rightness of their path.

Persecution would also have engendered a strong sense of the need to pull together. As Jesus's execution nears he tells his followers, 'When a strong man armed keepeth his palace, his goods are in peace: But when a stronger than he shall come upon him, and overcome him, he taketh from him all his armour wherein he trusted, and divideth his spoils' (10:43).

Although there is something to the idea that persecution leads to an increased emphasis on in- and out-groups, it is unlikely to be the whole story. Division is a theme of too much of Jesus's teaching to be dismissed as mere adornment. There is a very strong Manichaean strand of 'us and them' in his moral thinking.

Such division is connected to Jesus's ideas of ultimate judgement. Some passages make it sound as though Jesus believed that ultimate judgement would be like that painted by Bosch and Brueghel, in which the saved are sent to heaven, the damned to hell. Most vividly, Jesus says, 'Fear him, which after he hath killed hath power to cast into hell; yea, I say unto you, Fear him' (Luke 12:5). However, we should be cautious about accepting the apparent obviousness of this reading in the context of a gospel which talks little of any life to come. As we have seen, Jesus said the Kingdom of God is within us. It is more consonant with the Gospel as a whole to see the judgement to come as some kind of unavoidable reckoning rather than a literal hell.

Whether Jesus believed in an afterlife or not, he is quite clear that the judgement to come would divide us absolutely. The Parable of the Weeds (7:16–21) is a good example of this. In this somewhat opaque tale, a man sows good wheat seeds but an enemy sows weeds among them. When a servant sees this, the master tells him not to try to pull up the young weeds as that would disturb the wheat too. He says, 'Let both grow together until the harvest: and in the time of harvest I will say to the reapers, Gather ye together first the weeds, and bind them in bundles to burn them: but gather the wheat into my barn.' The message here seems clear enough: for a long time the good and the bad will coexist, but there will be a reckoning in which the weeds are burned and the wheat harvested, the bad get their come-uppance and the good flourish.

Perhaps the most disturbing such parable concerns the Tenants in the Vineyard (7:28–39). A landowner lets out his vineyards and when the time comes for him to collect his share of the harvest, he sends some servants to take it. But the tenants kill every one, and those whom he subsequently sends, even in the end his son. The tale is a clear allegory for the ways in which the religious authorities have rejected the truth, even when it comes in the form of the son, Jesus. We know this is how the parable was understood because we are told the chief priests and the scribes 'perceived that he had spoken this parable against them' and so 'the same hour sought to lay hands on him'.

The parable makes it easy to understand why the religious authorities were frightened by it. Jesus quotes Psalm 118:22, 'The stone the builders rejected has become the capstone'. This means that Jesus, whom the scribes and Pharisees rejected, would become the head of a new movement. But Jesus adds a gruesome coda to the Psalm verse: 'Whosoever shall fall upon that stone shall be broken; but on whomsoever it shall fall, it will grind him to powder' (7:37).

It is not rare for Jesus to use such extreme language. The Parable of the Talents ends with the lines 'cast ye the unprofitable servant into outer darkness: there shall be weeping and gnashing of teeth. But those mine enemies, which would not that I should reign over them, bring hither, and slay them before me' (7:62). Jesus is not literally advocating slaying enemies or grinding them to dust. But he chooses these metaphors deliberately. He could equally have had the wicked simply end up empty-handed or alone. In portraying them as violently destroyed he is emphasising that people must pick the right side, and pointing to the dire consequences of not doing so.

These passages flatten the moral high ground established by the preaching of forgiveness. If in the long run your enemies will be smitten anyway it is hardly an act of great kindness to turn the other cheek in the short term. Non-judgement and forgiveness lose their savour when they come with the promise that revenge is a dish best served cold.

Even if we believe that the vengeful tone of many of these sayings is hyperbolic, it is still troubling the way Jesus emphasises how so many are not going to be saved: 'strait is the gate, and narrow is the way, which leadeth unto life, and few there be that find it' (4:2–3). In one short parable he says, 'A net was cast into the sea, and gathered of every kind: Which, when it was full, they drew to shore, and sat down, and gathered the good into vessels, but cast the bad away' (9:10). Likewise in the Parable of the Ten Virgins (7:74–81, five of them were wise and brought oil for their lamps as they awaited the bridegroom. But five were foolish and did not, and after hours of waiting, their lamps had burned out. When they asked the wise virgins to let them have some of their oil they were refused. So the five wise ones were let into the feast and the five foolish ones were not. This is a clear allegory for salvation, with Jesus as the bridegroom. At its ending, Jesus comes across as harsh and unforgiving. The foolish virgins plead, 'Lord, Lord, open to us,' but the bridegroom replies, 'Verily I say unto you, I know you not.'

The same message is conveyed in a short parable about the master of the house, who at one point shuts his doors (4:3). People knock at them, saying, 'Lord, Lord, open unto us', but the master answers, 'I know you not whence ye are; depart from me, all ye workers of iniquity.' This alludes to the threat of a final judgement and the need to repent in time. The image of a God disowning the sinners he had created and refusing them entry to his house seems deplorable, an Old Testament God of wrath and vengeance, not the supposedly New Testament one of love and forgiveness.

However, if we read this teaching in secular terms it has no such inhumane cruelty. It becomes instead a stark reminder about the finitude of life. If death is the end and no heaven awaits, to say that there will come a time when it is too late for the change of heart we all need to live life well is no more than a starkly honest description of the truth. If we want to reform we have to start now. We do not have the luxury of eternity to get it right.

This secular version of unavoidable judgement may lack the vindictiveness of the religious alternative but it retains a lot of its harshness. It also retains a scepticism about human goodness that makes the failure of most people to heed the word all too inevitable, best summed up in the Parable of the Sower (7:1–15), in which a sower scatters a lot of seed, most of which does not grow. Some falls by the wayside and is quickly brushed away. Some falls among stones, where it is received but only shallowly, so lacking deep roots it fails to grow to maturity. Some falls among thorns and is crowded out by them. These portray the three main reasons why human beings do not heed the word: wickedness, shallowness and the distraction of less important concerns. This does not so much describe three kinds of human being as three aspects of human nature.

The Gospel's dim view of *Homo sapiens* is most evident when it shows us how we act. The whole story of the passion is one of how pathetic people are. The crowds go from zealous supporters to baying masses in a matter of days. Even though the scribes and Pharisees repeatedly say they fear the crowd if they try to arrest Jesus, such is their devotion, in the end the mob turns against him in an instant: 'And they all forsook him, and fled' (12:41). Even Peter denies him thrice, despite – when being warned he would – insisting with apparent sincerity that he would never be so callow (12:55–58).

For all Jesus tells us that the meek and the poor are blessed, his life and teaching paint a sorry picture of humanity. As we have already seen, such is his distrust of people's capacity to understand him that he deliberately uses parables to hide his message, not to make it clearer. Only the disciples, hardly paragons of wisdom and virtue themselves, are 'given to know the mysteries of the Kingdom of Heaven' and he explains to them the meaning of the parables in private (7:8–27).

The idea that most humans are unable to get Jesus's message and few will be saved in time is disturbing enough. What's worse is the strong suggestion that, when it comes to salvation, the world seems to be capricious. Christian teaching often emphasises the importance of grace. We are not saved by our own efforts, since they are never enough to raise us out of sin. We depend upon the grace of God to be saved, purely by his mercy and not by our own endeavours.

This reassuring aspect of Jesus's teaching becomes troubling when it is translated into secular terms. Nature offers no providential salvation. The closest it gets to grace is when blind chance deals us good fortune rather than bad.

The difference between the doctrine of divine, purposeful grace and the naturalistic idea of chance would seem to be as clear as night and day. However, in Jesus's teaching there is sometimes a strong stress on the almost random nature of salvation. In the Parable of the Workers in the Vineyard (7:63–73), workers are hired at different times of the day so some work for all of it, some half and some only a few hours. Yet they are all paid the same. The positive message here is of the mercy of grace: even sinners who repent late in life will receive the same forgiveness as those who have lived well throughout it. The conclusion, 'So the last shall be first, and the first last', is another iteration of the familiar inversion of the temporal order which offers hope for the most wretched.

However, taken as a whole, the parable is saying more than this. It is rejecting conventional ideas of merit altogether and embracing what in worldly terms can only be described as indifference to justice. The vineyard owner refuses to be held to any standard of justice other than his right to do as he pleases with what he owns: 'Is it not lawful for me to do what I will with mine own?' In the secular reading of this we can see a warning that we cannot rely on justice to be done in this world. The world will turn as it does, blind to whether it is fair to us or not.

Most importantly, we are told 'many are called, but few are chosen'. The word 'chosen' indicates that it is not in our power to be saved or not, which is precisely what the parable suggests. But nor is it the case that people will be chosen on the basis of any merit. Divine grace and nature's chance turn out to be equally indifferent to justice and merit.

The Parable of Talents (7:51–62) is another tale that sits uncomfortably with the view that Jesus believed salvation would be fair. A nobleman gives three servants some money to look after. The first got five talents, the second two and the last one (a talent was a measure of gold). The first two servants traded and doubled their master's money. The third, however, was afraid of losing the little he had been entrusted with. He told his master he was a 'hard man' who 'takest up that thou layedst not down, and reapest that thou didst not sow'. So he went and hid the talent in the earth. The nobleman was angry with him and gave the one talent he had to the man who already had ten.

The parable is peculiar. The clearest and most comforting take-home message is that we all ought to make the most of what is given to us, large or small. It's like Marx's phrase, 'from each according to his abilities'. In the parable, the nobleman says, 'For unto whomsoever much is given, of him shall be much required: and to whom men have committed much, of him they will ask the more.' This is a matter of making the best use not merely of material resources but of our capabilities. Indeed, it is because of this parable that the English word 'talent' means gifts or abilities.

This sounds reasonable enough. But given Jesus's praise of the meek, you might expect that he would have told the story with the servant who was given five talents burying them and show the person given just one making the most of it. Making more of less would be more praiseworthy than making best use of more. That would chime with the story of the widow whose meagre offering at the temple exceeded that of the rich because 'all these have of their abundance cast in unto the offerings of God: but she of her penury hath cast in all the living that she had, even all her living' (6:9). But that is the opposite of what happens with the servants. The moral of the story is in fact 'For unto every one that hath shall be given, and he shall have abundance: but from him that hath not shall be taken away even that which he hath' (7:61).

We can make this consistent with the rest of Jesus's teaching by imagining that he is telling us different things about different stages in our development. His pronouncements about the inversion of the existing order tell us that those who are rich and prosperous now will in the long run be worse off than those who are poor and humble. The teachings that seem to contradict this tell us that once the wheat and the chaff have been separated, the good will see their rewards multiply while the bad's losses will be compounded. The judgement on us will be harsh, even if we understand that judgement to be no more than our fate in this world.

The message makes even more sense if we understand what judgement means in more secular terms. I have argued that

Jesus is most concerned with transformation of the self and that the Kingdom of Heaven is a mode of being rather than a transcendental place we might end up in. If that is right we should never read any parables that talk of rewards and punishments as though those were external goods. The 'rewards' of virtue are not measured in wealth or health but in how the nature of our existence is transformed.

This counters the sense of injustice several parables convey. The workers in the vineyard who are hired first, the servant who received the fewest talents and the dutiful son who stays with his father while the prodigal leaves home all seem to get a raw deal. But what if the message is that Jesus is not talking about external rewards at all? If you are good, living a good life becomes all the reward you need. If others take longer to reach that state but, having done so, enjoy the same rewards as you, then you have nothing to complain about. You should be pleased if someone who is not good becomes good and should not feel you deserve anything extra for having been good all along. These parables are perhaps not so much telling us that ultimate rewards are unfair but that we should get away from thinking about worldly rewards being some kind of payback for virtue.

One final aspect of Jesus's doctrine of division is harder to understand from a contemporary secular perspective. Jesus says a lot about how we should live but he also seems to think that the single most important thing we can do is to take him as our master. Jesus commands that people follow him. There are simply too many verses that say this to deny it: for example, 'He that gathereth not with me scattereth' (10:44) and 'Ye are my friends, if ye do whatsoever I command you' (5:18). Not only that, but Jesus makes it clear that following him requires giving up everything else: 'whosoever he be of you that forsaketh not all that he hath, he cannot be my disciple' (4:13). This passage goes on to make it clear that following Jesus is not easy: 'Whosoever will come after me, let him deny himself, and take up his cross, and follow me' (4:14). The price of doing so, we are later told, could even be death: 'He that findeth his life shall lose it: and he that loseth his life for my sake shall find it' (10:54).

The call to follow Jesus is perhaps what makes it most difficult to see him as no more than a great moral teacher. 'It's very easy as a twenty-first-century progressive person to say look at his progressive gender politics, how he's telling us not to be so obsessed about nationhood and is quite rude about the nuclear family,' says Elizabeth Oldfield. 'But he's not just dissolving it all, saying no forms of belonging, no forms of identity. He's saying *new* forms of belonging and identity around *me*, around *my* kingdom.'

In the Gospel, it is all too clear that he saw himself as founding a new movement centred on himself. It is not enough to follow his teaching; it is necessary to follow him. One reason for this is that Jesus never appeared to be talking to future generations. It seems incontrovertible that the Jesus of the four Gospels believed some kind of end times were coming soon, if not in his lifetime then in the lifetimes of his followers. Everything would become clear soon enough: 'For there is nothing covered, that shall not be revealed; neither hid, that shall not be known. Therefore whatsoever ye have spoken in darkness shall be heard in the light; and that which ye have spoken in the ear in closets shall be proclaimed upon the housetops' (11:34).

The more evangelical wings of Christianity emphasise an exclusivity in Jesus's teaching that more liberal branches find problematic. One of their most-used verses is John 14:6: 'I am the way, the truth, and the life: no man cometh unto the Father, but by me.' However figuratively we interpret this, the central message that Jesus and Jesus alone must be followed comes through loud and clear in the Gospel. Those who see Jesus as just one among many moral teachers are ignoring the fact that he himself believed he was much more special than that.

One advantage of secular moral philosophy is that we are not obliged to take on every aspect of a wise teacher's system. We can choose to set aside the Jesus cult and take away much of the rest. In the case of his teachings on division, what is taken away is dark and troubling. Few are able to understand the true path and follow it. Few will develop into the virtuous people they are meant to be and so be 'saved'. And our fate is not entirely within our control. Fate and chance are indifferent to justice and mercy.

Jesus is often portrayed as the prophet of hope. Yet to me his vision is a bleak one. Nonetheless, in its secular version it paints a picture of the harsh reality of the world which is more convincing than the traditional religious interpretations in which we rely on a sometimes capricious and unjust God to save us.

10

GOOD WITHOUT GOD

In May 1924, a fourteen-year-old boy was kidnapped and murdered in Chicago. It was not just another killing in a city with a notoriously high homicide rate. The murderers had an unusual and chilling motive. They were two wealthy students who simply wanted to demonstrate their intellectual superiority. One, Nathan Leopold, had become fascinated by Nietzsche's concept of the Übermensch, the 'overman' who rejected society's values and created his own. Leopold thought he and Richard Loeb were two such superior specimens of human kind and that their victim, Bobby Franks, was a dispensable member of the mindless herd.

Nietzsche is most famous for declaring, 'God is dead.' This isn't as glib or straightforward as it sounds. In *Thus Spoke Zarathustra* he has a madman say these lines, adding that 'it is we who have killed him'. Still, it is incontrovertible that Nietzsche wanted a godless 'transvaluation of all values' in which the 'slave morality' of Christianity, which preaches submission, is replaced by a heroic commitment to overcoming.

Any Nietzsche scholar will tell you that to interpret this as a call to gratuitous homicide is a gross distortion of his philosophy. In Patrick Hamilton's play *Rope*, based on the Leopold and Loeb case, the professor who taught the murderers about Nietzsche complains, 'You've given my words a meaning that I never dreamed of!' But for many, the murder of Bobby Franks is the appalling logical consequence of overthrowing a morality based on the divine and replacing it with a fully human one. The protesting professor ends up expressing deep remorse for ever having endorsed the ideas his students twisted. 'Tonight you've made me ashamed of every concept I ever had of superior or inferior beings.'

Even if we don't think that without God we are doomed to murderous amorality, a great many people do worry that without a divine foundation, morality can have no robust basis. It would be like the house made of sand in Jesus's parable that is washed away by the first strong tide of human anger or desire. We may accept that we can make sense of Jesus's teachings as a secular moral philosophy, but if we take away the divine ground on which it stands, what holds it up?

The question is naive if it assumes that the idea of the good requires a belief in God. It is little wonder many assume this necessity, because much moral teaching in the Christian world has appealed to nothing more than divine authority. It was how I was taught the difference between right and wrong at my Catholic primary school. I had to do what I was told because that was what God wanted, and since God was my creator I had better not question it. After all, he was going to judge me at some point and he wasn't going to answer questions from me about why I ought to have listened to him.

In the Hebrew Bible, morality is usually delivered by divine command, with no questions asked. Consider how the Ten Commandments were delivered to the Israelites. Moses is given no reasons why the principles God commands are good ones. It is enough that God commands them. God calls Moses up to Mount Sinai and tells him, 'Thus shalt thou say to the house of Jacob, and tell the children of Israel' (Exodus 19:3). Moses then descends, 'called for the elders of the people, and laid before their faces all these words which the Lord commanded him'; in response they tell him, 'All that the Lord hath spoken we will do' (Exodus 19:7–8). When he ascends once more to receive what we now know as the Ten Commandments, even though there are clearly at least eleven, the people see 'the thunderings, and the lightnings, and the noise of the trumpet, and the mountain smoking' (Exodus 20:18). That is all the reason they needed to obey.

Few believe in the historical accuracy of this story. We would also be right to doubt the claims made by most people across history to have spoken on behalf of God. Nonetheless, many people do believe that for a moral teacher to speak with any authority, what they say has to gain its legitimacy from a divine source. If that is right, take the Christ out of Jesus and you are left with no more than someone with strong opinions which lack authority.

The crudest version of the idea that morality is grounded in the will of God or gods does not stand up to scrutiny. This divine command theory says that right and wrong are determined by God's fiat alone. One powerful Christian argument against divine command theory is that Jesus himself doesn't seem to endorse it. His case for reform of the law rejects the idea that moral laws can be justified by a simple appeal to authority, or implemented by a straightforward reference to a rule book. He does not make his case for real goodness by stating that 'God says so' or 'it is written'. As we have seen throughout this study, Jesus argues his case in many of the same ways as secular moral theorists.

There are some suggestions in the Gospel that in teaching by example Jesus is consciously rejecting divine command theory. On one occasion, for example, the chief priests and the scribes challenge Jesus, saying, 'By what authority doest thou these things?' This is a trap. If he answers, 'God,' they could accuse him of blasphemy. Any other answer, however, would expose his lack of legitimacy. But Jesus replies by setting them his own trap, asking them if John the Baptist acted under the authority of God or man. For political reasons they can't answer. To say he had divine authority would acknowledge John's authority, but to deny that authority overtly would agitate his many followers. Jesus then tells them, 'Neither do I tell you by what authority I do these things' (10:13–16).

This incident is sometimes read as showing how clever Jesus is at avoiding the snares set for him. But it would seem very odd for Jesus to refuse to claim the authority he has simply because he is scared of the consequences. The story makes more sense if we see it as showing how Jesus rejects the idea that he needs to claim any authority at all. The context helps explain why. When Jesus asks the scribes and priests about their authority it provokes them to think about political considerations. This shows how the very notion of authority is tied in with questions of politics and power. Likewise divine command is a form of moral authority that is essentially rooted in power, in this case omnipotence. Jesus has no time for political power of any kind, as we have seen. The only authority which Jesus can claim is his example.

Possibly the most powerful objection to divine command

theory is also the oldest one. In the *Euthyphro*, Plato asks whether the gods command what is good because it is good or what they command is good because they command it. The second option can be swiftly ruled out. It cannot be the case that rape and torture, for example, are only bad because the gods say they are. A good god could not make these terrible things good just by declaring that they were. That leaves only the first option: the gods command what is good *because* it is good. But that means that the goodness or badness of things does not depend on any gods. In monotheistic terms, the good, not God, grounds morality.

Plato's argument has always struck me as elegant and compelling. The Euthyphro dilemma should make it clear that nothing is added to the reality of goodness by giving it a divine source. All that is lost is the assurance that goodness will be upheld and will ultimately win. Take away God and you take away the moral enforcer, but you don't take away morality itself.

However, although every sensible person should agree that 'because God says so' is no justification for a moral principle, the broader idea that morality requires some kind of transcendent source is not so easily swept aside. 'Transcendent' is a slippery concept that is used more often than it is understood. At minimum it refers to something that is both greater than and other from ourselves, something that cannot be found purely in the physical world of the here and now.

The Euthyphro dilemma may demolish the idea that God's will determines what is good, but it doesn't show that morality lacks a transcendent source. It might even suggest the opposite, since it points to a source of goodness independent of God. If that source were nothing more than human culture or evolution, why would it have any more force than God's will? Surely it needs to belong to some higher realm?

Plato certainly thought it did. For him the eternal form of the good existed at the highest level of reality, above and beyond the finite and corruptible things of the material world. In most traditions, the good at least appears to be above and beyond the human. Confucius talked of following the 'way of heaven', while the Daoists thought of the *dào*, the way, as existing eternally. Fantasy fiction often draws on the idea of an ultimate good to create its own myths, such as 'the force' in *Star Wars*.

If there is some kind of transcendent source of goodness, then it might even be possible to reconnect it with God. The Euthyphro dilemma renders the good and God asunder because it assumes a distinction between the gods as divine commanders-in-chief and goodness as a moral quality. This was easy to do with the gods of ancient Greece, who were like human beings with superpowers. The God of many Christians today is a lot less anthropomorphic. For them, there is a sense that God doesn't just *do* good, he *is* the good.

This is difficult to understand if we think of God as some kind of person, with beliefs, desires and agency. For many Christians it is important that God has a kind of personhood. But for plenty of others this way of thinking about God is merely the best method we have of grasping the mystery of the divine, which is in some sense a purposive agent but in ways we cannot fathom. Others go further and say the whole idea of God is simply a personification of the good, a kind of metaphor to help us to conceive of what is ultimately inconceivable. For many who take any of these views, God and transcendent goodness are in some sense fused.

There are, then, at least two ways for people to reject the crude idea that the good is what God commands, while holding on to the idea that goodness has some transcendent source. The first is that God and the good are in some sense one and the same. The second is that Jesus has some kind of special insight into the nature of absolute goodness and that is what gives his teachings their authority. Neither is credible from a secular viewpoint, but within the context of faith either or both could make some sense.

In any case, to argue that *The Godless Gospel* lacks foundations it is not enough to show that rooting Jesus's teachings in a transcendent source of goodness is *coherent*. You have to show that his morality *requires* such a source. The consensus of the experts I consulted was that it does. One member who articulated this explicitly was John Cottingham. When I first met Cottingham he was not a religious man. It was only later in his life that he found his faith, becoming a Roman Catholic a few years ago. In his writings he has repeatedly emphasised the need for some kind of transcendence for life to be meaningful and for morality to have its power. Little wonder, then, that he believes that without such a transcendent basis Jesus's morality would lose its force: 'The authoritative nature of Jesus's teaching is underpinned not so much because he is the messiah but because unless there is an eternal source of value the requirement to be just, merciful and compassionate is hard to justify.'

Cottingham speaks for many when he says he 'can't conceive of the naturalistic universe of physics and then the good. I don't see where it would fit. You can't base it just on human nature, which seems to be self-evidently a ragbag of contradictory principles. If our impulses to the good were just one among many natural impulses, then they wouldn't have the right kind of status to *require* us to act.'

One problem I have with this is that it is hard to have any clear idea of what kind of real thing 'objective goodness' could be. I don't believe in spooky non-natural forces. I can accept that ultimate reality might be beyond our comprehension, but I am not prepared to commit to a vague concept of absolute, objective goodness on no more than an intuitive feeling that morality requires it.

Still, we might justifiably ask for some reason to believe that morality is *real*. But it seems to me that there are better ways of understanding the reality of goodness without any need of an objective transcendent reality. In East Asian thought, for example, their conceptions of the good seem to be more integrated into the natural world. Confucius did talk about the 'way of heaven' (*tiān*), but this did not seem to be a reference to any supernatural realm. Rather, *tiān* seemed to refer to the natural order of things. Similarly, Daoism is a philosophy centred on nature and its concept of the *dào* is better understood as the universal principle that governs all of nature rather than as a supernatural force that somehow intervenes in it. I'm not suggesting that either *dào* or *tiān* is a concept that the modern secular mind can take on wholesale, but they do point to the possibility of understanding goodness as both real and fully part of the natural world.

Our twenty-first-century, scientifically informed version of natural goodness would see it as comparable to things like love or beauty. These certainly exist, but they don't turn up in physics textbooks or under a microscope. Most of us accept that, like all the phenomena of consciousness, they emerge from the workings of embodied, socialised human brains. We don't yet know how this happens but we can be pretty sure that these marvellous bodies and brains are made up of nothing more than the stuff of physics. Love and beauty are as real as anything that has emerged from the complex arrangements of matter, like stars, chairs or sounds. Love and beauty have the capacity to fill us with joy or break our hearts. They even have some relation to truth, since we can be mistaken about what we love, even if beauty is to some extent in the eye of the beholder. We can believe all this without insisting that either needs a transcendent source. Why can't the same be true of goodness?

Cottingham suggested that our moral impulses would be without solid foundation if they were based in nothing more than our evolved psychology. But if you believe in evolution *everything* we think and feel is *based in* our evolved psychology. It didn't get transplanted in our brains by aliens. Buying into the evolutionary story does not force you to believe that morality is *nothing more than* an evolved response. The wonder of evolution is that it can give rise to things that take on a meaning and value that are greater than simply evolutionary advantage. We make music solely thanks to evolved auditory sense organs and brain circuits, but Beethoven's late quartets are more than *just* evolved noises. As the neurophilosopher Patricia Churchland points out, science shows us time and again how 'beautiful things emerge from rather ugly sources'.[1]

One very good reason for believing that morality is real is that it is concerned with things that most certainly exist. When you see someone suffer unnecessarily you are observing something all too real. There is a sense in which if you do not agree that this is bad, then there is something about the world that you are just not getting. I cannot believe it is necessary to add to this some kind of transcendent substrate. I am sure that when Cottingham sees scenes of cruelty on the news he is responding directly to the suffering as a human being. He does not need to ask whether his reaction comes with a transcendental certificate of authenticity.

To me, the demand for a transcendent basis for ethics is little more than intellectual table-thumping. Because some find it intolerable or inconceivable that morality doesn't come with some kind of objective external validation, they simply bang the table and insist it must do so. Such arguments from personal incredulity have no force. Cottingham offers plenty of reasons why he cannot accept that we are 'no more than a strange cosmic excrescence', but I find none of them convincing. Ultimately, although many find the belief that human life is without intrinsic purpose intolerable, that is no counter-argument against it.[2]

If we accept that morality does not require a transcendent foundation, Jesus could be a moral teacher even without any belief that he has some kind of hotline to the divine. He would be in good company, since most of the world's moral philosophers proposed their theories without appeal to an ultimate authority. They still, however, needed to make a case for how they understood good and bad, right and wrong. Without some kind of claim to special authority or divine revelation, what else can a moral teacher appeal to?

The short answer is reason. Until I went to university, the teaching of morality had been confined to the religious studies syllabus. When I started learning about moral philosophy, I found that you most certainly could not appeal to religious authority to back up your case. You needed arguments. Having been raised in a culture in which religion seemed to own ethics, this was a difficult transition to make. It was hard to see how you could *argue* for a moral position. It wasn't simply a matter of establishing the facts. Even with our best knowledge of animal consciousness or foetal development, there are disagreements about the ethics of eating meat or abortion.

I struggled with moral philosophy and it turned out to be my lowest-graded paper in my final exams. In retrospect, I think my problem was that I understood the demand for rationality too narrowly. I was looking for proofs, conclusive arguments, and not surprisingly I didn't find them. I have since learned to be more modest in what I hope reason can do in ethics. In short, a rational approach to ethics requires providing *reasonable reasons* to support your claims. Both adjective and noun are required in this formula. There are many *reasons* that could be presented to justify a moral claim, but many would not even begin to qualify as *reasonable*. 'Accept my moral judgement or else' might work as a threat, but it provides no reason sincerely to accept the moral claims in question. 'I know it's good because everyone says it is' is a similarly unreasonable claim. Any serious moral teacher must provide reasonable reasons for someone to accept their teachings and not simply assert them.

This leaves the question open as to what makes reasons reasonable. Unfortunately, there is no clear and precise answer to that. If there were we'd have no moral disagreement and morality would have become a science. The frustration and difficulty of moral philosophy are precisely that we can agree enough on what constitutes good reasons to engage in discussion but not enough to come to anything like complete consensus.

If the alternative to appeals to authority is rational moral argument, on the face of it, Jesus doesn't look like a great moral teacher. We don't see him presenting formal arguments for his moral positions and his teachings do not form a systematic whole. But the kinds of arguments archetypically put forward in philosophy textbooks are not the only reasonable reasons for accepting a moral claim. Scratch the surface of moral philosophy and you find that the giving of reasonable reasons involves much more than presenting logical arguments.

Consider how one of the most common forms of argument in moral philosophy today is to appeal to a thought experiment or hypothetical case study. For instance, in 'Famine, Affluence, and Morality', one of the most influential papers on moral philosophy in the twentieth century, Peter Singer wrote, 'if I am walking past a shallow pond and see a child drowning in it, I ought to wade in and pull the child out. This will mean getting my clothes muddy, but this is insignificant, while the death of the child would presumably be a very bad thing.' The story is not an argument, but reading it is supposed to establish a general principle: 'if it is in our power to prevent something very bad from happening, without thereby sacrificing anything else of comparable moral importance, we ought, morally, to do it.' This principle entails that comfortable Westerners should sacrifice anything that is remotely luxurious and use the money instead to prevent starvation and easily curable illnesses in poorer parts of the world.[3]

Many of Jesus's teachings follow exactly the same structure. He tells parables, from which his listeners are intended to draw out implications for how they live their lives. The main difference between Jesus's style and that of modern philosophers is that he often leaves his listeners to work out the wider lesson for themselves. Reading the Gospel is therefore not like reading a modern treatise on moral philosophy in which all we have to do is follow the argument. It is instead something that requires us to think for ourselves. In that sense, it is perhaps more deeply philosophical for being less overtly philosophical.

There is another reason why the absence of overt moral arguments in Jesus's teachings does not make him inherently unphilosophical. In order to be able to draw out general principles from parables and thought experiments and to exercise good judgement when doing so, you need more than the ability to make logical inferences. You also need to *attend* very carefully to how the world really is and to respond to the salient aspects of it. The basis of Singer's pond thought experiment, for example, is not an argument but an invitation to attend. If we do so we find ourselves unable to deny that the right thing to do is to wade in and save the child. We *see* this before articulating any moral principle. The general rule about preventing something bad if it is easily in our power to do so is something we rationally formulate to make sense of our moral experience. The principle does not shape that experience itself. Principles are codifications of moral responses.

There are many reasons for thinking that ethics is always ultimately a matter of attending and responding appropriately. The role of reason is simply to turn these responses into general principles, to check our responses for consistency, and to draw out the consequences of these principles to make sure they are indeed the right ones. Reason is a tool for improving our moral judgement.

If we accept this more modest role for rationality in moral thinking we have to accept that it cannot give us a reason to be moral in the first place. There have been philosophers like Immanuel Kant who disagree and argue that morality can be grounded in reason alone, but few have been persuaded by his or others' attempts to do so.

If we cannot reason our way to knowledge of what is good how do we know what is? Philosophers have disagreed, but many of them end up saying words to the effect that you know good and bad when you see them. At least you do if you look carefully enough. For example, the early-twentieth-century Cambridge moral philosopher G. E. Moore argued that 'good' is real but it can never be defined in terms of anything else. To say, as some utilitarians do, that the good is simply that which increases happiness is mistaken because 'good' and 'happy' do not mean the same thing. It is always an open question whether happiness is good. Is the happiness of a sadist good, for example? 'Good' is real but indefinable and not one among the many things found in nature. There is no way to know what it is other than to see it. In a similar way, people can give you examples of yellow things and point you towards them, but yellowness is something you have to see for yourself and cannot be defined in terms of anything else. At root, the good is known by a kind of intuition.

The Scottish Enlightenment philosopher David Hume took a more down-to-earth view. He thought that the good could be defined in naturalistic terms. We call good anything that is 'useful to society, or useful or agreeable to the person himself'.[4] Our motivation to do good comes not from reason but from 'the natural sentiment of benevolence', which 'engages us to pay to the interests of mankind and society'.[5]

In many ways Moore and Hume profoundly disagreed. Moore thought good was an undefinable part of a non-natural reality, Hume that it was a definable part of the natural world. But in another vital aspect they agreed: the ultimate basis of any identification of something as good or bad, right or wrong, is not an argument but an observation which requires a non-rational capacity – either intuition (Moore) or moral sentiment (Hume).

This picture of morality helps explain how we see moral change usually coming about. For example, I once interviewed an atheist lesbian single mother called Renee in a small town in Texas. Of all her marginalised identities, being an atheist was by far the most problematic. She thought the explanation was simply a matter of familiarity: 'If somebody finds out that I'm a lesbian, they would say, I have an aunt or a sister who's a lesbian, but if someone finds out I'm an atheist, they don't know how to deal with it. They don't even know what an atheist is. I've been here ten years now and don't know anybody in the whole county who's an atheist.' I think Renee is right and that the reason LGBT+ rights have advanced so much in America is not because activists won a moral argument but because as people came to know more and more gay people their experience showed them there was nothing wicked about them.

There are many moral philosophies where there is no argument offered to justify the notion of the good being used. Confucian ethics, for example, concerns itself only with what is required to create a good society and has no interest in metaphysical conceptions of goodness. When it comes to determining what is a good society, it is assumed that we recognise that harmony is better than disharmony, prosperity better than poverty, peace better than war.

Similarly, the utilitarianism of the nineteenth-century philosopher John Stuart Mill posits that happiness is good and pain bad, but there is no real argument for this. He simply suggests that, if you think about it, happiness is the only thing we believe is good in itself and pain the only thing that is bad in itself.

The absence of any argument from Jesus for what fundamentally makes actions right or wrong is not therefore a good reason to dismiss his moral teachings as nothing more than a series of instructions issued by decree. For him to be taken seriously as a moral teacher we need only be persuaded that he is skilled at making us attend carefully to what goodness is. It is certainly clear that he himself believed in the need for such good 'moral vision': 'The light of the body is the eye: therefore when thine eye is single [sees clearly], thy whole body also is full of light; but when thine eye is evil, thy body also is full of darkness' (2:17).

Modern Western philosophy has come to think of 'seeing clearly' as being primarily a matter of ascertaining facts and reasoning logically from them. This has little or nothing to do with ethics. But there is no shortage of philosophers who have made a connection between acute understanding and being good. In Indian philosophy, the orthodox schools are known as *darśanas*, the root word of which literally means 'to see'. Another Sanskrit word, meaning 'the science of enquiry' – what we would broadly call philosophy – is *ānvīkṣikī*, which originally meant something like 'looking at'.

Even in Western philosophy, there has remained a current of thought that attributes an ethical dimension to accurate seeing. Aristotle wrote, 'pay no less attention to the unproved assertions and opinions of experienced and older people than to demonstrations of fact; because they have an insight from their experience which enables them to see correctly.'[6] More idiosyncratic is an interesting remark Wittgenstein made suggesting that logic and ethics were inseparable. 'How can I be a logician before I'm a decent human being?' he asked in a letter to Bertrand Russell. Wittgenstein's biographer Ray Monk explains the connection as resting on the fact that 'If he's going to think clearly about logic, he's got to remove the things getting in the way of clear thought.' That clarity of thought requires honesty about yourself. Hence 'Wittgenstein also said that in philosophy what is required is not intelligence but will.'[7]

But what is it that we see clearly when we are attending to the world in the appropriately ethically way? In the Gospel, Jesus constantly asks us to be mindful of two things. The first is our own moral development, something we have seen that Jesus repeatedly focuses on. The second is the needs and sufferings of others. Jesus is not an abstract moral theoretician who coldly dishes out injunctions. In several of his parables, people are shown to be motivated to do the right thing not by principle but by a powerfully emotional sympathetic response to need and suffering. In the Parable of the Unforgiving Servant, 'the lord of that servant was moved with compassion, and loosed him, and forgave him the debt' (8:38). When the father of the prodigal son saw he had returned he 'had compassion, and ran, and fell on his neck, and kissed him' (8:49). When the Good Samaritan saw the man left for dead by thieves 'he had compassion on him' (9:21). Jesus himself is shown to respond emotionally to the plight of others, such as when he saw a crowd of his followers 'and was moved with compassion toward them, because they were as sheep not having a shepherd' (8:14).

Experience shows us that compassion is very often the driver of moral change. Take, for example, the 1972 publication of Nick Ut's famous photograph of a horribly burnt young girl, Kim Phuc, fleeing a napalm attack in South Vietnam. This single image did more to shift public opinion on the injustice of the war than any amount of dispassionate analysis. Similarly, nothing countered hostility to refugees in Europe more than the photo of the drowned three-year-old Syrian Kurd Alan Kurdi in 2015.

Jesus's emphasis on compassion has a strong parallel with the idea of moral sympathy that was developed in eighteenth-century Scotland by Francis Hutcheson, Adam Smith and, as we saw earlier, David Hume. In slightly different ways, all three argued that morality is based on nothing more than a capacity to identify with the feelings of others. We 'feel their pain' to some degree and therefore seek to remove that pain. We share their joy and so are motivated to do what we can to ensure that those around us are happy.

A concern for others is a natural instinct that it pleases us to exercise. As Hume said, 'every act of virtue or friendship is attended with a secret pleasure'. This might sound like little more than selfishness: we want to relieve the pain of others only because it pains us, and we want to increase their happiness only because that makes us happy. But Hume insists he is not saying that we are motivated to do good only because it gives us this pleasure. The arrow of causation points the other way: 'I feel a pleasure in doing good to my friend, because I love him; but do not love him for the sake of that pleasure.'[8] It is only because we have a 'virtuous sentiment or passion' that acting on it gives us pleasure. Someone who bears only ill will can get no pleasure at all from helping others and might even delight in their suffering.

Raw compassion is not enough by itself to lead us to goodness. Rather, it must be attentive compassion, sympathy that is sensitive to context and practicalities. Unreflective, inattentive compassion is often little more than a projection of our own emotions on to others, or bad guesses as to what they would want. This kind of naive, sentimental compassion can have bad consequences. Imagining that others must be feeling embarrassed because we would be in their situation, for example, can make them feel worse, not better. Responding without thinking can also be counterproductive, such as when we send unwanted and unnecessary gifts to people in need that end up being stacked in warehouses unused, as happened after one mass killing at a school in America. Jesus said nothing explicit about how attentive compassion differs from the inattentive kind. But by his example he modelled the right kind of attentiveness.

Jesus didn't conform to most people's stereotype of a moral teacher, issuing judgements with certainty and claims to authority. When asked what people should do, he usually simply told them that they already had the commandments. Sometimes he didn't speak at all. When people asked who he was or by what authority he spoke, he batted the question back and asked others what they thought. He spoke in riddles, which we prefer to call 'parables'. And like Socrates, he didn't write down a single word, perhaps because, as the son of a carpenter in a society where over 95 per cent of the people were illiterate, he couldn't write.[9]

Nonetheless, there can be little doubt that, stripped of his divine status, the Jesus of *The Godless Gospel* is still a bona fide moral teacher. He does not ask us to accept his teaching on the basis of mere authority but rather invites us to attend to the needs of others, to his own example and to our own frailties. He wants us to think for ourselves, which is why his parables require us to work out their meaning.

Ironically, Jesus's morality is not typically taught as he himself taught it. Rather, it is delivered with a clarity and certainty that speak of absolute authority. For centuries in Christendom, 'Jesus said' has prefixed claims and instructions that are supposed to put them beyond question.

If any doubt remains that Jesus counts as a moral teacher, just ask yourself how you learned your moral values. Most people would answer that they were taught by their parents or guardians, and by their community. Hardly anyone cites a teacher who is an expert in ethics. Nor do they mean that their parents sat them down and made them follow a home-schooling syllabus on right and wrong. The way in which morality is actually taught is complex and diffuse. We give children some clear dos and don'ts. We tell them stories in which they can see the difference between being a good person and being a wicked one. We try to set a good example, to teach them politeness by modelling politeness and so on. We also try to make sure they spend their time in environments that we think will build moral character rather than erode it. There is nothing systematic in this process and nor does it rest on any clear fundamental principle. No wonder, then, that when children ask why they should behave as we're telling them to do we find it hard to come up with a clear answer.

Everything included in this account of how we actually

acquire our moral values identifies an important characteristic of the kind of moral teacher who speaks to people directly rather than who writes treatises. First, they will have a clear sense of what is right and wrong in many situations. Second, they will appreciate that rules are not enough and people have to develop a moral sensibility of their own. To do that, teachers often use stories which enable people to see right and wrong in action and to imagine themselves facing similar dilemmas. Third, they will practise what they preach, modelling goodness, in part because showing is more powerful than telling. They will also hope and encourage others to act as exemplars and will encourage people to avoid dangerous temptations. Fourth, unlike most parents, they will have something clear to say about what the point of being good is. They will have a conception of the *summum bonum*, the highest good towards which right action aims.

Anyone familiar with the life and teachings of Jesus will recognise him in this description, even if they do not recognise his divinity.

CONCLUSION

There have been times when I've wondered whether the whole project of this book is misguided. One such moment came when Karen Kilby suggested that Jesus did not offer 'a complete ethics' and probably wasn't interested in expounding a universal moral code. After all, most scholars agree that Jesus was speaking with an expectation that the end times were near. 'He doesn't seem to me to be setting up the pattern to go on for the next two thousand years. To me there seems to be an immediacy in his challenge to the people he is addressing.'

But another thing she said shortly afterwards did more than just reassure me, it helped me see the best way to look at Jesus's teaching today: 'I experience Jesus's teaching as something that grabs me, challenges me and shakes me up.' That for me gets to the essence of Jesus's enduring significance. We may decide that other more complete moral philosophies provide a better basis for our actions. But his teachings offer a much-needed challenge to our moral thinking that shakes us out of any complacency.

'It's like the way sourdough works,' Kilby explains. 'You

have this invisible leaven in it and then you've got the under-lying flour. I think of the flour as some kind of general human wisdom, culture or moral system. The leaven is the Gospel. The Gospel doesn't work on its own, in a vacuum. If you just try to base everything on that and that alone you can't really make it work, or you'll be deluding yourself. So I don't think of it as a whole system in itself but as a transformative element that can embed itself in any culture.'

This looks to me like the right way to frame *The Godless Gospel* for today. We can't simply uproot Jesus's moral teaching from its first-century Palestine context and replant it in the present day. But we can follow its spirit, rather than its letter, which is surely the most authentic way to take it anyway. And in its spirit we find a series of moral challenges rather than a complete moral system.

The first challenge is to 'turn from the powerful to the powerless', as Kilby puts it. As someone who finds Aristotle's ideal of the good life compelling, I consider this extremely useful. Aristotle offers an attractive vision of human flourishing which involves living according to our nature as completely and fully as possible. Great if you have the resources and abilities needed to flourish, but there is no blessing in being poor if you don't. In Aristotle's day, human flourishing was an ethic for Athenian aristocrats. Today, flourishing is within the grasp of more people than ever before. But the poor are still with us, in their billions. Jesus reminds us that to ignore them and focus solely on our own flourishing is to show a profound lack of compassion.

Another of his essential challenges is our need for humility. Humility makes us less judgemental, more forgiving and more aware of our dependence on others. 'At the heart of Jesus's ethics is fundamental human brokenness,' says Elizabeth Oldfield. 'As a starting point for ethics that's quite a good place. The limits of our self-understanding and the depths of our ability for self-deception mean that we need to live in a community of practice. Ethics is not something that can happen with one person. The whole human only comes alive in healthy relationships because we feel each other's brokenness.'

Jesus also challenges us to commit to what is good and true, even if that means turning our backs on what is pleasant and easy. In a culture where people profess to detest tax-avoiding international companies but still buy their goods and services regularly because it's so convenient, that's a hard call. But there is something joyous in recognising goodness as the most important thing in the world and fully devoting yourself to it. Jesus captured this in two analogies: 'When a man hath found treasure hid in a field, he hideth, and for joy thereof goeth and selleth all that he hath, and buyeth that field. A merchant man, seeking goodly pearls, when he had found one pearl of great price, went and sold all that he had, and bought it' (9:8–9). When you find the right way, you give up everything for it.

Finally, Jesus challenges us to aim high, higher than we can ever actually reach: 'Be ye therefore perfect' (2:45). This runs counter to a widely accepted ethical principle, attributed to Kant, that *ought* implies *can*. In other words, you can only say that someone is morally obliged to do something if they are actually capable of doing so. This looks sensible. For example, you can't be responsible for saving someone's life if there is no way you could actually save them. How, then, can ethics in the Christian context mean, as Simon Critchley puts it, that *ought* implies *cannot*?[1]

Because it is right that morality always asks more of us than we are able to give. Falling short is inevitable. Jesus is asking us to be perfect, not magicians. He is not saying we ought to do actions that are simply impossible. He is saying we ought to strive to become better people than we are capable of becoming.

This would not sound odd in many contexts other than in morality. Sports people and artists, for example, often say they strive for perfection but know they can't reach it. We tend to admire this aspiration and understand that it reflects a seriousness of intent rather than an insane belief in the impossible. It is perhaps an indictment of the shallowness of our age that we do not treat our moral growth as seriously as we do our sporting, professional or creative development.

It is a pity that contemporary Christianity seems unwilling or unable to emphasise the radical toughness of Jesus's teaching. There is too much gentle Jesus meek and mild, or what one evangelical once described to me as the 'Jesus is my boyfriend' way of thinking. 'Jesus is morally demanding in a way that requires penitence, self-examination and soul-searching into the motivation of our actions, especially in relation to aggression, violence and attitudes towards the other,' says Brian Mountford. 'There is a big dumbing-down culture in the Church of England, primarily directed towards the intellectual content of faith, but occasionally spilling over into moral compromise on political and fiscal issues, as we try to keep our place in the national establishment.'

And yet Mountford also sees that 'people in a trivialising society are still thirsty for something more serious and more morally and intellectually demanding'. Secular humanism is often unable to provide this. I always wince when I remember the poster campaign on the side of London buses that read: 'There's probably no God. Now stop worrying and enjoy your life.' It felt so frivolous. Religion at its best brings some gravitas to life, to the question of how we ought to live. Philip Larkin captured this in his poem 'Church Going', in which he called the church a 'serious house on serious earth' which addresses a 'hunger in himself to be more serious'.

You don't need to turn to religion to feed this hunger. If religions tend to exhibit more moral seriousness it is largely because they have a greater sense that we are accountable to something other than ourselves. I believe this feeling of accountability is something that the godless can and should feel too. We are also accountable: to our society, our family, our own conscience and to our moral sympathy. Whenever compassion allows us to really feel the suffering of others, we are instinctively moved to do something about it and recognise that there is something unjustifiable in simply focusing on our own selfish needs.

We don't need to believe that the good to which we are accountable is divine or transcendent. Both theologians and philosophers can be too caught up in abstruse metaphysical complexities. Many worry that unless goodness has some kind of independent objective reality, morality is hollow and baseless. But those people are surely taking too dim a view of themselves and others. Do religious people really think that they would stop caring about others if they stopped believing in God? We don't need to obsess about the ultimate nature of the good to feel its force. Love and goodness are real enough to be of supreme importance even if they have no existence beyond this planet.

The Godless Gospel is challenging, but in a way it boils down to principles that are simple enough. A stripped-down secular version of the Lord's Prayer (6:39) can be reduced to three things:

> Give us day by day our daily bread.
> And forgive us our sins; for we also forgive every one
>   that is indebted to us.
> And lead us not into temptation; but deliver us from
>   evil.

The prayer is framed as an address to a higher power. The godless could understand this simply as a means of recognising that we are not entirely self-sufficient, that we need the help of others and are in some sense answerable for our actions. The prayer could be turned into a mantra, an address to ourselves:

> May we have our daily bread.
> And have our sins forgiven; as we also forgive every
> one that is indebted to us.
> And may we not be led into temptation; but be
> delivered from evil.

It is important that this mantra is addressed to 'us' rather than to 'me'. I think it is an essential part of Jesus's teaching that we live in a moral community and although the transformation of the self is the key goal this can't be achieved by the self alone.

The first line is both a wish and a reminder of the modesty of our needs and those of others. We are vulnerable creatures of flesh and blood and we cannot do anything without the basic necessities of life. But we don't *need* more than these. Nice though it might be to have the everyday luxuries modern life affords, we should not covet them. That would cultivate acquisitiveness, selfishness, materialism and dissatisfaction with what we have.

At the same time, thinking about our basic needs reminds us that not everyone has them met. Jesus's challenge not to turn our backs on the sick, the hungry and the destitute has to be taken seriously. To work on our moral development, which is the subject of the rest of the brief mantra, we also have to address the pressing needs of those around us.

The second line is a call to forgive and a wish to be forgiven. As we have seen, this is not a matter of dispensing absolution, erasing wrongs like a moral wet wipe. It is primarily a matter of refraining from judgement and of re-establishing relationships. We forgive not because we overlook wrongdoing. We forgive because we know we are all deeply flawed and we have as much reason to seek forgiveness from others as we do to demand it of them. To refuse forgiveness means to stand in judgement of others. Although we have to judge *what* is right or wrong, we have no right to say *who* is good or bad. When we remain in judgement and don't move on to forgiveness we become distracted from our primary task of reforming ourselves and we become too fixated on the reform of others. Also, where there is no forgiveness, there are broken relationships. Life is too short and our bonds are too precious to allow such disruptions to last any longer than is necessary.

The third line is simply a resolution to resist evil. It is interesting that this is framed negatively. It is not a question of doing good but of not doing bad. As a piece of moral psychology I think this is astute. Too often we think the challenge of being good is to do great acts, such as becoming an aid worker or volunteering at a homeless shelter. But the world would be a far better place if we simply refrained from doing wrong, even if we did nothing heroic. If you don't fall for temptations, such as deceit, dishonesty, malicious revenge and cruel gossip, you live a good, decent life. Galen's maxim 'First do no harm' is not just for physicians.

The importance of resisting evil is played out in a lot of the films of the Coen brothers. Many of these feature three archetypes: people of simple goodness, people who succumb to temptation and psychopaths. The last of these are simply beyond our comprehension. The first two are remarkably similar and represent the vast bulk of humanity. In their films, as in life, most of the people who lie, steal or kill are not at heart 'bad people', different from the rest of us. Rather they allow themselves to be tempted, step by step, down a path that leads to ruin. In *Fargo*, for example, Jerry is an ordinary guy struggling to maintain the standard of living for his family which they and his wife's side of the family expect. He doesn't want much, just a little more self-respect, which he misguidedly identifies with his ability to bring home the bacon. So he succumbs to the first small temptation of a little creative accounting, until the credit company catches up with him. This leads to a staged kidnapping of his wife to extract a ransom from her father, who is after all a wealthy son of a bitch who has the money and snobbishly looks down on Jerry, a used car salesman. The plan goes wrong, with fatal consequences. Jerry didn't need a good moral theory to prevent this happening. He just needed to resist the slow erosion of his moral character by a series of small, understandable temptations. If only at such key moments he had remembered *may we not be led into temptation; but be delivered from evil.*

Powerful though these moral teachings are, there still remains a question: what holds them all together? Why follow them? Every ethical system answers this question with an explicit or implicit notion of the *summum bonum*, the greatest good towards which right action leads us. In utilitarianism this is the greatest happiness of the greatest number, in Aristotle human flourishing, in Buddhism the end of suffering. In many religious ethics the *summum bonum* is life in paradise or some kind of union with the divine, as in the Indic idea of a return to the ultimate oneness of *Brahman*.

When I asked my theologian interviewees what they thought the *summum bonum* of Jesus's teaching was, their answers invariably had some kind of secular version. For Brian Mountford, the *summum bonum* is 'self-giving love'. This is something he finds resonates even with those with no religion: 'I talk to the ungodly most often at wedding services and I think an important theme of marriage is self-giving love. I usually try to develop that into a more community, national and international interpretation of what to act selflessly might actually add up to for society, and the response I get is always enthusiastic and affirmative.'

Keith Ward has a similar conception of the *summum bonum* to which Jesus's teachings point: 'a community in which people serve each other and are filled with the love of God'. Lucy Winkett also conceives of the *summum bonum* as a 'future that is discernible, that is nearly here, and is realisable in the everyday. It's not waiting for you when you're dead. Jesus called this the *basileia*, the kingdom or commonwealth of God. The picture he often used was of a meal or a banquet where everyone is welcome and where all are fed equally. There's an equal sharing of the earth's bounty, where people are different from one another but the poor are especially welcome.'

Karen Kilby sums up the *summum bonum* as 'Love of God and neighbour. As human societies we're always marginalising, stratifying and creating patterns of oppression. The moral life is always in resistance to this. Its end is people flourishing in community with one another, as imaged by a shared meal.'

It doesn't take too much imagination to conceive of this kind of ultimate good in secular terms. It sounds very much like many other conceptions of the just society. For lots of the religious, however, this love supreme can't be rooted in nothing more than human imperfection. 'All there is comes from the dust of the big bang,' says Mountford. 'Therefore I find it difficult to believe our notions of good and love are simply inventions of the human mind and that they're not somehow embedded in the stuff of the universe.'

It is also true that without God our capacity to realise this

'Kingdom of God' is extremely limited. That's why Elizabeth Oldfield says that if you completely secularise Jesus's teaching 'it doesn't quite leave you with enough hope to carry on. Maybe what the transcendent part gives you is the resilience and joy.' Winkettt echoes these thoughts: 'There are some things that are simply not resolvable in life. There is a belief that there is some kind of way of reconciling those things after death. Without that, living with your mistakes can be bleaker.' Similarly, Kilby says, 'I think for Christianity to work it has to include trust in a radically unthinkable eschatological activity of God to redeem all that is clearly not good in this world.'

I can see why Christians would think the Gospel needs God. Without a resurrection, without divine assistance, humanity will never be able to fully overcome its weaknesses and limitations. But I think the lack of a deity makes *The Godless Gospel* even more challenging and credible than the religious version. It takes more seriously the same themes and ideas that Christianity has stressed. Human beings are broken, 'fallen' creatures. Instead of imagining that we can be fully healed, we need to accept that this is how we are and we need to make the best of it. We recognise that goodness demands more of us than we can give. Instead of imagining that God can bridge the gap between who we are and who we ideally ought to be, we simply have to try to do our best, being forgiving of ourselves and others when we fail. The poor will always be with us. Instead of allowing thoughts of a utopian Kingdom of Heaven to come to reassure us that everything will be OK in the end, we have even more reason to do what we can now, before it is too late for those presently suffering. Sometimes love for others and the commitment to live with integrity require us to give up our own lives. Instead of imagining a resurrection that diminishes the seriousness of this, we should see the sacrifice as real and final, a testament to humanity's capacity for true selfless, self-emptying love.

In many ways I find this godless Gospel truer to the spirit of Jesus's teaching than the version in which God is the great cosmic guarantor, there to ensure a happy ending. Jesus never promised a land of milk and honey and never made his path sound easy. He warned that many are called but few are chosen, and he insisted that the Kingdom of Heaven is within us, that great love required laying down our lives. He did not seek to set up a cosy, established church but led something more akin to what the former Bishop of Edinburgh Richard Holloway calls an 'underground guerrilla movement'. Jesus remains as much a countercultural force in our lifetimes as he was in his own.

We don't know what the historical Jesus really thought but I wonder whether his original message was just too hard to take. When his life ended on the cross, that should have been the defining example of how seriously he took the idea of sacrifice and the need to live well, even if it meant living a shorter life. Over time, however, his followers needed a happier ending. They added a resurrection, ignored what he said about the Kingdom of Heaven being within us and imagined it as world to come. They made his teaching more palatable and more attractive, but in doing so they enfeebled it.

Christians say that Jesus died for us. It is perhaps time for him to die once more, this time for good, in order that what matters most in his message can rise again.

PART TWO

The Godless Gospel

A NOTE ON THE TEXT

The editing of *The Godless Gospel* was an imperfect and flawed process, much like the editing of the original Gospels. Not only were there many more gospels in circulation than were selected for the New Testament, we can be sure that the versions of Matthew, Mark, Luke and John we have now contain idiosyncratic choices by writers and copiers as well as transcription errors. While I hope there are none of the latter in this godless Gospel, it would seem more likely that there are in fact a few.

Although I have removed from this godless Gospel all mentions of prophecies, God, miracles and so on, some religious references remain: for instance, to prayer and the sabbath. In such cases I believe it is easy enough to make sense of what is said without assuming the reality of a transcendent God. These passages make it clear that there is no simple fact of the matter as to what in the Gospels should be counted as essentially religious in content. Judgements must be made.

In a very few cases where it seems to make sense, I have replaced 'God' with 'good'. Other than that I have not changed the wording. I chose the King James Version for the simple reason that it is widely agreed to be the most poetic. I have consulted other translations considered more literally accurate to help avoid misunderstanding of the text's meaning.

Many of the same stories appear in more than one Gospel. To avoid repetition I have created hybrid versions for *The Godless Gospel* which omit no elements without duplication. The sources are provided at the end of the book. The references given often contain much more than has been selected but they should include all that has been.

I have retained the original chronology when possible and desirable. However, the original Gospels place many events at different times. Most notably, Jesus cleanses the temple at the start of his ministry in John but at the end in Matthew, Mark and Luke. So I did not worry about playing with the chronology of events and teachings that had no specific context in Jesus's life and have grouped such passages together thematically.

I THE BEGINNING

THE BIRTH OF JESUS

¹ The beginning of the gospel of Jesus.

² It came to pass in the days of Herod the king, that there went out a decree from Caesar Augustus that all the world should be taxed. And all went to be taxed, every one into his own city. ³ And Joseph also went up from Galilee, out of the city of Nazareth, into Judaea, unto the city of David, which is called Bethlehem (because he was of the house and lineage of David); To be taxed with Mary his espoused wife, being great with child.

⁴ And so it was, that, while they were there, the days were accomplished that she should be delivered. And she brought forth her firstborn son, and wrapped him in swaddling clothes, and laid him in a manger; because there was no room for them in the inn.

CHILDHOOD

⁵ And the child grew, and waxed strong in spirit, filled with wisdom. ⁶ Now his parents went to Jerusalem every year at the feast of the passover. And when he was twelve years old, they went up to Jerusalem after the custom of the feast.

⁷ And when they had fulfilled the days, as they returned, the child Jesus tarried behind in Jerusalem; and Joseph and his mother knew not of it. ⁸ But they, supposing him to have been in the company, went a day's journey; and they sought him among their kinsfolk and acquaintance. And when they found him not, they turned back again to Jerusalem, seeking him.

⁹ And it came to pass, that after three days they found him in the temple, sitting in the midst of the doctors, both hearing them, and asking them questions. And all that heard him were astonished at his understanding and answers. And Jesus increased in wisdom and stature.

JESUS BEGINS HIS TEACHING

¹⁰ And Jesus himself began to be about thirty years of age. ¹¹ He returned from Jordan, and went into the wilderness. And in those days he did eat nothing: and when they were ended, he afterward hungered. ¹² And when had ended all the temptation, Jesus returned into Galilee.

¹³ From that time Jesus began to preach, and to say, Repent: for the Kingdom of Heaven is at hand. ¹⁴ And he taught in their synagogues, being glorified of all and there went out a fame of him through all the region round about.

¹⁵ And when he came to Nazareth, where he had been brought up, he taught them in their synagogue, insomuch that they were astonished, and said, Whence hath this man this

wisdom? [16] Is not this the carpenter's son, the son of Mary, the brother of James, and Joses, and of Juda, and Simon? And his sisters, are they not all with us? Whence then hath this man all these things?

[17] And they were offended in him. But Jesus said unto them, A prophet is not without honour, save in his own country, and among his own kin, and in his own house.

[18] And all they in the synagogue, when they heard these things, were filled with wrath, And rose up, and thrust him out of the city, and led him unto the brow of the hill whereon their city was built, that they might cast him down headlong.

[19] But he passing through the midst of them went his way, And came down to Capernaum, a city of Galilee which is upon the sea coast, in the borders of Zabulon and Nephthalim, and taught them on the sabbath days. [20] And they were astonished at his doctrine: for his word was with power. And the fame of him went out into every place of the country round about.

[21] And when it was day, he departed and went into a desert place: and the people sought him, and came unto him, and stayed him, that he should not depart from them. [22] And he said unto them, I must preach the Kingdom of Heaven to other cities also: for therefore am I sent. And he preached in the synagogues of Galilee.

JESUS CALLS HIS DISCIPLES

[23] And Jesus, walking by the sea of Galilee, saw two brethren, Simon called Peter, and Andrew his brother, casting a net into the sea: for they were fishers. And he saith unto them, Follow me, and I will make you fishers of men. And straightway they forsook their nets, and followed him.

[24] When he had gone a little farther thence, he saw James

the son of Zebedee, and John his brother, who also were in the ship mending their nets, and he called them. And they left their father Zebedee in the ship with the hired servants, and followed him.

²⁵ And they went into Capernaum; and straightway on the sabbath day he entered into the synagogue, and taught. ²⁶ And forthwith, when they were come out of the synagogue, they entered into the house of Simon and Andrew, with James and John.

²⁷ And in the morning, rising up a great while before day, he went out, and departed into a solitary place, and there prayed. ²⁸ And Simon and they that were with him followed after. He called unto him his twelve disciples, that they should be with him, and that he might send them forth to preach. ²⁹ Now the names of the twelve apostles are these; The first, Simon, whom he surnamed Peter, and Andrew his brother; James the son of Zebedee, and John his brother, and he surnamed them Boanerges, which is, The sons of thunder; Philip, and Bartholomew; Thomas, and Matthew the tax collector; James the son of Alphaeus, and Lebbaeus, whose surname was Thaddaeus; Simon the Canaanite, called the zealot, and Judas Iscariot, who also betrayed him.

³⁰ And he said unto them, Let us go into the next towns, that I may preach there also: for therefore came I forth. And he went about all the cities and villages, teaching in their synagogues.

2 THE SERMON ON THE MOUNT

THE BEATITUDES

¹ And there followed him great multitudes of people from
Galilee, and from Decapolis, and from Jerusalem, and
from Judaea, and from the sea coast of Tyre and Sidon,
and from beyond Jordan. And seeing the multitudes, he went
up into a mountain: and when he was set, his disciples came
unto him: And he opened his mouth, and taught them, saying,

² Blessed be ye poor: for yours is the Kingdom of Heaven.

³ Blessed are the poor in spirit and pure in heart.

⁴ Blessed are they that mourn: for they shall be comforted.

⁵ Blessed are ye that hunger now: for ye shall be filled.

⁶ Blessed are ye that weep now: for ye shall laugh.

⁷ Blessed are the meek: for they shall inherit the earth.

⁸ Blessed are they which do hunger and thirst after righteousness: for they shall be filled.

[9] Blessed are the merciful: for they shall obtain mercy.

[10] Blessed are the peacemakers: for they shall be called the children of God.

[11] Blessed are ye, when men shall hate you, and when they shall separate you from their company, and shall reproach you, and cast out your name as evil, for my sake. Rejoice ye in that day, and leap for joy: for, behold, your reward is great.

[12] But woe unto you that are rich! for ye have received your consolation.

Woe unto you that are full! for ye shall hunger. Woe unto you that laugh now! for ye shall mourn and weep.

[13] Woe unto you, when all men shall speak well of you! for so did their fathers to the false prophets.

[14] Blessed are they which are persecuted for righteousness' sake.

Blessed are ye, when men shall revile you, and persecute you, and shall say all manner of evil against you falsely.

[15] Ye are the salt of the earth: but if the salt have lost his savour, wherewith shall it be salted? It is neither fit for the land, nor yet for the dunghill; it is thenceforth good for nothing, but to be cast out, and to be trodden under foot of men. He that hath ears to hear, let him hear.

THE LIGHT OF THE WORLD

[16] Ye are the light of the world. A city that is set on an hill cannot be hid. Neither do men light a candle, and put it under a bushel, but on a candlestick; and it giveth light unto all that are in the house.

[17] The light of the body is the eye: therefore when thine eye

is single*, thy whole body also is full of light; but when thine eye is evil, thy body also is full of darkness. Take heed therefore that the light which is in thee be not darkness.

[18] If thy whole body therefore be full of light, having no part dark, the whole shall be full of light, as when the bright shining of a candle doth give thee light. [19] Let your light so shine before men, that they may see your good works. [20] For there is nothing hid, which shall not be manifested; neither was any thing kept secret, but that it should come abroad.

FULFILLING THE LAW

[21] Think not that I am come to destroy the law: I am not come to destroy, but to fulfil. For verily I say unto you, one jot or one tittle shall in no wise pass from the law, till all be fulfilled.

[22] Whosoever therefore shall break one of these least commandments, and shall teach men so, he shall be called the least: but whosoever shall do and teach them, the same shall be called great. [23] For I say unto you, your righteousness must exceed the righteousness of the scribes and Pharisees.

[24] Ye have heard that it was said of them of old time, Thou shalt not kill; and whosoever shall kill shall be in danger of the judgment: But I say unto you, That whosoever is angry with his brother without a cause shall be in danger of the judgment: and whosoever shall say to his brother, Raca,† shall be in danger of the council: but whosoever shall say, Thou fool, shall be in danger of hell fire.

[25] Therefore if thou bring thy gift, and there rememberest

---

* Sees clearly.
† An insult, 'empty-headed' or 'foolish'.

that thy brother hath ought against thee; Leave there thy gift, and go thy way; first be reconciled to thy brother, and then come and offer thy gift. ²⁶ Agree with thine adversary quickly, while thou art in the way with him; lest at any time the adversary deliver thee to the judge, and the judge deliver thee to the officer, and thou be cast into prison. Verily I say unto thee, Thou shalt by no means come out thence, till thou hast paid the uttermost farthing.

²⁷ Ye have heard that it was said by them of old time, Thou shalt not commit adultery: But I say unto you, That whosoever looketh on a woman to lust after her hath committed adultery with her already in his heart. ²⁸ And if thy right eye offend thee, pluck it out, and cast it from thee: for it is profitable for thee that one of thy members should perish, and not that thy whole body should be cast into hell. ²⁹ And if thy right hand offend thee, cut it off, and cast it from thee: for it is profitable for thee that one of thy members should perish, and not that thy whole body should be cast into hell. ³⁰ And if thy foot offend thee, cut it off: it is better for thee to enter life halt or maimed, than having two feet to be cast into hell.

³¹ Woe unto the world because of offences! for it must needs be that offences come; but woe to that man by whom the offence cometh!

³² It hath been said, Whosoever shall put away his wife, let him give her a writing of divorcement: But I say unto you, That whosoever shall put away his wife, saving for the cause of fornication, causeth her to commit adultery: and whosoever shall marry her that is divorced committeth adultery.

³³ Again, ye have heard that it hath been said by them of old time, Thou shalt not forswear thyself, but shalt perform unto the Lord thine oaths: But I say unto you, Swear not at all; neither by heaven Nor by the earth: neither by Jerusalem.

[34] Neither shalt thou swear by thy head, because thou canst not make one hair white or black. But let your communication be, Yea, yea; Nay, nay: for whatsoever is more than these cometh of evil.

LOVE THINE ENEMIES

[35] Ye have heard that it hath been said, An eye for an eye, and a tooth for a tooth: But I say unto you, That ye resist not evil: but whosoever shall smite thee on thy right cheek, turn to him the other also. [36] And if any man will sue thee at the law, and take away thy coat, let him have thy cloak also. And whosoever shall compel thee to go a mile, go with him twain. Give to him that asketh thee, and from him that would borrow of thee turn not thou away.

[37] Ye have heard that it hath been said, Thou shalt love thy neighbour, and hate thine enemy. But I say unto you which hear, Love your enemies, do good to them which hate you, bless them that curse you, do good to them that hate you, despitefully use you, and persecute you.

[38] And as ye would that men should do to you, do ye also to them likewise. [39] For if ye love them which love you, what thank have ye? for sinners also love those that love them. And if ye do good to them which do good to you, what thank have ye? for sinners also do even the same.

[40] And if ye lend to them of whom ye hope to receive, what thank have ye? for sinners also lend to sinners, to receive as much again. And if ye salute your brethren only, what do ye more than others? do not even the tax collectors so? [41] But love ye your enemies, and do good, and lend, hoping for nothing again; and your reward shall be great, and ye shall be the children of the Highest.

[42] Thou shalt love thy neighbour as thyself. There is none other commandment greater than this.

[43] A new commandment I give unto you, That ye love one another; as I have loved you, that ye also love one another. By this shall all men know that ye are my disciples, if ye have love one to another.

[44] Greater love hath no man than this, that a man lay down his life for his friends.

[45] Be ye therefore merciful. Be ye therefore perfect.

3 THE SERMON ON THE MOUNT CONTINUED

DO NOT SOUND A TRUMPET BEFORE THEE

¹ Take heed that ye do not your alms before men, to be seen of them. Therefore when thou doest thine alms, do not sound a trumpet before thee, as the hypocrites do in the synagogues and in the streets, that they may have glory of men. Verily I say unto you, They have their reward. But when thou doest alms, let not thy left hand know what thy right hand doeth: That thine alms may be in secret.

² And when thou prayest, thou shalt not be as the hypocrites are: for they love to pray standing in the synagogues and in the corners of the streets, that they may be seen of men. Verily I say unto you, They have their reward. But when ye pray, use not vain repetitions, as the heathen do: for they think that they shall be heard for their much speaking. Be not ye therefore like unto them.

[3] Moreover when ye fast, be not, as the hypocrites, of a sad countenance: for they disfigure their faces, that they may appear unto men to fast. Verily I say unto you, They have their reward. But thou, when thou fastest, anoint thine head, and wash thy face; That thou appear not unto men to fast.

TAKE NO THOUGHT FOR YOUR LIFE

[4] Lay not up for yourselves treasures upon earth, where moth and rust doth corrupt, and where thieves break through and steal: For where your treasure is, there will your heart be also. [5] No man can serve two masters: for either he will hate the one, and love the other; or else he will hold to the one, and despise the other. Ye cannot serve good and mammon. [6] Therefore I say unto you, Take no thought for your life, what ye shall eat, or what ye shall drink; nor yet for your body, what ye shall put on. Is not the life more than meat, and the body than raiment?

[7] Behold the fowls of the air: for they sow not, neither do they reap, nor gather into barns. Are ye not much better than they? Which of you by taking thought can add one cubit unto his stature? [8] And why take ye thought for raiment? Consider the lilies of the field, how they grow; they toil not, neither do they spin: And yet I say unto you, That even Solomon in all his glory was not arrayed like one of these.

[9] Therefore take no thought, saying, What shall we eat? or, What shall we drink? or, Wherewithal shall we be clothed? But seek ye first righteousness; and all these things shall be added unto you. [10] Take therefore no thought for the morrow: for the morrow shall take thought for the things of itself. Sufficient unto the day is the evil thereof.

JUDGE NOT, THAT YE BE NOT JUDGED

[11] Can the blind lead the blind? shall they not both fall into the ditch? [12] The disciple is not above his master: but every one that is perfect shall be as his master.

[13] And how canst thou say to thy brother, Brother, let me pull out the mote that is in thine eye, when thou thyself beholdest not the beam that is in thine own eye? Thou hypocrite, cast out first the beam out of thine own eye, and then shalt thou see clearly to pull out the mote that is in thy brother's eye.

[14] Judge not, that ye be not judged: condemn not, that ye be condemned: forgive, that ye be forgiven: [15] For with what judgment ye judge, ye shall be judged: and with what measure ye mete, it shall be measured to you again.*

SEEK, AND YE SHALL FIND

[16] Give, and it shall be given unto you; good measure, pressed down, and shaken together, and running over, shall men give into your bosom. For with the same measure that ye mete withal it shall be measured to you again.

[17] And he said unto them, Which of you shall have a friend, and shall go unto him at midnight, and say unto him, Friend, lend me three loaves; For a friend of mine in his journey is come to me, and I have nothing to set before him? And he from within shall answer and say, Trouble me not: the door is

---

* Matthew uses the formula 'Judge not, that ye be not judged', Luke 'Judge not, and ye shall not be judged', extending this to condemnation and forgiveness. I have adopted Matthew's 'that ye be not' in place of 'and ye shall not be'.

now shut, and my children are with me in bed; I cannot rise and give thee.

18 I say unto you, Though he will not rise and give him, because he is his friend, yet because of his importunity he will rise and give him as many as he needeth. 19 And I say unto you, Ask, and it shall be given you; seek, and ye shall find; knock, and it shall be opened unto you. 20 If thou canst believe, all things are possible to him that believeth.

21 Therefore I say unto you, What things soever ye desire, when ye pray, believe that ye receive them, and ye shall have them. For every one that asketh receiveth; and he that seeketh findeth; and to him that knocketh it shall be opened. 22 What man is there of you, whom if his son ask bread, will he give him a stone? Or if he ask a fish, will he give him a serpent? Or if he shall ask an egg, will he offer him a scorpion? 23 Therefore all things whatsoever ye would that men should do to you, do ye even so to them.

KNOW THEM BY THEIR FRUITS

24 Beware of false prophets, which come to you in sheep's clothing, but inwardly they are ravening wolves. 25 Ye shall know them by their fruits. For of thorns men do not gather figs, nor of a bramble bush gather they grapes. 26 Even so every good tree bringeth forth good fruit; but a corrupt tree bringeth forth corrupt fruit. For a good tree bringeth not forth corrupt fruit; neither doth a corrupt tree bring forth good fruit. Every tree that bringeth not forth good fruit is hewn down, and cast into the fire.

27 A good man out of the good treasure of his heart bringeth forth that which is good; and an evil man out of the evil treasure of his heart bringeth forth that which is evil: for of the abundance of the heart his mouth speaketh.

[28] The thief cometh not, but for to steal, and to kill, and to destroy: I am come that they might have life, and that they might have it more abundantly.

[29] Many will say to me, Lord, Lord, have we not prophesied in thy name? and in thy name done many wonderful works? And then will I profess unto them, I never knew you: depart from me, ye that work iniquity. And why call ye me, Lord, Lord, and do not the things which I say?

[30] Therefore whosoever heareth these sayings of mine, and doeth them, I will liken him unto a wise man, which built an house, and digged deep, and laid the foundation on a rock: and the flood arose, the winds blew, and the stream beat vehemently upon that house, and could not shake it: for it was founded upon a rock. [31] And every one that heareth these sayings of mine, and doeth them not, shall be likened unto a foolish man, which built his house upon the sand: And the rain descended, and the floods came, and the winds blew, and beat upon that house; and it fell: and great was the fall of it.

[32] And it came to pass, when Jesus had ended these sayings, the people were astonished at his doctrine. For he taught them as one having authority, and not as the scribes.

4 FOLLOWING JESUS

THE NARROW GATE

¹ Jesus went through the cities and villages, teaching, and journeying toward Jerusalem. Then said one unto him, Lord, are there few that be saved? And he said unto them, ² Enter ye in at the strait gate: for wide is the gate, and broad is the way, that leadeth to destruction, and many there be which go in thereat: Because strait is the gate, and narrow is the way, which leadeth unto life, and few there be that find it.

³ When once the master of the house is risen up, and hath shut to the door, and ye begin to stand without, and to knock at the door, saying, Lord, Lord, open unto us; and he shall answer and say unto you, I know you not whence ye are: ⁴ Then shall ye begin to say, We have eaten and drunk in thy presence, and thou hast taught in our streets. But he shall say, I tell you, I know you not whence ye are; depart from me, all ye workers of iniquity.

⁵ And they shall come from the east, and from the west, and

from the north, and from the south, and shall sit down in the Kingdom of Heaven. And, behold, there are last which shall be first, and there are first which shall be last.

⁶ Then said Jesus to those Jews which believed on him, If ye continue in my word, then are ye my disciples indeed; And ye shall know the truth, and the truth shall make you free.

⁷ They answered him, We be Abraham's seed, and were never in bondage to any man: how sayest thou, Ye shall be made free? Jesus answered them, Verily, verily, I say unto you, Whosoever committeth sin is the servant of sin.

THE PRICE OF DISCIPLESHIP

⁸ And it came to pass, that, as they went in the way, a certain man said unto him, Lord, I will follow thee whithersoever thou goest. And Jesus said unto him, Foxes have holes, and birds of the air have nests; but I hath not where to lay mine head.

⁹ And he said unto another, Follow me. But he said, suffer me first to go and bury my father. Jesus said unto him, Let the dead bury their dead: but go thou and preach the Kingdom of Heaven.

¹⁰ And another also said, I will follow thee; but let me first go bid them farewell, which are at home at my house. And Jesus said unto him, If any man come to me, and hate not his father, and mother, and wife, and children, and brethren, and sisters, yea, and his own life also, he cannot be my disciple. No man, having put his hand to the plough, and looking back, is fit for the kingdom of God.

¹¹ For which of you, intending to build a tower, sitteth not down first, and counteth the cost, whether he have sufficient to finish it? Lest haply, after he hath laid the foundation, and is not able to finish it, all that behold it begin to mock him, Saying,

This man began to build, and was not able to finish. ¹² Or what king, going to make war against another king, sitteth not down first, and consulteth whether he be able with ten thousand to meet him that cometh against him with twenty thousand? Or else, while the other is yet a great way off, he sendeth an ambassage, and desireth conditions of peace.

¹³ So likewise, whosoever he be of you that forsaketh not all that he hath, he cannot be my disciple.

And when he had called the people unto him with his disciples also, he said unto them, Whosoever will come after me, let him deny himself, and take up his cross, and follow me. ¹⁴ For whosoever shall be ashamed of me and of my words, of him shall I be ashamed. For whosoever will save his life shall lose it; but whosoever shall lose his life for my sake and the gospel's, the same shall save it. ¹⁵ For what shall it profit a man, if he shall gain the whole world, and lose himself or be cast away? Or what shall a man give in exchange for his soul?

THE PARABLE OF THE FEAST

¹⁶ Then said he also to him that bade him, When thou makest a dinner or a supper, call not thy friends, nor thy brethren, neither thy kinsmen, nor thy rich neighbours; lest they also bid thee again, and a recompence be made thee. ¹⁷ But when thou makest a feast, call the poor, the maimed, the lame, the blind: And thou shalt be blessed; for they cannot recompense thee. ¹⁸ And when one of them that sat at meat with him heard these things, he said unto him, Blessed is he that shall eat bread in the Kingdom of Heaven.

¹⁹ And Jesus spake unto them again by parables, and said, A certain king made a marriage for his son, And sent forth his servants to call them that were bidden to the wedding: But they

made light of it, and went their ways, one to his farm, another to his merchandise.

²⁰ Again, he sent forth other servants, saying, Tell them which are bidden, Behold, I have prepared my dinner: my oxen and my fatlings are killed, and all things are ready: come unto the marriage. ²¹ They all with one consent began to make excuse. The first said unto him, I have bought a piece of ground, and I must needs go and see it: I pray thee have me excused. And another said, I have bought five yoke of oxen, and I go to prove them: I pray thee have me excused. And another said, I have married a wife, and therefore I cannot come. ²² And the remnant* took his servants, and entreated them spitefully, and slew them.

But when the king heard thereof, he was wroth: and he sent forth his armies, and destroyed those murderers, and burned up their city. ²³ Then saith he to his servants, The wedding is ready, but they which were bidden were not worthy. Go ye therefore into the streets and lanes of the city, and as many as ye shall find, bid to the marriage. Bring in hither the poor, and the maimed, and the halt, and the blind.

²⁴ So those servants went out into the highways, and gathered together all as many as they found, both bad and good. And the servant said, Lord, it is done as thou hast commanded, and yet there is room.

²⁵ And the lord said unto the servant, Go out into the highways and hedges, and compel them to come in, that my house may be filled. For I say unto you, That none of those men which were bidden shall taste of my supper.

²⁶ And when the king came in to see the guests, he saw there

---

* The rest of the invited guests.

a man which had not on a wedding garment: [27] And he saith unto him, Friend, how camest thou in hither not having a wedding garment? And he was speechless. [28] Then said the king to the servants, Bind him hand and foot, and take him away, and cast him into outer darkness, there shall be weeping and gnashing of teeth. [29] For many are called, but few are chosen. And many that are first shall be last; and the last first.

5 TEACHINGS AT CAPERNAUM

HUMILITY

[1] Now when he had ended all his sayings in the audience of the people, he entered into Capernaum. [2] And a certain centurion's servant, who was dear unto him, was sick, and ready to die. And when he heard of Jesus, he sent unto him the elders of the Jews, beseeching him that he would come. [3] And when they came to Jesus, they besought him instantly, saying that he was worthy for whom he should do this: For he loveth our nation, and he hath built us a synagogue.

[4] Then Jesus went with them. And when he was now not far from the house, the centurion sent friends to him, saying unto him, Lord, trouble not thyself: for I am not worthy that thou shouldest enter under my roof: Wherefore neither thought I myself worthy to come unto thee. [5] For I also am a man set under authority, having under me soldiers, and I say unto one,

Go, and he goeth; and to another, Come, and he cometh; and to my servant, Do this, and he doeth it.

⁶ When Jesus heard these things, he marvelled at him, and turned him about, and said unto the people that followed him, I say unto you, I have not found so great faith, no, not in Israel. ⁷ And he put forth a parable to those which were bidden, when he marked how they chose out the chief rooms; saying unto them, When thou art bidden of any man to a wedding, sit not down in the highest room; lest a more honourable man than thou be bidden of him; And he that bade thee and him come and say to thee, Give this man place; and thou begin with shame to take the lowest room. ⁸ But when thou art bidden, go and sit down in the lowest room; that when he that bade thee cometh, he may say unto thee, Friend, go up higher: then shalt thou have worship in the presence of them that sit at meat with thee. ⁹ For whosoever exalteth himself shall be abased; and he that humbleth himself shall be exalted.

¹⁰ And he spake another parable unto certain which trusted in themselves that they were righteous, and despised others: ¹¹ Two men went up into the temple to pray; the one a Pharisee, and the other a publican. ¹² The Pharisee stood and prayed thus with himself, God, I thank thee, that I am not as other men are, extortioners, unjust, adulterers, or even as this publican. I fast twice in the week, I give tithes of all that I possess. ¹³ And the tax collector, standing afar off, would not lift up so much as his eyes unto heaven, but smote upon his breast, saying, God be merciful to me a sinner.

¹⁴ I tell you, this man went down to his house justified rather than the other: for every one that exalteth himself shall be abased; and he that humbleth himself shall be exalted.

MASTERS AND SERVANTS

[15] Then he called his twelve disciples together and said he unto them, The harvest truly is great, but the labourers are few. [16] But which of you, having a servant plowing or feeding cattle, will say unto him by and by, when he is come from the field, Go and sit down to meat? [17] And will not rather say unto him, Make ready wherewith I may sup, and gird thyself, and serve me, till I have eaten and drunken; and afterward thou shalt eat and drink? [18] Doth he thank that servant because he did the things that were commanded him? I trow not.* So likewise ye, when ye shall have done all those things which are commanded you, say, We are unprofitable servants: we have done that which was our duty to do.

Ye are my friends, if ye do whatsoever I command you. [19] Ye know that the princes of the Gentiles exercise dominion over them, and they that are great exercise authority upon them. [20] But it shall not be so among you: but whosoever will be great among you, let him be your minister; And whosoever will be chief among you, let him be your servant.

[21] And supper being ended, He riseth from supper, and laid aside his garments; and took a towel, and girded himself. After that he poureth water into a bason, and began to wash the disciples' feet, and to wipe them with the towel wherewith he was girded.

[22] Then cometh he to Simon Peter: and Peter saith unto him, Lord, dost thou wash my feet? [23] Jesus answered and said unto him, What I do thou knowest not now; but thou shalt know hereafter.

---

* I think not.

²⁴ Peter saith unto him, Thou shalt never wash my feet. Jesus answered him, If I wash thee not, thou hast no part with me.

²⁵ Simon Peter saith unto him, Lord, not my feet only, but also my hands and my head.

²⁶ Jesus saith to him, He that is washed needeth not save to wash his feet, but is clean every whit: and ye are clean, but not all. ²⁷ For he knew who should betray him; therefore said he, Ye are not all clean.

²⁸ So after he had washed their feet, and had taken his garments, and was set down again, he said unto them, Know ye what I have done to you? Ye call me Master and Lord: and ye say well; for so I am. If I then, your Lord and Master, have washed your feet; ye also ought to wash one another's feet. ²⁹ For I have given you an example, that ye should do as I have done to you. Verily, verily, I say unto you, The servant is not greater than his lord; neither he that is sent greater than he that sent him. If ye know these things, happy are ye if ye do them. ³⁰ Henceforth I call you not servants; for the servant knoweth not what his lord doeth: but I have called you friends; for all things that I have heard of my Father I have made known unto you.

³¹ If the world hate you, ye know that it hated me before it hated you. If ye were of the world, the world would love his own: but because ye are not of the world, but I have chosen you out of the world, therefore the world hateth you. ³² Remember the word that I said unto you, The servant is not greater than his lord. If they have persecuted me, they will also persecute you; if they have kept my saying, they will keep yours also.

INSTRUCTING THE APOSTLES

³³ Verily, verily, I say unto you, Except a corn of wheat fall into the ground and die, it abideth alone: but if it die, it bringeth

forth much fruit. ³⁴ He that loveth his life shall lose it; and he that hateth his life in this world shall keep it. ³⁵ If any man serve me, let him follow me; and where I am, there shall also my servant be.

³⁶ Go your ways: behold, I send you forth as lambs among wolves. Take nothing for thy journey, save a staff only; no scrip,* no bread, no money in your purse: But be shod with sandals; and not put on two coats: and salute no man by the way.

³⁷ And into whatsoever house ye enter, first say, Peace be to this house. And if the son of peace be there, your peace shall rest upon it: if not, it shall turn to you again. ³⁸ And in the same house remain, eating and drinking such things as are set before you: for the labourer is worthy of his hire. Go not from house to house. ³⁹ And whosoever shall not receive you, nor hear you, when ye go out of that city, shake off the very dust from your feet for a testimony against them. ⁴⁰ Cast not ye your pearls before swine, lest they trample them under their feet, and turn again and rend you.

⁴¹ Ye know that they which are accounted to rule over the Gentiles exercise lordship over them; and their great ones exercise authority upon them. But so shall it not be among you: but whosoever will be great among you, shall be your minister: And whosoever of you will be the chiefest, shall be servant of all.

⁴² And they went out through the towns, and preached that men should repent.

---

* A bag.

6 TRAVELS AND TEACHINGS

CRUMBS FROM THEIR MASTERS' TABLE

¹ Then Jesus went thence, and departed into the coasts of Tyre and Sidon. And, behold, a woman of Canaan came out of the same coasts, and cried unto him, saying, Have mercy on me, O Lord, thou son of David; my daughter is grievously vexed.

² But he answered her not a word.

³ And his disciples came and besought him, saying, Send her away; for she crieth after us. But he answered and said, I am not sent but unto the lost sheep of the house of Israel.

⁴ Then came she, saying, Lord, help me. But he answered and said, It is not meet to take the children's bread, and to cast it to dogs. ⁵ And she said, Truth, Lord: yet the dogs eat of the crumbs which fall from their masters' table.

Then Jesus answered and said unto her, O woman, great is thy faith: be it unto thee even as thou wilt.

⁶ And Jesus departed from thence, and came nigh unto the

sea of Galilee; and went up into a mountain, and sat down there. And great multitudes came unto him.

TRUE CHARITY

[7] Then in the audience of all the people he said unto his disciples, Beware of the scribes, which desire to walk in long robes, and love greetings in the markets, and the highest seats in the synagogues, and the chief rooms at feasts; Which devour widows' houses, and for a shew make long prayers: the same shall receive greater damnation.

[8] And he looked up, and saw how the people cast money into the treasury: and many that were rich cast in much. And he saw also a certain poor widow casting in thither two mites. [9] And he said, Of a truth I say unto you, that this poor widow hath cast in more than they all: For all these have of their abundance cast in unto the offerings of God: but she of her penury hath cast in all the living that she had, even all her living.

[10] And it came to pass, as he spake these things, a certain woman of the company lifted up her voice, and said unto him, Blessed is the womb that bare thee, and the paps which thou hast sucked. [11] But he said, Yea rather, blessed are they that hear the word, and keep it.

THE EYE OF THE NEEDLE

[12] And when he was gone forth into the way, there came one running, and kneeled to him, and asked him, Good Master, what shall I do that I may inherit life?

[13] And Jesus said unto him, Why callest thou me good? there is none good: but if thou wilt enter into life, keep the commandments.

[14] He saith unto him, Which?

Thou knowest the commandments, Do not commit adultery, Do not kill, Do not steal, Do not bear false witness, Defraud not, Honour thy father and mother. Thou shalt love thy neighbour as thyself.

[15] And he answered and said unto him, Master, all these have I observed from my youth: what lack I yet?

[16] Then Jesus beholding him loved him, and said unto him, One thing thou lackest: if thou wilt be perfect, go thy way, sell whatsoever thou hast, and give to the poor: and come, take up the cross, and follow me.

[17] But when the young man heard that saying, he went away sorrowful: for he had great possessions.

[18] And Jesus looked round about, and saith unto his disciples, How hardly shall they that have riches enter into the Kingdom of Heaven!

[19] And the disciples were astonished at his words. But Jesus answereth again, and saith unto them, Children, how hard is it for them that trust in riches to enter into the Kingdom of Heaven! And again I say unto you, it is easier for a camel to go through the eye of a needle, than for a rich man to enter into the Kingdom of Heaven.

[20] And they were astonished out of measure, saying among themselves, Who then can be saved?

[21] And Jesus looking upon them saith, all things are possible.

TRUE RICHES

[22] And one of the company said unto him, Master, speak to my brother, that he divide the inheritance with me.

[23] And he said unto him, Man, who made me a judge or a divider over you? Take heed, and beware of covetousness: for a

man's life consisteth not in the abundance of the things which he possesseth.

²⁴ And he spake a parable unto them, saying, The ground of a certain rich man brought forth plentifully: And he thought within himself, saying, What shall I do, because I have no room where to bestow my fruits? ²⁵ And he said, This will I do: I will pull down my barns, and build greater; and there will I bestow all my fruits and my goods. And I will say to my soul, Soul, thou hast much goods laid up for many years; take thine ease, eat, drink, and be merry.

²⁶ Thou fool, this night thy soul shall be required of thee: then whose shall those things be, which thou hast provided?

So is he that layeth up treasure for himself, and is not rich. ²⁷ Sell that ye have, and give alms; provide yourselves bags which wax not old, a treasure in the heavens that faileth not, where no thief approacheth, neither moth corrupteth. Let your loins be girded about, and your lights burning.*

MARTHA AND MARY

²⁸ Now it came to pass, as they went, that he entered into a certain village: and a certain woman named Martha received him into her house. And she had a sister called Mary, which also sat at Jesus' feet, and heard his word.

²⁹ But Martha was cumbered about much serving, and came to him, and said, Lord, dost thou not care that my sister hath left me to serve alone? bid her therefore that she help me.

³⁰ And Jesus answered and said unto her, Martha, Martha, thou art careful and troubled about many things. But one thing

---

* Meaning 'be ready'.

is needful: and Mary hath chosen that good part, which shall not be taken away from her.

SUFFER THE LITTLE CHILDREN

[31] At the same time came the disciples unto Jesus, saying, Who is the greatest?

And he sat down, and called the twelve, and saith unto them, If any man desire to be first, the same shall be last of all, and servant of all.

[32] And he took a child, and set him in the midst of them: and when he had taken him in his arms, he said unto them, become as little children. Whosoever therefore shall humble himself as this little child, the same is greatest. [33] And whosoever shall receive one such little child in my name receiveth me: and whosoever shall receive me, receiveth not me, but him that sent me. For he that is least among you all, the same shall be great; and he that is not against us is on our part. [34] And whosoever shall offend one of these little ones, it is better for him that a millstone were hanged about his neck, and that he were drowned in the depth of the sea.

Suffer the little children to come unto me, and forbid them not: for of such is the Kingdom of Heaven. [35] Verily I say unto you, Whosoever shall not receive the Kingdom of Heaven as a little child, he shall not enter therein. [36] And he took them up in his arms, laid his hands on them, and departed thence.

PRAYER

[37] And when he had sent the multitudes away, he went up into a mountain apart to pray: and when the evening was come, he was there alone. [38] And it came to pass, that, as he was praying

in a certain place, when he ceased, one of his disciples said unto him, Lord, teach us to pray.

[39] And he said unto them, When ye pray, say,

Give us day by day our daily bread. And forgive us our sins; for we also forgive every one that is indebted to us. And lead us not into temptation; but deliver us from evil.

7 PARABLES

THE PARABLE OF THE SOWER

[1] The same day went Jesus out of the house, and sat by the sea side. And great multitudes were gathered together unto him, so that he went into a ship, and sat in the sea; and the whole multitude stood on the shore.

[2] And he spake many things unto them in parables, saying, Behold, a sower went forth to sow; [3] And it came to pass, as he sowed, some seeds fell by the way side, and they were trodden down, and the fowls of the air came and devoured them up: [4] Some fell upon stony places, where they had not much earth: and forthwith they sprung up, because they had no depth of earth and lacked moisture: But when the sun was up, they were scorched; and because they had no root, they withered away. [5] And some fell among thorns; and the thorns sprung up, and choked them, and they yielded no fruit: [6] But other fell into good ground, and brought forth fruit, some an hundredfold, some sixtyfold, some thirtyfold.

[7] And when he had said these things, he cried, If any man have ears to hear, let him hear.

[8] And when he was alone, the disciples came, and said unto him, Why speakest thou unto them in parables? He answered and said unto them,

[9] Unto you it is given to know the mysteries of the Kingdom of Heaven: Take heed therefore how ye hear, for with what measure ye mete, it shall be measured to you: and unto you that hear shall more be given. For whosoever hath, to him shall be given, and he shall have more abundance: but whosoever hath not, from him shall be taken away even that which he seemeth to have. [10] Therefore speak I to them in parables: because they seeing see not; and hearing they hear not, neither do they understand. For this people's heart is waxed gross, and their ears are dull of hearing, and their eyes they have closed; lest at any time they should see with their eyes and hear with their ears, and should understand with their heart, and should be converted. [11] But blessed are your eyes, for they see: and your ears, for they hear.

And he said unto them, Know ye not this parable? and how then will ye know all parables? [12] Now the parable is this: The seed is the word. And these are they by the way side, where the word is sown; but when they have heard, evil cometh immediately, and taketh away the word that was sown in their hearts. [13] They which are sown on stony ground, when they hear, receive the word with joy; and these have no root, and so endure but for a time, and in time of temptation, affliction or persecution fall away. [14] And that which fell among thorns are they, which, when they have heard, go forth, and are choked with cares and riches and pleasures of this life, and bring no fruit to perfection. [15] But that on the good ground are they, which in an honest and good heart, having heard the word, keep it, and bring forth fruit with patience.

THE PARABLE OF THE WEEDS

¹⁶ Another parable put he forth unto them, saying, a man sowed good seed in his field: ¹⁷ But while men slept, his enemy came and sowed weeds among the wheat, and went his way. But when the blade was sprung up, and brought forth fruit, then appeared the weeds also.

¹⁸ So the servants of the householder came and said unto him, Sir, didst not thou sow good seed in thy field? from whence then hath it weeds?

¹⁹ He said unto them, An enemy hath done this. The servants said unto him, Wilt thou then that we go and gather them up?

²⁰ But he said, Nay; lest while ye gather up the weeds, ye root up also the wheat with them. ²¹ Let both grow together until the harvest: and in the time of harvest I will say to the reapers, Gather ye together first the weeds, and bind them in bundles to burn them: but gather the wheat into my barn.

THE PARABLES OF THE MUSTARD SEED AND THE YEAST

²² Another parable put he forth unto them, saying, Whereunto shall we liken the Kingdom of Heaven? or with what comparison shall we compare it? ²³ It is like a grain of mustard seed, which indeed is the least of all seeds: but when it is grown, it is the greatest among herbs, and becometh a tree, and shooteth out great branches; so that the fowls of the air may lodge under the shadow of it.

²⁴ So is the Kingdom of Heaven, as if a man should cast seed into the ground; And should sleep, and rise night and day, and the seed should spring and grow up, he knoweth not how. ²⁵ For the earth bringeth forth fruit of herself; first the blade, then

the ear, after that the full corn in the ear. But when the fruit is brought forth, immediately he putteth in the sickle, because the harvest is come.

²⁶ Another parable spake he unto them; And again he said, Whereunto shall I liken the Kingdom of Heaven? It is like yeast, which a woman took and hid in three measures of meal, till the whole was leavened.

²⁷ All these things spake Jesus unto the multitude in parables, as they were able to hear it, and without a parable spake he not unto them. But when they were alone, he expounded all things to his disciples.

THE PARABLE OF THE TENANTS IN THE VINEYARD

²⁸ Hear another parable: A certain man planted a vineyard, and set an hedge about it, and digged a winepress in it, and built a tower, and let it out to tenants, and went into a far country: ²⁹ And when the time of the fruit drew near, he sent to the tenants servants, that he might receive from the husbandmen of the fruit of the vineyard. And the tenants took his servants, and beat one, and killed another, and stoned another.

³⁰ Again, he sent other servants more than the first: and they did unto them likewise. ³¹ And again he sent another; and him they killed, and many others; beating some, and killing some.

³² Then said the lord of the vineyard, What shall I do? I will send my beloved son: it may be they will reverence him when they see him.

³³ But when the tenants saw the son, they reasoned among themselves, This is the heir; come, let us kill him, and let us seize on his inheritance. And they caught him, and cast him

out of the vineyard, and slew him. ³⁴ What therefore shall the lord of the vineyard do unto them?

³⁵ They say unto him, He will miserably destroy those wicked men, and will let out his vineyard unto other husbandmen, which shall render him the fruits in their seasons.

³⁶ Jesus saith unto them, Did ye never read in the scriptures? And he beheld them, and said, What is this then that is written, The stone which the builders rejected, the same is become the head of the corner? ³⁷ Whosoever shall fall upon that stone shall be broken; but on whomsoever it shall fall, it will grind him to powder.

³⁸ And the chief priests and the scribes the same hour sought to lay hands on him; and they feared the people: for they perceived that he had spoken this parable against them. ³⁹ And they watched him, and sent forth spies, which should feign themselves just men, that they might take hold of his words, that so they might deliver him unto the power and authority of the governor.

THE PARABLE OF THE UNJUST STEWARD

⁴⁰ And he said also unto his disciples, There was a certain rich man, which had a steward; and the same was accused unto him that he had wasted his goods. ⁴¹ And he called him, and said unto him, How is it that I hear this of thee? give an account of thy stewardship; for thou mayest be no longer steward.

⁴² Then the steward said within himself, What shall I do? for my lord taketh away from me the stewardship: I cannot dig; to beg I am ashamed. I am resolved what to do, that, when I am put out of the stewardship, they may receive me into their houses.

⁴³ So he called every one of his lord's debtors unto him, and

said unto the first, How much owest thou unto my lord? And he said, An hundred measures of oil. And he said unto him, Take thy bill, and sit down quickly, and write fifty.

[44] Then said he to another, And how much owest thou? And he said, An hundred measures of wheat. And he said unto him, Take thy bill, and write fourscore.

[45] And the lord commended the unjust steward, because he had done wisely: for the children of this world are in their generation wiser than the children of light. [46] And I say unto you, Make to yourselves friends of the mammon of unrighteousness; that, when ye fail, they may receive you into everlasting habitations. [47] He that is faithful in that which is least is faithful also in much: and he that is unjust in the least is unjust also in much. [48] If therefore ye have not been faithful in the unrighteous mammon, who will commit to your trust the true riches? And if ye have not been faithful in that which is another man's, who shall give you that which is your own? [49] No servant can serve two masters: for either he will hate the one, and love the other; or else he will hold to the one, and despise the other. Ye cannot serve the good and mammon.

[50] And the Pharisees also, who were covetous, heard all these things: and they derided him.

And he said unto them, Ye are they which justify yourselves before men; for that which is highly esteemed among men is abomination in the sight of the good.

THE PARABLE OF THE TALENTS

[51] A nobleman travelling into a far country called his own servants, and delivered unto them his goods. And unto one he gave five talents, to another two, and to another one; to every man according to his several ability; and straightway took his

journey. [52] But his citizens hated him, and sent a message after him, saying, We will not have this man to reign over us.

[53] Then he that had received the five talents went and traded with the same, and made them other five talents. And likewise he that had received two, he also gained other two. [54] But he that had received one went and digged in the earth, and hid his lord's money.

[55] And it came to pass, that when he was returned, having received the kingdom, then he commanded these servants to be called unto him, to whom he had given the money, that he might know how much every man had gained by trading.

[56] And so he that had received five talents came and brought other five talents, saying, Lord, thou deliveredst unto me five talents: behold, I have gained beside them five talents more.

His lord said unto him, Well done, thou good and faithful servant: thou hast been faithful over a few things, I will make thee ruler over many things: enter thou into the joy of thy lord.

[57] He also that had received two talents came and said, Lord, thou deliveredst unto me two talents: behold, I have gained two other talents beside them.

His lord said unto him, Well done, good and faithful servant; thou hast been faithful over a few things, I will make thee ruler over many things: enter thou into the joy of thy lord.

[58] Then he which had received the one talent came and said, Lord, I knew thee that thou art an hard man: thou takest up that thou layedst not down, and reapest that thou didst not sow. And I was afraid, and went and hid thy talent in the earth: lo, there thou hast that is thine.

[59] His lord answered and said unto him, Out of thine own mouth will I judge thee, thou wicked servant. Thou knewest that I reap where I sowed not, and gather where I have not strawed: Thou oughtest therefore to have put my money into

the bank, and then at my coming I should have received mine own with interest. ⁶⁰ Take therefore the talent from him, and give it unto him which hath ten talents.

And they said unto him, Lord, he hath ten talents.

⁶¹ For unto every one that hath shall be given, and he shall have abundance: but from him that hath not shall be taken away even that which he hath. For unto whomsoever much is given, of him shall be much required: and to whom men have committed much, of him they will ask the more. ⁶² And cast ye the unprofitable servant into outer darkness: there shall be weeping and gnashing of teeth. But those mine enemies, which would not that I should reign over them, bring hither, and slay them before me.

THE PARABLE OF THE WORKERS IN THE VINEYARD

⁶³ A man that is an householder went out early in the morning to hire labourers into his vineyard. And when he had agreed with the labourers for a penny a day, he sent them into his vineyard. ⁶⁴ And he went out about the third hour, and saw others standing idle in the marketplace, And said unto them; Go ye also into the vineyard, and whatsoever is right I will give you. And they went their way. ⁶⁵ Again he went out about the sixth and ninth hour, and did likewise. ⁶⁶ And about the eleventh hour he went out, and found others standing idle, and saith unto them, Why stand ye here all the day idle? They say unto him, Because no man hath hired us. He saith unto them, Go ye also into the vineyard; and whatsoever is right, that shall ye receive.

⁶⁷ So when even was come, the lord of the vineyard saith unto his steward, Call the labourers, and give them their hire,

beginning from the last unto the first. [68] And when they came that were hired about the eleventh hour, they received every man a penny.

[69] But when the first came, they supposed that they should have received more; and they likewise received every man a penny. [70] And when they had received it, they murmured against the goodman of the house, Saying, These last have wrought but one hour, and thou hast made them equal unto us, which have borne the burden and heat of the day.

[71] But he answered one of them, and said, Friend, I do thee no wrong: didst not thou agree with me for a penny? Take that thine is, and go thy way: I will give unto this last, even as unto thee. [72] Is it not lawful for me to do what I will with mine own? Is thine eye evil, because I am good? [73] So the last shall be first, and the first last: for many be called, but few chosen.

THE PARABLE OF THE TEN VIRGINS

[74] Ten virgins, which took their lamps, and went forth to meet the bridegroom. And five of them were wise, and five were foolish. [75] They that were foolish took their lamps, and took no oil with them: But the wise took oil in their vessels with their lamps.

[76] While the bridegroom tarried, they all slumbered and slept. [77] And at midnight there was a cry made, Behold, the bridegroom cometh; go ye out to meet him. Then all those virgins arose, and trimmed their lamps. [78] And the foolish said unto the wise, Give us of your oil; for our lamps are gone out.

[79] But the wise answered, saying, Not so; lest there be not enough for us and you: but go ye rather to them that sell, and buy for yourselves. [80] And while they went to buy, the

bridegroom came; and they that were ready went in with him to the marriage: and the door was shut.

[81] Afterward came also the other virgins, saying, Lord, Lord, open to us. But he answered and said, Verily I say unto you, I know you not.*

_____

* This and the Parable of the Talents are about the Son of man coming again so may have no ethical message.

8 AMONG SINNERS

LEVI THE TAX COLLECTOR

[1] And again he entered into Capernaum after some days; and it was noised that he was in the house. And he went forth again by the sea side; and all the multitude resorted unto him, and he taught them. [2] And as he passed by, he saw Levi the son of Alphaeus sitting at the receipt of custom, and said unto him, Follow me. And he arose and followed him.

[3] And Levi made him a great feast in his own house: and there was a great company of tax collectors and sinners that sat down with Jesus and his disciples: for there were many, and they followed him. [4] And when the scribes and Pharisees saw him eat with publicans and sinners, they said unto his disciples, How is it that he eateth and drinketh with publicans and sinners?

[5] When Jesus heard it, he saith unto them, They that are whole have no need of the physician; but they that are sick. But go ye and learn what that meaneth, I will have mercy, and

not sacrifice: I came not to call the righteous, but sinners to repentance.

ZACCHAEUS THE TAX COLLECTOR

[6] And Jesus entered and passed through Jericho. And, behold, there was a man named Zacchaeus, which was the chief among the tax collectors, and he was rich. [7] And he sought to see Jesus who he was; and could not for the press, because he was little of stature. And he ran before, and climbed up into a sycomore tree to see him: for he was to pass that way.

[8] And when Jesus came to the place, he looked up, and saw him, and said unto him, Zacchaeus, make haste, and come down; for to day I must abide at thy house. [9] And he made haste, and came down, and received him joyfully.

[10] And when they saw it, they all murmured, saying, That he was gone to be guest with a man that is a sinner.

[11] And Zacchaeus stood, and said unto the Lord: Behold, Lord, the half of my goods I give to the poor; and if I have taken any thing from any man by false accusation, I restore him fourfold.

[12] And Jesus said unto him, This day is salvation come to this house. For I am come to seek and to save that which was lost. [13] Come unto me, all ye that labour and are heavy laden, and I will give you rest. Take my yoke upon you, and learn of me; for I am meek and lowly in heart: and ye shall find rest unto your souls. For my yoke is easy, and my burden is light.

LOST SHEEP

[14] And Jesus, when he came out, saw much people, and was moved with compassion toward them, because they were as

sheep not having a shepherd: and he began to teach them many things. Then drew near unto him all the tax collectors and sinners for to hear him. [15] And the Pharisees and scribes murmured, saying, This man receiveth sinners, and eateth with them.

[16] And he spake this parable unto them, saying, What man of you, having an hundred sheep, if he lose one of them, doth not leave the ninety and nine in the wilderness, and go after that which is lost, until he find it? [17] And if so be that he find it, verily I say unto you, he rejoiceth more of that sheep, than of the ninety and nine which went not astray. And when he cometh home, he calleth together his friends and neighbours, saying unto them, Rejoice with me; for I have found my sheep which was lost. [18] I say unto you, that likewise joy shall be over one sinner that repenteth, more than over ninety and nine just persons, which need no repentance.

[19] Either what woman having ten pieces of silver, if she lose one piece, doth not light a candle, and sweep the house, and seek diligently till she find it? And when she hath found it, she calleth her friends and her neighbours together, saying, Rejoice with me; for I have found the piece which I had lost. [20] Likewise, I say unto you, there is joy over one sinner that repenteth. For I am come to save that which was lost.

[21] I am the good shepherd, and know my sheep, and am known of mine. The good shepherd giveth his life for the sheep. [22] But he that is an hireling, and not the shepherd, whose own the sheep are not, seeth the wolf coming, and leaveth the sheep, and fleeth: and the wolf catcheth them, and scattereth the sheep. The hireling fleeth, because he is an hireling, and careth not for the sheep. [23] And other sheep I have, which are not of this fold: them also I must bring, and they shall hear my voice; and there shall be one fold, and one shepherd.

FORGIVENESS

²⁴ And he entered into a ship, and passed over, and came into his own city. ²⁵ And, behold, they brought to him a man sick of the palsy, lying on a bed: and Jesus seeing their faith said unto the sick of the palsy; Son, be of good cheer; thy sins be forgiven thee.

²⁶ And, behold, certain of the scribes said within themselves, This man blasphemeth.

²⁷ And Jesus knowing their thoughts said, Verily I say unto you, All sins shall be forgiven unto the sons of men, and blasphemies wherewith soever they shall blaspheme. Wherefore think ye evil in your hearts? ²⁸ Ye may know that the Son of man hath power on earth to forgive sins. ²⁹ Take heed to yourselves: If thy brother trespass against thee, rebuke him; and if he repent, forgive him.

³⁰ Then came Peter to him, and said, Lord, how oft shall my brother sin against me, and I forgive him? till seven times?

³¹ Jesus saith unto him, I say not unto thee, Until seven times: but, Until seventy times seven. And if he trespass against thee seven times in a day, and seven times in a day turn again to thee, saying, I repent; thou shalt forgive him. ³² Moreover if thy brother shall trespass against thee, go and tell him his fault between thee and him alone: if he shall hear thee, thou hast gained thy brother. ³³ But if he will not hear thee, then take with thee one or two more, that in the mouth of two or three witnesses every word may be established. ³⁴ And if he shall neglect to hear them, tell it unto the church: but if he neglect to hear the church, let him be unto thee as an heathen man and a tax collector.

THE PARABLE OF THE UNFORGIVING SERVANT

[35] A certain king would take account of his servants. [36] And when he had begun to reckon, one was brought unto him, which owed him ten thousand talents. [37] But forasmuch as he had not to pay, his lord commanded him to be sold, and his wife, and children, and all that he had, and payment to be made. The servant therefore fell down, and worshipped him, saying, Lord, have patience with me, and I will pay thee all. [38] Then the lord of that servant was moved with compassion, and loosed him, and forgave him the debt.

[39] But the same servant went out, and found one of his fellow servants, which owed him an hundred pence: and he laid hands on him, and took him by the throat, saying, Pay me that thou owest. And his fellow servant fell down at his feet, and besought him, saying, Have patience with me, and I will pay thee all. [40] And he would not: but went and cast him into prison, till he should pay the debt. [41] So when his fellow servants saw what was done, they were very sorry, and came and told unto their lord all that was done.

[42] Then his lord, after that he had called him, said unto him, O thou wicked servant, I forgave thee all that debt, because thou desiredst me: Shouldest not thou also have had compassion on thy fellow servant, even as I had pity on thee? [43] And his lord was wroth, and delivered him to the tormentors, till he should pay all that was due unto him.

THE PARABLE OF THE PRODIGAL SON

[44] And he said, A certain man had two sons: And the younger of them said to his father, Father, give me the portion of goods that falleth to me. And he divided unto them his living. [45] And

not many days after the younger son gathered all together, and took his journey into a far country, and there wasted his substance with riotous living.

And when he had spent all, there arose a mighty famine in that land; and he began to be in want. 46 And he went and joined himself to a citizen of that country; and he sent him into his fields to feed swine. And he would fain have filled his belly with the husks that the swine did eat: and no man gave unto him.

47 And when he came to himself, he said, How many hired servants of my father's have bread enough and to spare, and I perish with hunger! 48 I will arise and go to my father, and will say unto him, Father, I have sinned against heaven, and before thee, And am no more worthy to be called thy son: make me as one of thy hired servants.

49 And he arose, and came to his father. But when he was yet a great way off, his father saw him, and had compassion, and ran, and fell on his neck, and kissed him.

50 And the son said unto him, Father, I have sinned against heaven, and in thy sight, and am no more worthy to be called thy son.

51 But the father said to his servants, Bring forth the best robe, and put it on him; and put a ring on his hand, and shoes on his feet: And bring hither the fatted calf, and kill it; and let us eat, and be merry: For this my son was dead, and is alive again; he was lost, and is found. And they began to be merry.

52 Now his elder son was in the field: and as he came and drew nigh to the house, he heard musick and dancing. And he called one of the servants, and asked what these things meant. 53 And he said unto him, Thy brother is come; and thy father hath killed the fatted calf, because he hath received him safe and sound. And he was angry, and would not go in: therefore came his father out, and intreated him.

[54] And he answering said to his father, Lo, these many years do I serve thee, neither transgressed I at any time thy commandment: and yet thou never gavest me a kid, that I might make merry with my friends: But as soon as this thy son was come, which hath devoured thy living with harlots, thou hast killed for him the fatted calf.

[55] And he said unto him, Son, thou art ever with me, and all that I have is thine. It was meet that we should make merry, and be glad: for this thy brother was dead, and is alive again; and was lost, and is found.

THE WOMAN TAKEN IN ADULTERY

[56] Jesus went unto the mount of Olives. And early in the morning he came again into the temple, and all the people came unto him; and he sat down, and taught them. [57] Whosoever putteth away his wife, and marrieth another, committeth adultery: and whosoever marrieth her that is put away from her husband committeth adultery.

[58] And the scribes and Pharisees brought unto him a woman taken in adultery; and when they had set her in the midst, They say unto him, Master, this woman was taken in adultery, in the very act. [59] Now Moses in the law commanded us, that such should be stoned: but what sayest thou?

This they said, tempting him, that they might have to accuse him. But Jesus stooped down, and with his finger wrote on the ground, as though he heard them not. [60] So when they continued asking him, he lifted up himself, and said unto them, He that is without sin among you, let him first cast a stone at her. And again he stooped down, and wrote on the ground.

[61] And they which heard it, being convicted by their own conscience, went out one by one, beginning at the eldest, even

unto the last: and Jesus was left alone, and the woman standing in the midst.

[62] When Jesus had lifted up himself, and saw none but the woman, he said unto her, Woman, where are those thine accusers? hath no man condemned thee?

[63] She said, No man, Lord. And Jesus said unto her, Neither do I condemn thee: go, and do wrong no more.

9 MORE PARABLES

THE FIRST PARABLE OF THE FIG TREE

[1] And he spake to them a parable; Behold the fig tree, and all the trees; When they now shoot forth, ye see and know of your own selves that summer is now nigh at hand. [2] So likewise ye, when ye see these things come to pass, know ye that the Kingdom of Heaven is nigh at hand.

THE PARABLE OF THE TWO SONS

[3] A certain man had two sons; and he came to the first, and said, Son, go work to day in my vineyard. [4] He answered and said, I will not: but afterward he repented, and went. [5] And he came to the second, and said likewise. And he answered and said, I go, sir: and went not.

[6] Whether of them twain did the will of his father? They say unto him, The first. Jesus saith unto them, Verily I say unto you, That the publicans and the harlots go into the kingdom of

God before you. ⁷ For John came unto you in the way of righteousness, and ye believed him not: but the tax collectors and
the harlots believed him: and ye, when ye had seen it, repented
not afterward, that ye might believe him.

THE PARABLE OF HIDDEN TREASURE

⁸ When a man hath found treasure hid in a field, he hideth, and
for joy thereof goeth and selleth all that he hath, and buyeth
that field. ⁹ A merchant man, seeking goodly pearls, when he
had found one pearl of great price, went and sold all that he
had, and bought it. ¹⁰ A net was cast into the sea, and gathered
of every kind: Which, when it was full, they drew to shore, and
sat down, and gathered the good into vessels, but cast the bad
away. ¹¹ Jesus saith unto them, Have ye understood all these
things? They say unto him, Yea, Lord.

¹² Then said he unto them, Therefore every scribe which
is instructed unto the Kingdom of Heaven is like unto a man
that is an householder, which bringeth forth out of his treasure
things new and old. ¹³ And it came to pass, that when Jesus had
finished these parables, he departed thence.

THE GOOD SAMARITAN

¹⁴ And, behold, a certain lawyer stood up, and tempted him,
saying, Master, what shall I do to inherit life?

¹⁵ He said unto him, What is written in the law? how readest
thou?

¹⁶ And he answering said, Thou shalt love thy neighbour as
thyself.

¹⁷ And he said unto him, Thou hast answered right: this do,
and thou shalt live.

¹⁸ But he, willing to justify himself, said unto Jesus, And who is my neighbour?

¹⁹ And Jesus answering said, A certain man went down from Jerusalem to Jericho, and fell among thieves, which stripped him of his raiment, and wounded him, and departed, leaving him half dead. ²⁰ And by chance there came down a certain priest that way: and when he saw him, he passed by on the other side. And likewise a Levite, when he was at the place, came and looked on him, and passed by on the other side. ²¹ But a certain Samaritan, as he journeyed, came where he was: and when he saw him, he had compassion on him, And went to him, and bound up his wounds, pouring in oil and wine, and set him on his own beast, and brought him to an inn, and took care of him. ²² And on the morrow when he departed, he took out two pence, and gave them to the host, and said unto him, Take care of him; and whatsoever thou spendest more, when I come again, I will repay thee.

²³ Which now of these three, thinkest thou, was neighbour unto him that fell among the thieves?

²⁴ And he said, He that shewed mercy on him. Then said Jesus unto him, Go, and do thou likewise.

THE SECOND PARABLE OF THE FIG TREE

²⁵ And on the morrow, when they were come from Bethany, he was hungry: And seeing a fig tree afar off having leaves, he came, if haply he might find any thing thereon: and when he came to it, he found nothing but leaves; for the time of figs was not yet. ²⁶ And Jesus answered and said unto it, No man eat fruit of thee hereafter for ever. And his disciples heard it.

²⁷ He spake also this parable; A certain man had a fig tree planted in his vineyard; and he came and sought fruit thereon,

and found none. [28] Then said he unto the dresser of his vineyard, Behold, these three years I come seeking fruit on this fig tree, and find none: cut it down; why cumbereth it the ground?

[29] And he answering said unto him, Lord, let it alone this year also, till I shall dig about it, and dung it: And if it bear fruit, well: and if not, then after that thou shalt cut it down.

[30] Either make the tree good, and his fruit good; or else make the tree corrupt, and his fruit corrupt: for the tree is known by his fruit.

[31] O generation of vipers, how can ye, being evil, speak good things? for out of the abundance of the heart the mouth speaketh. A good man out of the good treasure of the heart bringeth forth good things: and an evil man out of the evil treasure bringeth forth evil things. [32] But I say unto you, That every idle word that men shall speak, they shall give account thereof. For by thy words thou shalt be justified, and by thy words thou shalt be condemned.

10 RADICAL PHILOSOPHIES

A WOMAN ANOINTS JESUS

¹ And being in Bethany in the house of Simon the leper, as he sat at meat, there came a woman in the city, which was a sinner, who brought an alabaster box of ointment of spikenard very precious; and she brake the box, and stood at his feet behind him weeping, and began to wash his feet with tears, and did wipe them with the hairs of her head, and kissed his feet, and anointed them with the ointment and poured it on his head.

² And there were some that had indignation within themselves, and said, Why was this waste of the ointment made? For it might have been sold for more than three hundred pence, and have been given to the poor. And they murmured against her.

³ Then saith one of his disciples, Judas Iscariot, Simon's son, which should betray him, Why was not this ointment sold for three hundred pence, and given to the poor?

⁴ This he said, not that he cared for the poor; but because he was a thief, and had the bag, and bare what was put therein.

⁵ Then said Jesus, Let her alone: against the day of my burying hath she kept this. For ye have the poor with you always, and whensoever ye will ye may do them good: but me ye have not always.

⁶ Now when a Pharisee saw it, he spake, saying, This man, if he were a prophet, would have known who and what manner of woman this is that toucheth him: for she is a sinner.

⁷ And Jesus answering said unto him, Simon, I have somewhat to say unto thee. And he saith, Master, say on.

⁸ There was a certain creditor which had two debtors: the one owed five hundred pence, and the other fifty. And when they had nothing to pay, he frankly forgave them both. Tell me therefore, which of them will love him most?

⁹ Simon answered and said, I suppose that he, to whom he forgave most. And he said unto him, Thou hast rightly judged.

¹⁰ And he turned to the woman, and said unto Simon, Seest thou this woman? I entered into thine house, thou gavest me no water for my feet: but she hath washed my feet with tears, and wiped them with the hairs of her head. ¹¹ Thou gavest me no kiss: but this woman since the time I came in hath not ceased to kiss my feet. My head with oil thou didst not anoint: but this woman hath anointed my feet with ointment. She hath wrought a good work on me. Verily I say unto you, Wheresoever this gospel shall be preached in the whole world, there shall also this, that this woman hath done, be told for a memorial of her. ¹² Wherefore I say unto thee, Her sins, which are many, are forgiven; for she loved much: but to whom little is forgiven, the same loveth little.

And he said to the woman; go in peace.

BY WHAT AUTHORITY?

¹³ And they come again to Jerusalem: And it came to pass, that on one of those days, as he taught the people in the temple, and preached the gospel, the chief priests and the scribes came upon him with the elders, And say unto him, By what authority doest thou these things? and who gave thee this authority to do these things?

¹⁴ And Jesus answered and said unto them, I will also ask of you one question, which if ye answer me, I in like wise will tell you by what authority I do these things. The baptism of John, was it from heaven, or of men? answer me.

¹⁵ And they reasoned with themselves, saying, If we shall say, From heaven; he will say, Why then did ye not believe him? But if we shall say, Of men; we fear the people; for all hold John as a prophet.

¹⁶ And they answered and said unto Jesus, We cannot tell. And Jesus answering saith unto them, Neither do I tell you by what authority I do these things.

THE SABBATH

¹⁷ And it came to pass, that he went through the corn fields on the sabbath day; and his disciples were an hungred, and began to pluck the ears of corn and to eat, rubbing them in their hands. ¹⁸ And the Pharisees said unto him, Behold, why do they on the sabbath day that which is not lawful? There are six days in which men ought to work, and not on the sabbath day.

¹⁹ And he said unto them, Have ye never read what David did, when he had need, and was an hungred, he, and they that were with him? How he went into the house of God in the days of Abiathar the high priest, and did eat the shewbread, which

is not lawful to eat but for the priests, and gave also to them which were with him?

20 Or have ye not read in the law, how that on the sabbath days the priests in the temple profane the sabbath, and are blameless? But I say unto you, That in this place is one greater than the temple, man is Lord also of the sabbath.

21 And he said unto them, The sabbath was made for man, and not man for the sabbath:

22 And he entered again into the synagogue; and there was a man there which had a withered hand. And they asked him, saying, Is it lawful to heal on the sabbath days? that they might accuse him.

23 And he said unto them, Thou hypocrites, doth not each one of you on the sabbath loose his ox or his ass from the stall, and lead him away to watering? What man shall there be among you, that shall have one sheep, and if it fall into a pit on the sabbath day, will he not lay hold on it, and lift it out? 24 How much then is a man better than a sheep? Is it lawful to do good on the sabbath days, or to do evil? to save life, or to kill? But they held their peace.

25 And he looked round about on them with anger, being grieved for the hardness of their hearts.

26 And the Pharisees went forth, and straightway took counsel with the Herodians against him, how they might destroy him.

THE LAW

27 Then came together unto him the Pharisees, and certain of the scribes, which came from Jerusalem. And when they saw some of his disciples eat bread with defiled, that is to say, with unwashen, hands, they found fault. 28 For the Pharisees, and all the Jews, except they wash their hands oft, eat not, holding the

tradition of the elders. And when they come from the market, except they wash, they eat not. And many other things there be, which they have received to hold, as the washing of cups, and pots, brasen vessels, and of tables.

²⁹ Then the Pharisees and scribes asked him, Why walk not thy disciples according to the tradition of the elders, but eat bread with unwashen hands?

³⁰ And the Lord said unto him, Now do ye Pharisees make clean the outside of the cup and the platter; but your inward part is full of ravening and wickedness. Ye fools, did not he that made that which is without make that which is within also? But rather give alms of such things as ye have; and, behold, all things are clean unto you.

³¹ Why do ye also transgress the commandment by your tradition? For God commanded, saying, Honour thy father and mother: and, He that curseth father or mother, let him die the death.

³² But ye say, Whosoever shall say to his father or his mother, It is a gift, by whatsoever thou mightest be profited by me; And honour not his father or his mother, he shall be free. Thus have ye made the commandment of none effect by your tradition.

³³ Ye hypocrites, This people draweth nigh unto me with their mouth, and honoureth me with their lips; but their heart is far from me, For laying aside the commandment, ye hold the tradition of men, as the washing of pots and cups: and many other such like things ye do. And he said unto them, Full well ye reject the commandment, that ye may keep your own tradition.

³⁴ And when he had called all the people unto him, he said unto them, Hearken unto me every one of you. If any man have ears to hear, let him hear and understand: There is nothing from without a man, that entering into him can defile him: Because it entereth not into his heart, but into the belly, and

goeth out into the draught, purging all meats? But the things which come out of him, those are they that defile the man.

[35] For from within, out of the heart of men, proceed evil thoughts, adulteries, fornications, murders, Thefts, covetousness, wickedness, deceit, lasciviousness, an evil eye, blasphemy, pride, foolishness: All these evil things come from within, and defile the man.

[36] Knowest thou that the Pharisees were offended, after they heard this saying? Let them alone: they be blind leaders of the blind. And if the blind lead the blind, both shall fall into the ditch.

[37] And he spake also a parable unto them; No man putteth a piece of a new garment upon an old; if otherwise, then both the new maketh a rent, and the piece that was taken out of the new agreeth not with the old.

[38] And no man putteth new wine into old bottles; else the new wine will burst the bottles, and be spilled, and the bottles shall perish. But new wine must be put into new bottles; and both are preserved. No man also having drunk old wine straightway desireth new: for he saith, The old is better.

[39] And from thence he arose, and went into the borders of Tyre and Sidon, and entered into an house, and would have no man know it: but he could not be hid.

FASTING

[40] Then came to him the disciples of John, saying, Why do we and the Pharisees fast oft, but thy disciples fast not?

[41] And Jesus said unto them, Can the children of the bridechamber mourn, as long as the bridegroom is with them? but the days will come, when the bridegroom shall be taken from them, and then shall they fast in those days.

SEEKERS OF SIGNS

[42] Some, tempting him, sought of him a sign from heaven. But he, knowing their thoughts, said unto them, Every kingdom divided against itself is brought to desolation; and a house divided against a house falleth. [43] When a strong man armed keepeth his palace, his goods are in peace: But when a stronger than he shall come upon him, and overcome him, he taketh from him all his armour wherein he trusted, and divideth his spoils. [44] He that is not with me is against me: and he that gathereth not with me scattereth.

[45] And when the people were gathered thick together, he began to say, This is an evil generation: they seek a sign; and there shall no sign be given it.

[46] And he said also to the people, When ye see a cloud rise out of the west, straightway ye say, There cometh a shower; and so it is. And when ye see the south wind blow, ye say, There will be heat; and it cometh to pass. [47] Ye hypocrites, ye can discern the face of the sky and of the earth; but how is it that ye do not discern this time? Yea, and why even of yourselves judge ye not what is right?*

COMING WITH A SWORD

[48] While he yet talked to the people, behold, his mother and his brethren stood without, desiring to speak with him. Then one said unto him, Behold, thy mother and thy brethren stand without, desiring to speak with thee.

[49] But he answered and said unto him that told him, Who

---

* Why do you not judge for yourselves what is right.

is my mother? and who are my brethren? [50] And he stretched forth his hand toward his disciples, and said, Behold my mother and my brethren! For whosoever shall do good, the same is my brother, and my sister, and mother.*

[51] Suppose ye that I am come to give peace on earth? I tell you, Nay; but rather division: I came not to send peace, but a sword. [52] For from henceforth there shall be five in one house divided, three against two, and two against three. The father shall be divided against the son, and the son against the father; the mother against the daughter, and the daughter against the mother; the mother in law against her daughter in law, and the daughter in law against her mother in law. And a man's foes shall be they of his own household.

[53] He that loveth father or mother more than me is not worthy of me: and he that loveth son or daughter more than me is not worthy of me. And he that taketh not his cross, and followeth after me, is not worthy of me. [54] He that findeth his life shall lose it: and he that loseth his life for my sake shall find it. [55] He that receiveth you receiveth me, and he that receiveth me receiveth him that sent me. He that receiveth a prophet in the name of a prophet shall receive a prophet's reward; and he that receiveth a righteous man in the name of a righteous man shall receive a righteous man's reward. [56] He that heareth you heareth me; and he that despiseth you despiseth me.

[57] And John answered and said, Master, we saw one acting in thy name; and we forbad him, because he followeth not with us.

[58] And Jesus said unto him, Forbid him not: for he that is not against us is for us.

---

* The original is 'For whosoever shall do the will of God', not 'do good'.

II TROUBLE IN JERUSALEM

ARRIVAL IN JERUSALEM

¹ And as they departed from Jericho, a great multitude followed him. And they brought a colt to Jesus, and cast their garments on him; and he sat upon him. And many spread their garments in the way: and others cut down branches off the trees, and strawed them in the way. ² And the multitudes that went before, and that followed, cried, saying, Hosanna to the son of David: Blessed is he that cometh in the name of the Lord; Hosanna in the highest.

³ And when he was come into Jerusalem, all the city was moved, saying, Who is this? And the multitude said, This is Jesus the prophet of Nazareth of Galilee.

⁴ And some of the Pharisees from among the multitude said unto him, Master, rebuke thy disciples.

⁵ And he answered and said unto them, I tell you that, if these should hold their peace, the stones would immediately cry out.

⁶ The Pharisees therefore said among themselves, Perceive ye how ye prevail nothing? behold, the world is gone after him.

THE CLEANSING OF THE TEMPLE

⁷ And Jesus went into the temple, And found in the temple those that sold oxen and sheep and doves, and the changers of money sitting: ⁸ And when he had made a scourge of small cords, he drove them all out of the temple, and the sheep, and the oxen; and poured out the changers' money, and overthrew the tables; and cast out all them that sold and bought in the temple, and the seats of them that sold doves, And would not suffer that any man should carry any vessel through the temple. ⁹ And he taught, saying unto them, Is it not written, My house shall be called of all nations the house of prayer? but ye have made it a den of thieves.

¹⁰ And the scribes and chief priests heard it, and sought how they might destroy him: And could not find what they might do: for all the people were astonished at his doctrine.

THE DESTRUCTION OF THE TEMPLE

¹¹ And as he went out of the temple, one of his disciples saith unto him, Master, see what manner of stones and what buildings are here!

¹² And Jesus answering said unto him, Seest thou these great buildings? there shall not be left one stone upon another, that shall not be thrown down. ¹³ Many false prophets shall rise, and shall deceive many. And because iniquity shall abound, the love of many shall wax cold. But he that shall endure unto the end, the same shall be saved. ¹⁴ And this gospel of the Kingdom of Heaven shall be preached in all the world for a witness unto all nations; and then shall the end come. Heaven and earth shall pass away, but my words shall not pass away.

¹⁵ And when he was demanded of the Pharisees, when the

Kingdom of Heaven should come, he answered them and said, The Kingdom of Heaven cometh not with observation: Neither shall they say, Lo here! or, lo there! for, behold, the Kingdom of Heaven is within you.

RENDER UNTO CAESAR

[16] Then went the Pharisees, and took counsel how they might entangle him in his talk. [17] And they sent out unto him their disciples with the Herodians, saying, Master, we know that thou art true, and teachest the way of truth, neither carest thou for any man: for thou regardest not the person of men. Tell us therefore, What thinkest thou? Is it lawful to give tribute unto Caesar, or not? Shall we give, or shall we not give?

[18] But Jesus perceived their wickedness, and said unto them, Why tempt ye me, ye hypocrites? [19] Shew me the tribute money. And they brought unto him a penny. And he saith unto them, Whose is this image and superscription?

[20] They say unto him, Caesar's. Then saith he unto them, Render therefore unto Caesar the things which are Caesar's.

[21] When they had heard these words, they marvelled, and left him, and went their way.

PHARISEES AND SADDUCEES

[22] The Pharisees also came unto him, tempting him, and saying unto him, Is it lawful for a man to put away his wife for every cause?

[23] And he answered and said unto them, Have ye not read, that he which made them at the beginning made them male and female, And said, For this cause shall a man leave father and mother, and shall cleave to his wife: and they twain shall

be one flesh? ²⁴ Wherefore they are no more twain, but one flesh. What therefore God hath joined together, let not man put asunder.

²⁵ They say unto him, Why did Moses then command to give a writing of divorcement, and to put her away?

²⁶ And Jesus answered and said unto them, Moses because of the hardness of your hearts suffered you to put away your wives: but from the beginning it was not so. ²⁷ And I say unto you, Whosoever shall put away his wife, except it be for fornication, and shall marry another, committeth adultery: and whoso marrieth her which is put away doth commit adultery.

²⁸ His disciples say unto him, If the case of the man be so with his wife, it is not good to marry.

²⁹ But he said unto them, All men cannot receive this saying, save they to whom it is given. For there are some eunuchs, which were so born from their mother's womb: and there are some eunuchs, which were made eunuchs of men: and there be eunuchs, which have made themselves eunuchs for the Kingdom of Heaven's sake. He that is able to receive it, let him receive it.

³⁰ The same day came to him the Sadducees, which say that there is no resurrection, and asked him, Saying, Master, Moses wrote unto us, If any man's brother die, having a wife, and he die without children, that his brother should take his wife, and raise up seed unto his brother. ³¹ There were therefore seven brethren: and the first took a wife, and died without children. And the second took her to wife, and he died childless. And the third took her; and in like manner the seven also: and they left no children, and died. Last of all the woman died also. Therefore in the resurrection whose wife of them is she? for seven had her to wife.

³² Jesus answered and said unto them, Ye do err. The good

is not the good of the dead, but of the living. The children of this world marry, and are given in marriage.

33 And when the multitude heard this, they were astonished at his doctrine.

THE HYPOCRITES

34 Then spake Jesus to the multitude, and to his disciples, saying For there is nothing covered, that shall not be revealed; neither hid, that shall not be known. Therefore whatsoever ye have spoken in darkness shall be heard in the light; and that which ye have spoken in the ear in closets shall be proclaimed upon the housetops. 35 And I say unto you my friends, Be not afraid of them that kill the body, and after that have no more that they can do.

36 Whereunto then shall I liken the men of this generation? and to what are they like? They are like unto children sitting in the marketplace, and calling one to another, and saying, We have piped unto you, and ye have not danced; we have mourned to you, and ye have not wept. 37 For John the Baptist came neither eating bread nor drinking wine; and ye say, He hath a devil. I come eating and drinking; and ye say, Behold a gluttonous man, and a winebibber, a friend of publicans and sinners! 38 But wisdom is justified* of all her children.

39 The scribes and the Pharisees sit in Moses' seat: All therefore whatsoever they bid you observe, that observe and do; but do not ye after their works: for they say, and do not. 40 For they bind heavy burdens and grievous to be borne, and lay them on men's shoulders; but they themselves will not move them with

---

* Proved right.

one of their fingers. ⁴¹ But all their works they do for to be seen of men: they make broad their phylacteries,* and enlarge the borders of their garments, And love the uppermost rooms at feasts, and the chief seats in the synagogues, And greetings in the markets, and to be called of men, Rabbi, Rabbi.

⁴² But be not ye called Rabbi; and all ye are brethren. Neither be ye called masters. But he that is greatest among you shall be your servant. ⁴³ And whosoever shall exalt himself shall be abased; and he that shall humble himself shall be exalted.

⁴⁴ But woe unto you, scribes and Pharisees, hypocrites! for ye shut up the Kingdom of Heaven against men: for ye neither go in yourselves, neither suffer ye them that are entering to go in.

⁴⁵ Woe unto you, Pharisees! for ye love the uppermost seats in the synagogues, and greetings in the markets.

⁴⁶ Woe unto you, scribes and Pharisees, hypocrites! for ye are as graves which appear not, and the men that walk over them are not aware of them.

⁴⁷ Woe unto you, scribes and Pharisees, hypocrites! for ye devour widows' houses, and for a pretence make long prayer: therefore ye shall receive the greater damnation.

⁴⁸ Woe unto you, scribes and Pharisees, hypocrites! for ye compass sea and land to make one proselyte, and when he is made, ye make him twofold more the child of hell than yourselves.

⁴⁹ Woe unto you, scribes and Pharisees, hypocrites! for ye pay tithe of mint and anise and cummin and rue and all manner of herbs, and have omitted the weightier matters of the law, judgment, mercy, and faith: these ought ye to have done, and

---

* Rolls of parchment containing passages from the Torah, enclosed in a case of black calfskin.

not to leave the other undone. Ye blind guides, which strain at a gnat, and swallow a camel.

⁵⁰ Woe unto you, scribes and Pharisees, hypocrites! for ye make clean the outside of the cup and of the platter, but within they are full of extortion and excess. Thou blind Pharisee, cleanse first that which is within the cup and platter, that the outside of them may be clean also.

⁵¹ Woe unto you, scribes and Pharisees, hypocrites! for ye are like unto whited sepulchres, which indeed appear beautiful outward, but are within full of dead men's bones, and of all uncleanness. Even so ye also outwardly appear righteous unto men, but within ye are full of hypocrisy and iniquity.

⁵² Woe unto you, scribes and Pharisees, hypocrites! because ye build the tombs of the prophets, and garnish the sepulchres of the righteous, And say, If we had been in the days of our fathers, we would not have been partakers with them in the blood of the prophets.

⁵³ Wherefore ye be witnesses unto yourselves, that ye are the children of them which killed the prophets. Fill ye up then the measure of your fathers. From the blood of Abel unto the blood of Zacharias which perished between the altar and the temple: verily I say unto you, It shall be required of this generation.

⁵⁴ Then answered one of the lawyers, and said unto him, Master, thus saying thou reproachest us also.

⁵⁵ And he said, Woe unto you also, ye lawyers! for ye lade men with burdens grievous to be borne, and ye yourselves touch not the burdens with one of your fingers.

⁵⁶ Woe unto you, lawyers! for ye have taken away the key of knowledge: ye entered not in yourselves, and them that were entering in ye hindered. Ye serpents, ye generation of vipers, how can ye escape damnation?

⁵⁷ O Jerusalem, Jerusalem, thou that killest the prophets,

and stonest them which are sent unto thee, how often would I have gathered thy children together, even as a hen gathereth her chickens under her wings, and ye would not! Behold, your house is left unto you desolate.

⁵⁸ And as he said these things unto them, the scribes and the Pharisees began to urge him vehemently, and to provoke him to speak of many things: Laying wait for him, and seeking to catch something out of his mouth, that they might accuse him.

THE CHIEF PRIESTS PLOT

⁵⁹ Then assembled together a council the chief priests, and the scribes, and the elders of the people, unto the palace of the high priest, who was called Caiaphas, and said, What do we? If we let him thus alone, all men will believe on him: and the Romans shall come and take away both our place and nation.

⁶⁰ And one of them, named Caiaphas, being the high priest that same year, said unto them, Ye know nothing at all, Nor consider that it is expedient for us, that one man should die for the people, and that the whole nation perish not.

⁶¹ Then from that day forth they took counsel together for to put him to death. But they said, Not on the feast day, lest there be an uproar among the people.

12 THE TRAP IS SET

JUDAS PLOTS WITH THE PRIESTS

¹ In the day time Jesus was teaching in the temple; and at night he went out, and abode in the mount that is called the mount of Olives. And all the people came early in the morning to him in the temple, for to hear him.

² Now the feast of unleavened bread drew nigh, which is called the Passover. And the chief priests and scribes sought how they might kill him; for they feared the people.

³ Judas surnamed Iscariot, being of the number of the twelve went his way, and communed with the chief priests and captains, and said unto them, What will ye give me, and I will deliver him unto you?

⁴ And they were glad, and covenanted to give him thirty pieces of silver. And he promised, and sought opportunity to betray him unto them in the absence of the multitude.

THE LAST SUPPER

⁵ And the first day of unleavened bread, his disciples went forth, and came into the city, and they made ready the passover. And in the evening, he sat down with the twelve. ⁶ And there was also a strife among them, which of them should be accounted the greatest.

⁷ And he said unto them, He that is greatest among you, let him be as the younger; and he that is chief, as he that doth serve. For whether is greater, he that sitteth at meat, or he that serveth? is not he that sitteth at meat? but I am among you as he that serveth. ⁸ Ye are they which have continued with me in my temptations. And he said unto them, With desire I have desired to eat this passover with you before I suffer.

⁹ And he took bread, and gave thanks, and brake it, and gave unto them, saying, This is my body which is given for you: this do in remembrance of me.

¹⁰ And he took the cup, and when he had given thanks, he gave it to them saying, This cup is the new testament in my blood, which is shed for many. And they all drank of it.

¹¹ And as they did eat, he said, Verily I say unto you, that one of you shall betray me. And they were exceeding sorrowful, and began every one of them to say unto him, Lord, is it I?

¹² And he answered and said unto them, It is one of the twelve, that dippeth with me in the dish.

¹³ Simon Peter then lying on Jesus' breast saith unto him, Lord, who is it? Jesus answered, He it is, to whom I shall give a sop, when I have dipped it. And when he had dipped the sop, he gave it to Judas Iscariot, the son of Simon.

¹⁴ Then Judas, which betrayed him, answered and said, Master, is it I? He said unto him, Thou hast said. That thou doest, do quickly.

¹⁵ Now no man at the table knew for what intent he spake this unto him. For some of them thought, because Judas had the bag, that Jesus had said unto him, Buy those things that we have need of against the feast; or, that he should give something to the poor.

¹⁶ He then having received the sop went immediately out: and it was night. And when they had sung an hymn, they went out into the mount of Olives.

THE MOUNT OF OLIVES

¹⁷ Simon Peter said unto him, Lord, whither goest thou? Jesus answered him, Whither I go, thou canst not follow me now; but thou shalt follow me afterwards.

¹⁸ Peter said unto him, Lord, why cannot I follow thee now? I will lay down my life for thy sake.

¹⁹ Then saith Jesus unto them, All ye shall be offended because of me this night.

²⁰ Peter answered and said unto him, Though all men shall be offended because of thee, yet will I never be offended. I am ready to go with thee, both into prison, and to death.

²¹ Jesus said unto him, Verily I say unto thee, thou shalt thrice deny that thou knowest me.

²² Peter said unto him, Though I should die with thee, yet will I not deny thee. Likewise also said all the disciples.

²³ And he said unto them, When I sent you without purse, and scrip, and shoes, lacked ye any thing? And they said, Nothing. Then said he unto them, But now, he that hath a purse, let him take it, and likewise his scrip: and he that hath no sword, let him sell his garment, and buy one.

²⁴ And they said, Lord, behold, here are two swords. And he said unto them, It is enough.

THE GARDEN OF GETHSEMANE

²⁵ Then cometh Jesus with them unto a place called Gethsemane, and saith unto the disciples, Sit ye here, while I go and pray yonder. ²⁶ And he took with him Peter and the two sons of Zebedee, and began to be sorrowful and very heavy. Then saith he unto them, My soul is exceeding sorrowful, even unto death: tarry ye here, and watch with me. ²⁷ And he went a little farther, and fell on his face, and prayed.

²⁸ And he cometh unto the disciples, and findeth them asleep, and saith unto Peter, What, sleepest thou? Could ye not watch with me one hour? Watch and pray, lest ye enter into temptation. The spirit indeed is willing, but the flesh is weak.

²⁹ He went away again the second time, and prayed more earnestly, and his sweat was as it were great drops of blood falling down to the ground. ³⁰ And when he returned, he found them asleep again: for their eyes were heavy, neither wist they what to answer him. And he left them, and went away again, and prayed the third time.

³¹ Then cometh he to his disciples, and saith unto them, Sleep on now, and take your rest: behold, the hour is at hand, and I am betrayed into the hands of sinners. Rise, let us be going: behold, he is at hand that doth betray me.

³² And while he yet spake, lo, Judas, one of the twelve, came, and with him a great multitude with lanterns, torches, swords and staves, from the chief priests and elders of the people. ³³ And he that betrayed him gave them a sign, saying, Whomsoever I shall kiss, that same is he; take him, and lead him away safely. And forthwith he came to Jesus, and said, Hail, master; and kissed him.

³⁴ And Jesus said unto him, Friend, wherefore art thou come? Betrayest thou the Son of man with a kiss?

[35] And Jesus said unto them, Whom seek ye?

[36] They answered him, Jesus of Nazareth. Jesus saith unto them, I am he: if therefore ye seek me, let these go their way:

[37] Then came they, and laid hands on Jesus and took him. [38] When they which were about him saw what would follow, they said unto him, Lord, shall we smite with the sword? And one of them that stood by drew a sword, and smote a servant of the high priest, and cut off his ear. The servant's name was Malchus.

[39] Then said Jesus unto him, Put up again thy sword into his place: for all they that take the sword shall perish with the sword.

[40] In that same hour said Jesus to the multitudes, Are ye come out as against a thief with swords and staves for to take me? I sat daily with you teaching in the temple, and ye laid no hold on me: but this is your hour, and the power of darkness.

[41] And they all forsook him, and fled. And they led Jesus away to the high priest: and with him were assembled all the chief priests and the elders and the scribes.

JESUS BEFORE CAIAPHAS

[42] Then the band and the captain and officers of the Jews led him away to Annas first; for he was father in law to Caiaphas, which was the high priest that same year. Now Caiaphas was he, which gave counsel to the Jews, that it was expedient that one man should die for the people. [43] The high priest then asked Jesus of his disciples, and of his doctrine.

[44] Jesus answered him, I spake openly to the world; I ever taught in the synagogue, and in the temple, whither the Jews always resort; and in secret have I said nothing. Why askest thou me? ask them which heard me, what I have said unto them: behold, they know what I said.

⁴⁵ And when he had thus spoken, one of the officers which stood by struck Jesus with the palm of his hand, saying, Answerest thou the high priest so?

⁴⁶ Jesus answered him, If I have spoken evil, bear witness of the evil: but if well, why smitest thou me?

⁴⁷ Now Annas had sent him bound unto Caiaphas the high priest, where the scribes and the elders were assembled. And Peter followed him afar off, even into the palace of the high priest: and he sat with the servants, and warmed himself at the fire.

⁴⁸ Now the chief priests, and elders, and all the council, sought false witness against Jesus, to put him to death; But found none: yea, though many false witnesses came, their witness agreed not together. At the last came two false witnesses, ⁴⁹ And said, This fellow said, I am able to destroy the temple of God, and within three days I will build another made without hands.

⁵⁰ And the high priest arose, and said unto him, Answerest thou nothing? what is it which these witness against thee?

⁵¹ But Jesus held his peace, and answered nothing. And the high priest answered and said unto him, I adjure thee by the living God, that thou tell us whether thou be the Christ, the Son of God.

⁵² Jesus saith unto him, Thou hast said.

⁵³ Then the high priest rent his clothes, saying, He hath spoken blasphemy; what further need have we of witnesses? behold, now ye have heard his blasphemy. What think ye? They answered and said, He is guilty of death.

⁵⁴ Then did they spit in his face, and to blindfold him, and buffeted him; and others smote him with the palms of their hands, Saying, Prophesy unto us, thou Christ, Who is he that smote thee?

PETER DENIES JESUS

55 Now Peter sat without in the palace: and a damsel saw Peter warming himself, looked upon him, and said, And thou also wast with Jesus of Nazareth. But he denied before them all, saying, woman, I know not what thou sayest.

56 And when he was gone out into the porch, another maid saw him, and said unto them that were there, This fellow was also with Jesus of Nazareth. And again he denied with an oath, I do not know the man.

57 And after a while came unto him they that stood by, and said to Peter, Surely thou also art one of them: for thou art a Galilaean, and thy speech betrayeth thee. Then began he to curse and to swear, saying, I know not this man of whom ye speak.

58 And Peter remembered the word of Jesus, which said unto him, thou shalt deny me. And he went out, and wept bitterly.

13 TRIAL AND EXECUTION

JESUS BEFORE PILATE AND HEROD

¹ Then led they Jesus from Caiaphas unto the hall of judgment, and delivered him to Pontius Pilate the governor. It was early; and they themselves went not into the judgment hall, lest they should be defiled; but that they might eat the passover.

² Then Judas, which had betrayed him, when he saw that he was condemned, repented himself, and brought again the thirty pieces of silver to the chief priests and elders, saying, I have sinned in that I have betrayed the innocent blood. And they said, What is that to us? see thou to that.

³ And he cast down the pieces of silver in the temple, and departed, and went and hanged himself.

⁴ And the chief priests took the silver pieces, and said, It is not lawful for to put them into the treasury, because it is the price of blood. And they took counsel, and bought with them the potter's field, to bury strangers in. Wherefore that field was called, The field of blood, unto this day.

⁵ And Jesus stood before the governor: and the governor asked him, saying, Art thou the King of the Jews? And Jesus said unto him, Thou sayest.

⁶ Pilate then went out unto them, and said, What accusation bring ye against this man?

⁷ They answered and said unto him, If he were not a malefactor, we would not have delivered him up unto thee.

⁸ Then said Pilate unto them, Take ye him, and judge him according to your law. The Jews therefore said unto him, It is not lawful for us to put any man to death: Then said Pilate to the chief priests and to the people, I find no fault in this man.

⁹ And they were the more fierce, saying, He stirreth up the people, teaching throughout all Jewry, beginning from Galilee to this place.

¹⁰ When Pilate heard of Galilee, he asked whether the man were a Galilaean. And as soon as he knew that he belonged unto Herod's jurisdiction, he sent him to Herod, who himself also was at Jerusalem at that time.

¹¹ And when Herod saw Jesus, he was exceeding glad: for he was desirous to see him of a long season, because he had heard many things of him; and he hoped to have seen some miracle done by him. ¹² Then he questioned with him in many words; but he answered him nothing.

¹³ And the chief priests and scribes stood and vehemently accused him. And Herod with his men of war set him at nought, and mocked him, and arrayed him in a gorgeous robe, and sent him again to Pilate.

¹⁴ And the same day Pilate and Herod were made friends together: for before they were at enmity between themselves.

¹⁵ Then Pilate entered into the judgment hall again, and called Jesus, and said unto him, Art thou the King of the Jews?

¹⁶ Jesus answered him, Sayest thou this thing of thyself, or did others tell it thee of me?

¹⁷ Pilate answered, Am I a Jew? Thine own nation and the chief priests have delivered thee unto me: what hast thou done?

¹⁸ Jesus answered, My kingdom is not of this world.

¹⁹ And Pilate asked him, Art thou the King of the Jews? And he answering said unto them, Thou sayest it. ²⁰ And the chief priests accused him of many things: but he answered nothing.

²¹ And Pilate asked him again, saying, Answerest thou nothing? behold how many things they witness against thee. ²² But Jesus yet answered nothing; so that Pilate marvelled.

²³ Pilate therefore said unto him, Art thou a king then? Jesus answered, Thou sayest that I am a king. I bear witness unto the truth. Every one that is of the truth heareth my voice.

²⁴ Pilate saith unto him, What is truth? And when he had said this, he went out again unto the Jews, and saith unto them, I find in him no fault at all. But ye have a custom, that I should release unto you one at the passover: will ye therefore that I release unto you the King of the Jews?

²⁵ Then cried they all again, saying, Not this man, but Barabbas. Now Barabbas was a robber, which lay bound with them that had made insurrection with him, who had committed murder in the insurrection.

²⁶ Then Pilate therefore took Jesus, and scourged him. And the soldiers platted a crown of thorns, and put it on his head, and they put on him a purple robe, And said, Hail, King of the Jews! and they smote him with their hands.

²⁷ Pilate therefore went forth again, and saith unto them, Behold, I bring him forth to you, that ye may know that I find no fault in him. Then came Jesus forth, wearing the crown of thorns, and the purple robe. And Pilate saith unto them, Behold the man!

²⁸ When the chief priests therefore and officers saw him, they cried out, saying, Crucify him, crucify him. Pilate saith unto them, Take ye him, and crucify him: for I find no fault in him.

²⁹ The Jews answered him, We have a law, and by our law he ought to die, because he made himself the Son of God.

³⁰ When Pilate therefore heard that saying, he was the more afraid; And went again into the judgment hall, and saith unto Jesus, Whence art thou? But Jesus gave him no answer. ³¹ Then saith Pilate unto him, Speakest thou not unto me? knowest thou not that I have power to crucify thee, and have power to release thee?

³² Jesus answered, Thou couldest have no power at all against me, except it were given thee: therefore he that delivered me unto thee hath the greater sin.

³³ And from thenceforth Pilate sought to release him: but the Jews cried out, saying, If thou let this man go, thou art not Caesar's friend: whosoever maketh himself a king speaketh against Caesar. ³⁴ When Pilate therefore heard that saying, he brought Jesus forth, and sat down in the judgment seat in a place that is called the Pavement, but in the Hebrew, Gabbatha. And it was the preparation of the passover, and about the sixth hour: and he saith unto the Jews, Behold your King!

³⁵ The chief priests answered, We have no king but Caesar. And the Jews cried out, Away with him, away with him, crucify him. Pilate saith unto them, Shall I crucify your King? Why, what evil hath he done? And they cried out the more exceedingly, Crucify him.

³⁶ When Pilate saw that he could prevail nothing, but that rather a tumult was made, he took water, and washed his hands before the multitude, saying, I am innocent of the blood of this just person: see ye to it.

³⁷ And so Pilate, willing to content the people, released unto them him that for sedition and murder was cast into prison, whom they had desired; but he delivered Jesus to their will, when he had scourged him, to be crucified. And they took Jesus, and led him away.

THE CRUCIFIXION

³⁸ Then the soldiers of the governor took Jesus into the common hall, called Praetorium, and gathered unto him the whole band of soldiers. And they stripped him, and put on him a scarlet robe. And when they had platted a crown of thorns, they put it upon his head, and a reed in his right hand: and they bowed the knee before him, and mocked him, saying, Hail, King of the Jews!

³⁹ And they spit upon him, and took the reed, and smote him on the head. And after that they had mocked him, they took the robe off from him, and put his own raiment on him, and led him away to crucify him.

⁴⁰ And as they came out, they compel one Simon a Cyrenian, who passed by, coming out of the country, the father of Alexander and Rufus, to bear his cross. ⁴¹ And there followed him a great company of people, and of women, which also bewailed and lamented him. But Jesus turning unto them said, Daughters of Jerusalem, weep not for me, but weep for your-selves, and for your children.

⁴² And when they were come unto a place called Golgotha, that is to say, a place of a skull, They gave him vinegar to drink mingled with myrrh: and when he had tasted thereof, he would not drink.

⁴³ Then the soldiers, when they had crucified Jesus, took his garments, and made four parts, to every soldier a part; and also

his coat: now the coat was without seam, woven from the top throughout. They said therefore among themselves, Let us not rend it, but cast lots for it.

44 And sitting down they watched him there; And set up over his head his accusation written, JESUS OF NAZARETH THE KING OF THE JEWS. This title then read many of the Jews: for the place where Jesus was crucified was nigh to the city: and it was written in Hebrew, and Greek, and Latin.

45 Then said the chief priests of the Jews to Pilate, Write not, The King of the Jews; but that he said, I am King of the Jews.

46 Pilate answered, What I have written I have written.

47 Now there stood by the cross of Jesus his mother, and his mother's sister, Mary the wife of Cleophas, and Mary Magdalene. 48 When Jesus therefore saw his mother, and the disciple standing by, whom he loved, he saith unto his mother, Woman, behold thy son! Then saith he to the disciple, Behold thy mother! And from that hour that disciple took her unto his own home.

49 Then were there two thieves crucified with him, one on the right hand, and another on the left. Then said Jesus, forgive them; for they know not what they do.

50 And one of the malefactors which were hanged railed on him, saying, If thou be Christ, save thyself and us. But the other answering rebuked him, saying, we receive the due reward of our deeds: but this man hath done nothing amiss.

51 And they that passed by reviled him, wagging their heads, And saying, Thou that destroyest the temple, and buildest it in three days, save thyself. If thou be the Son of God, come down from the cross.

52 Likewise also the chief priests mocking him, with the scribes and elders, said, He saved others; himself he cannot save. If he be the King of Israel, let him now come down from

the cross, and we will believe him. He trusted in God; let him deliver him now, if he will have him: for he said, I am the Son of God.

[53] Now from the sixth hour there was darkness over all the land unto the ninth hour. And about the ninth hour Jesus cried with a loud voice. [54] Some of them that stood there, when they heard that, said, This man calleth for Elias. And straightway one of them ran, and took a spunge, and filled it with vinegar, and put it on a reed, and gave him to drink, saying, Let alone; let us see whether Elias will come to take him down.

[55] Jesus, when he had cried again with a loud voice, said, It is finished, and yielded up the ghost.

BURIAL

[56] And all his acquaintance, and the women that followed him from Galilee, stood afar off, beholding the things which were done, smote their breasts, and returned. [57] And many women were there beholding afar off, which followed Jesus from Galilee, ministering unto him: Among which was Mary Magdalene, and Mary the mother of James and Joses, and the mother of Zebedee's children.

[58] When the even was come, there came a rich man of Arimathaea, named Joseph, who also himself was Jesus' disciple: [59] He went to Pilate, and begged the body of Jesus. And Pilate marvelled if he were already dead: and calling unto him the centurion, he asked him whether he had been any while dead. And when he knew it of the centurion, he gave the body to Joseph.

[60] And there came also Nicodemus, which at the first came to Jesus by night, and brought a mixture of myrrh and aloes, about an hundred pound weight.

[61] And when Joseph had taken the body, he wrapped it in a clean linen cloth with the spices, And laid it in his own new tomb, which he had hewn out in the rock: and he rolled a great stone to the door of the sepulchre, and departed.

[62] And there was Mary Magdalene, and the other Mary, sitting over against the sepulchre.

PART ONE: NOTES

INTRODUCTION

1 Pew Research Center, 'The Changing Global Religious Landscape', 5 April 2017, https://www.pewforum.org/2017/04/05/the-changing-global-religious-landscape/.

2 Barna Group, 'What Do Americans Believe About Jesus? 5 Popular Beliefs', 1 April 2015, https://www.barna.com/research/what-do-americans-believe-about-jesus-5-popular-beliefs/.

3 Data from Christian Research (www.christian-research.org) cited in Jonathan Petre, 'One third of clergy do not believe in the Resurrection', *Daily Telegraph*, 31 July 2002.

4 John Harris's National Conversations podcast: Richard Dawkins, 24 October 2011.

5 ComRes BBC English regions miracles poll, 30 September 2018, www.comresglobal.com.

6 Ruth Gledhill, 'Archbishop of Westminster attacks atheism but says nothing on child abuse', *The Times*, 22 May 2009.

7 Pope Emeritus Benedict XVI, 'The Church and the scandal of sexual abuse', www.catholicnewsagency.com, 10 April 2019.

8 Voltaire, 'Épître à l'auteur du nouveau livre *Des Trois Imposteurs*' (Letter to the author of the new book *The Three Impostors*) (1769).

9 'Religion is on the decline – yet our society is underpinned by faith', *Spectator*, 9 September 2017.

10 C. S. Lewis, *Mere Christianity* (Geoffrey Bles, 1952), p. 41.

11 Albert Schweitzer, *The Quest of the Historical Jesus* (A. & C. Black, 1911), p. 4.

I A REVOLUTION OF THE SOUL

1 New Revised Standard Version: most translations do not use a version of 'emptying', but the original Greek word is the verb form of *kenosis*, *kenóō*, 'to empty'.

2 A QUESTION OF CHARACTER

1 Xunzi 2, in Philip J. Ivanhoe and Bryan W. Van Norden (eds.), *Readings in Classical Chinese Philosophy*, 2nd edn (Hackett, 2005), p. 261.

2 Note that the source Gospels also add, 'Thou shalt love the Lord thy God with all thy heart, and with all thy soul, and with all thy strength, and with all thy mind.' The excision of this for *The Godless Gospel* need not be as significant an edit as it might at first appear. As another interviewee, Elizabeth Oldfield, said, 'There is at least one school that would say that loving God and loving neighbour are the same thing. If God is revealed to us primarily in creation and through other people, when we love creation and other people we are loving God.'

3 *Analects* 7.8, in James Legge, *The Chinese Classics*, Vol. 1 (Oxford University Press, 1893), p. 197.

4 Bankei Yōtaku, 'The Unborn', in James W. Hesig, Thomas P. Kasulis and John C. Maraldo (eds.), *Japanese Philosophy: A Sourcebook* (University of Hawai'i Press, 2011), p. 199.

5 Akeel Bilgrami, 'Gandhi's Religion and Its Relation to His Politics', in J. M. Brown and A. Parel (eds.), *The Cambridge Companion to Gandhi* (Cambridge University Press, 2011), pp. 93–116.

6 *Bhagavad-Gītā*, 3:21, in Sarvepalli Radhakrishnan and Charles A. Moore (eds.), *A Sourcebook in Indian Philosophy* (Princeton University Press, 1957), p. 114.

7 *Mahābhārata*, Book 12: Santi Parva, §75, www.sacred-texts.com/hin/m12/m12a074.htm.

8 *Analects* 2.3, in Ivanhoe and Van Norden (eds.), *Readings in Classical Chinese Philosophy*, p. 5.

9 *Dhammapāda*, Verse 54.

10 Qur'ān, 33:21.

11 Lucy Winkett pointed me to this.

12 'Dialogue between His Holiness the Dalai Lama and Fr Laurence Freeman about the Teacher and Disciple in Sarnath, Varanasi', www.dalailama.com, 13 January 2013.

3 A REVOLUTION OF THE LAW

1 John Cottingham, *How Can I Believe?* (SPCK, 2018), p. 33.
2 Immanuel Kant, 'On a Supposed Right to Lie from Philanthropy', 8:425, in Mary Gregor (trans. and ed.), *Immanuel Kant: Practical Philosophy* (Cambridge University Press, 1996), p. 613.
3 Immanuel Kant, *Groundwork for the Metaphysic of Morals*, Section 1, in Gregor, ibid., pp. 7–8.
4 Section 2, ibid., p. 44.
5 Ibid., p. 38.

4 THE RENUNCIATION OF THE WORLD

1 Diogenes Laertius, *The Lives of the Eminent Philosophers*, translated by Pamela Mensch and edited by James Miller (Oxford University Press, 2018), Book 6:58, p. 286.
2 Prologue to *The Rule of St Benedict* (516).
3 Nicholas Griffin (ed.), *The Selected Letters of Bertrand Russell: The Public Years, 1914–1970* (Routledge, 2001), Letter 334, p. 199.
4 Robin Fox, 'Calcutta Perspective: Mother Teresa's care for the dying', Robin Fox, *Lancet*, 17 September 1994: doi.org/10.1016/S0140-6736(94)92353-1.
5 Serge Larivée, Carole Sénéchal and Geneviève Chénard, 'Les côtés ténébreux de Mère Teresa', *Studies in Religion/Sciences Religieuses*, 42(3), 1 September 2013, pp. 319–45: doi.org/10.1177/0008429812469894.
6 Runar M. Thorsteinsson, *Jesus as Philosopher: The Moral Sage in the Synoptic Gospels* (Oxford University Press, 2018).
7 'Vijaya Sutta: Vijaya' (SN 5.4), translated by Bhikkhu Bodhi, *Access to Insight* (BCBS edn), 13 June 2010, www.accesstoinsight.org.
8 Plato, *Phaedo*, translated by Benjamin Jowett, http://classics.mit.edu/Plato/phaedo.htm.
9 Roland J. Teske, 'The aim of Augustine's proof that God truly is', *International Philosophical Quarterly*, Vol. 26, No. 3 (1986), pp. 253–68.
10 Brendan Cox, 'Carrying on Jo's work against hate', *New York Times*, 23 September 2016.
11 Aristotle, *Nichomachean Ethics*, translated by J. A. K. Thomson (Penguin, 1996), 3.9.
12 Peter Singer, 'Famine, affluence, and morality', *Philosophy and Public Affairs*, Vol. 1, No. 1 (Spring 1972), pp. 229–43 (rev. edn).
13 Brian Mountford, *Christian Atheist* (O-Books, 2011), p. 51.

5 THE RENUNCIATION OF POLITICS

1 Rowan Williams, 'Time for us to challenge the idols of high finance', *Financial Times*, 1 November 2011.
2 'Dean Ison reflects on Occupy – one year on', stpauls.co.uk, 12 October 2012.
3 Giles Fraser, 'My hopes for the Occupy St Paul's drama that puts me on the stage', *Guardian*, 24 May 2015.
4 Giles Fraser, 'The Saturday interview: Justin Welby', *Guardian*, 21 July 2012.
5 Plato, *Crito*, 49c.
6 See Daniel C. Maguire, *Christianity without God* (SUNY Press, 2014), pp. 87–90.
7 Guru Arjan Dev, *Guru Granth Sahib: Raga Gauri*.
8 See Maguire, *Christianity without God*, p. 84.

6 MAKING YOURSELF HUMBLE

1 Bertrand Russell, 'The Superior Virtue of the Oppressed', *Unpopular Essays* (Routledge, 1950).
2 Viktor Frankl, *Man's Search for Meaning* (Pocket Books, 1959), p. 90.
3 *Testament of Jean Meslier* (1729) at www.marxists.org.
4 Albert Camus, 'The Myth of Sisyphus' (1942), in *The Myth of Sisyphus and Other Essays* (Alfred A. Knopf, 1955).

7 NON-JUDGEMENT

1 Letter 211 (423 CE), at www.newadvent.org/fathers/1102211.htm.
2 Mohandas K. Gandhi, *An Autobiography: The Story of My Experiments with Truth*, Part 4, Section 9: *A Tussle with Power*, at www.columbia.edu/itc/mealac/pritchett/oolitlinks/gandhi/.
3 *Analects* 4.25, in Philip J. Ivanhoe and Bryan W. Van Norden (eds.), *Readings in Classical Chinese Philosophy*, 2nd edn (Hackett, 2005), p. 13.
4 Aristotle, *Nichomachean Ethics*, 1169b35–1170a24, translated by J. A. K. Thomson (Penguin, 1996), p. 305.
5 *Sutrakritanga*, 1.11.33.
6 Thanks to John Cottingham for the pointer.

8 AGAINST FAMILY VALUES

1 Harriet Sherwood, 'Gay marriage vote could hit Methodist links with Church of England', *Guardian*, 30 June 2019.
2 Harriet Sherwood, 'Anglican church risks global schism over homosexuality', *Guardian*, 12 January 2016.
3 'Whether it's gay or straight, sex outside marriage is wrong', *Anglican mainstream*, 17 March 2013, and Lucy Kellaway, 'Lunch with the FT: Justin Welby', *Financial Times*, 10 May 2013.

10 GOOD WITHOUT GOD

1 Patricia Churchland, *Conscience* (W. W. Norton, 2019), p. 43.
2 John Cottingham, *How Can I Believe?* (SPCK, 2018), p. 7.
3 Peter Singer, 'Famine, Affluence, and Morality', *Philosophy and Public Affairs*, Vol. 1, No. 1 (Spring 1972), pp. 229–43.
4 David Hume, *An Enquiry concerning the Principles of Morals* (1751), Section VIII, available at davidhume.org/texts.
5 Ibid., Section V, Part 1.
6 Aristotle, *Nichomachean Ethics*, 1143b11–14, translated by J. A. K. Thomson (Penguin, 1996), p. 220.
7 Ray Monk, 'The Dark Side', in Julian Baggini and Jeremy Stangroom (eds.), *What Philosophers Think* (Continuum, 2003), p. 165.
8 David Hume, 'Of the Dignity or Meanness of Human Nature', in *Essays, Moral, Political, and Literary, Part 1* (1741), available at davidhume.org/texts.
9 See Daniel C. Maguire, *Christianity without God* (SUNY Press, 2014), p. 67.

CONCLUSION

1 See Simon Critchley, *Infinitely Demanding* (Verso, 1997), though the phrase 'ought implies cannot' was said in an interview with the *Philosophers' Magazine*, Issue 40 (1st Quarter 2008).

PART TWO: SOURCE REFERENCES FROM THE FOUR GOSPELS

7 PARABLES

8 AMONG SINNERS

9 MORE PARABLES

10 RADICAL PHILOSOPHIES

11 TROUBLE IN JERUSALEM

12 THE TRAP IS SET

13 TRIAL AND EXECUTION

ACKNOWLEDGMENTS

I am indebted to Clare Carlisle, John Cottingham, Karen Kilby, Brian Mountford, Elizabeth Oldfield, Nick Spencer, Keith Ward and Lucy Winkett, who gave up their time to talk to me about the moral teachings of Jesus and help ensure that I wasn't profoundly misunderstanding them. I have had terrific support from everyone at Granta, especially my editor, Bella Lacey. Lesley Levene did a terrific copy-editing job under challenging circumstances and David Worthington has again provided a very thorough index. I'm delighted that James Jones has come up with another excellent cover. I'm also indebted to the sales team at the Independent Alliance, who actually get my books on shelves. At home, Antonia Macaro continues to provide emotional support, intellectual challenge and daily delight.

INDEX